LIFE AND LOSS

A Guide to Help Grieving Children

Third Edition

Linda Goldman

 Routledge
Taylor & Francis Group

NEW YORK AND LONDON

This edition published 2014
by Routledge
711 Third Avenue, New York, NY 10017

and by Routledge
27 Church Road, Hove, East Sussex BN3 2FA

First edition published by Brunner-Mazel 1994
Second edition published by Routledge 2000

Library of Congress Cataloging-in-Publication Data

Goldman, Linda, 1946–
Life and loss : a guide to help grieving children / Linda Goldman. — Third Edition.
    pages cm
  Includes bibliographical references and index.
 1. Grief in children.   2. Loss (Psychology) in children.   3. Children—
Counseling of.   I. Title.
BF723.G75G65   2013
155.9'37083—dc23   2013003426

ISBN: 978-0-415-85389-7 (hbk)
ISBN: 978-0-415-63080-1 (pbk)
ISBN: 978-0-203-09733-5 (ebk)

Typeset in Dutch
by Apex CoVantage, LLC

Printed and bound in the United States of America by Sheridan Books, Inc. (a Sheridan Group Company).

LIFE AND LOSS

This item
the

Many clinicians and caring adults recognize that denying or ignoring grief issues in children leaves them feeling alone and that acknowledging loss is a crucial part of a child's healthy development. Really dealing with loss in productive ways, however, is sometimes easier said than done. For decades, *Life and Loss* has been the book clinicians have relied on for a full and nuanced presentation of the many issues with which grieving children grapple, as well as an honest exploration of the interrelationship between unresolved grief, educational success, and responsible citizenry. The third edition of *Life and Loss* brings this exploration firmly into the 21st century and makes a convincing case that children's grief is no longer restricted only to loss-identified children. Children's grief is now endemic; it is global. *Life and Loss* is not just the book clinicians and caring adults need to understand grief in today's society—it is the book they need in order to work with it in constructive ways.

Linda Goldman is the author of several books, including *Breaking the Silence: A Guide to Helping Children With Complicated Grief* and *Raising Our Children to Be Resilient: A Guide to Helping Children Cope With Trauma in Today's World*. She has been an educator in the public school system as a teacher and counselor for almost 20 years and has a private grief-therapy practice in Chevy Chase, Maryland. She also teaches as an adjunct professor in schools and universities.

Dedication

This book is dedicated to the children of the world and the child within each of us.

Contents

Preface

The Universal Child in a Grieving World

The new millennium ushered in exciting new technology, global communication, and increased social awareness of our planet and the interconnectedness of its people. Youngsters have sharpened their skills of intuition as thought transmission flashes instantaneously with modern technology. The ability to communicate ideas by e-mail, texting, blogging, and surfing the Internet has created a new world whereby girls and boys are immediately linked to a global community.

These enormous arenas of change are highlighted in this third edition of *Life and Loss*. They also produce challenges for our children. Natural disasters, terrorism, school shootings, violence, politics, and mature sexuality are made to seem normal as they inundate television and the Internet. Media brings distant alarming incidents, threats, and catastrophes into our homes and graphically imprints sounds and images onto our children's vulnerable, open minds. With information accessibility and overload becoming a part of modern culture, difficult and inappropriate data appear with the click of a channel or a mouse.

Privacy has diminished for kids growing up with Facebook, Twitter, and other social media. Communication with vast numbers of people is now possible, ranging from "friending" to cyberbullying and secret disclosure—underscoring the new paradigm that there are no secrets in today's world. This loss of privacy for our young people emerges out of the very scientific advancements so inherent in their surroundings. We, as caring adults, have a responsibility to meet the ever-changing challenges of each generation.

Today's children, and those of tomorrow, are grieving children. These children are not only those who have lost a toy, a pet, a secret, a home, or a parent, but are also the majority of our existing young people living in diverse life situations.

The world and daily life are changing rapidly. Young people often feel unprotected by the adult world, and their safety in school, outside the home, and even inside their homes may be threatened. Their ability to visualize a fulfilling future is becoming more limited. Our concern for our children's school performance and social and emotional well-being needs to address the huge, hidden realm of life issues that distract and preoccupy their thoughts and feelings.

Children's grief is not the isolated problem of children with identified loss. Children's grief is endemic—it is global. It is the norm, not the exception. Our goal is to learn to identify grief in its many forms and work with it constructively. We need to protect, prepare, and support our youth to live their lives fully and grieve death and loss as parts of a timeless journey of life in their complex universe of technology and change. As long as we deny any issue of grief or loss, at-risk young people emerge in a lonely environment. By our acknowledgment of their losses, children will feel we are affirming their reality. One of our primary challenges is to recognize the breadth and scope of the issues involving and related to grief and to emphasize the interrelationship between unresolved grief, emotional challenges, educational success, and responsible adulthood.

This third edition of *Life and Loss* includes a chapter on the losses often assumed or felt with varying family issues. The world has become a melting pot of cultures, religions, and family structures that include adoption, deployment, divorce, immigration, and all different kinds of families. It is essential to incorporate into grief work the concept of the loss of the idealized family. Acknowledging issues of imprisonment, deportation, blended families, and same-sex parenting enables us to instill core concepts that help eliminate idealized stereotyping and recognize the diversity of family structures so inherent in these modern times.

The universal child no longer has a family unit of only a mom, dad, brother, and sister. Today's child may live with a grandparent, stepsisters, a brother of a different race or nationality, or two dads or two moms. Inclusion devoid of stereotyping is key in meeting the needs of an ever-growing multicultural and diverse population of family systems.

In beginning to lay the groundwork, parents, educators, therapists, clergy, physicians, and all caring professionals need to take a fresh look at the present model used for mental health and learning. Acknowledgment of the relationship between repressed grief, ability to learn, and self-growth is essential. The emergence of a therapeutic educational paradigm for the grieving child based on this obvious connection has been slow in coming. *Life and Loss, 3rd Edition,* presents new models for grief support revolving around death and other losses that allow children to freely express their process and feel supported by peers and caring adults.

This new paradigm that relates decreased quality of learning to the shutdown of traumatized children needs to be brought out into the light of day. Let's look at today's world . . . today's needs . . . today's children . . . with a new way of seeing.

Children, parents, and professionals need to receive comprehensive trainings, resources, and supports to work with the groundswell of today's grief and loss issues. Only then can we create an international grief community capable of safeguarding all of its children.

Too often, unresolved grief in children not only leads to an inability to learn but also results in overwhelming and powerful emotions that get trapped, many times in destructive ways. Young people may project their unrecognized grief feelings outward onto the world in the form of homicide, violence, and abuse, or they may project inward onto themselves as self-hatred and possible suicide ideation and completion. Our goal is to help them release these feelings to grow to become productive adults.

The future of the planet rests on creating today and tomorrow's children who do not become the criminals, the homeless, the uneducated, the drug addicted, or the abandoned. If young people carry unacknowledged grief issues to such an extreme, they can become a detriment to themselves as well as society. Unfortunately, this is the path of all too many of today's youth. We must move forward in the 21st century to support children in becoming a global society capable of carrying humankind safely through the years to come.

Creating a society of productive human beings demands work. This work includes using evolving systems that allow a child's grief to be *expressed* rather than repressed. Only then can the inner growth of the child light the way to his or her emotional maturity, inner wisdom and responsible place as a universal citizen of the world.

Acknowledgments

Special thanks to . . .
Michael and Jonathan for their ever-loving support
Murshida Carol Conner for her immeasurable guidance
Kevin Kentfield and Carol Feiken for their beautiful photography
M.A. Lucas, Risa Garon, Jimmy Venza, Stephanie Handel,
Mani Sherier, Shirley Enebrad, The Burns Family, Lauren Redmond-Hoel
Emilio Parga, and Bonnie Carroll for their heartfelt contribution
Deepti Agarwal, Natalie Larkin, Anna Moore, and Sam Rosenthal for their patience and
expert editing
And to Henry, Tashi, and Lucy for being the most loyal friends in the animal kingdom.

Introduction

This book is written for and about children. It is also written for and about adults who want to help kids work through their issues of loss and grief. As a mom, wife, daughter, friend, teacher, therapist, educator, and pet owner, I am very aware of the importance of open communication, expressing feelings, and access to helpful resources during sensitive times in a child's life. My goal in creating this guide was to empower parents, educators, clergy, and health care professionals to acknowledge and respect children's loss and grief issues in an informed, open, and loving way, reducing the fear and denial often associated with these topics.

Each chapter of this guide includes suggestions that allow the mind, heart, and common sense to work together to create a caring environment for kids.

This guide is user friendly. One can open to any page and find useful information. Pictures are placed throughout the book as a reminder of the child's world and ways for adults to enter it. The reader may be surprised to see so many photographs showing children in a lighthearted fashion. These pictures illustrate how much time children spend with play and fantasy, no matter what their life circumstances or inner feelings may be. An active, playing child can still be a grieving child. Children escape and deny just as adults do, and often their mode of working through grief is play.

Real-life anecdotes have been chosen to illustrate typical situations. A section follows each story with practical ideas on how to help a child understand each situation and adjust to the change. Ways to prepare for grief, resources to use, and follow-up activities are included. This simplified but structured approach is beneficial in working with a wide range of circumstances. The basic ideas can be modified and expanded to fit new challenges that arise in the life of a child.

The title, *Life and Loss: A Guide to Help Grieving Children*, was chosen for several reasons. While we need to recognize death as an important part of life, it is only one of many losses children experience. Whether over a broken toy, a broken leg, a broken home, or a broken heart, children grieve and mourn. Moving, divorce, adoption, deportation, deployment, and illness are a few of the many issues interwoven into the threads of grief work that exist side by side with the death of a loved one (pet, friend, neighbor, sibling, parent, or grandparent). In today's world, we must also address the issues of violence, abuse, homicide, and suicide that impact our children's everyday lives.

The third edition of *Life and Loss* includes updated resources, websites, research from the past 12 years, and current information on loss of privacy and intimacy (Internet, secrecy exposed, cyberbullying), the digital age, pet death and loss, online memorializing, and children's grief-support groups. Two new chapters on *family loss issues* include discussions of diversity, divorce, adoption, immigration, deployment, imprisonment, and all different kinds of families.

In the first chapter, the stage of understanding is set by providing loss and grief statistics leading into the 21st century. It explores the categories of childhood losses, emphasizing the loss of a future and protection for today's children. A new loss so current for today's children is the loss of privacy and intimacy with exposure to social media and the Internet. Suggestions on how to help are presented. The remaining chapters develop a

deeper understanding of concepts that underlie Chapter 1. The myths of loss and grief with which we, as caring adults, have been reared and then pass on to our children are explored in Chapter 2. We need to acknowledge these myths and replace them with facts.

The four psychological tasks of grief are explained in Chapter 3. Material is provided to create an understanding of each task. Limiting clichés are replaced by more appropriate responses. The child's developmental understanding from birth to adolescence is presented. Ways to commemorate are offered. The story of Star, a pet dog that has died, offers practical ideas for real life situations.

Identifying behaviors associated with grief and loss is the first step in actively working with children's needs. Chapter 4 discusses this and then presents grief resolution techniques that can be used at home, in school, or on the playground, such as storytelling, letter writing, children's questions, drama, artwork, music, crafts, and other projective techniques that access and expand grief work with children. Introducing social media as an avenue for children's grief work will be explored. Computer folders for memory work, web support groups, memorializing online, and memory e-mails can be used effectively with standard cautions for children on the Internet.

Chapter 5 is a special story that provides a needed answer to the questions of what to say when a child wants to say good-bye to a dying person. Through one mother's experience, we are provided with a world of knowledge, and then we broaden her ideas to include a general format for other loss and grief issues. Resources for children who are living with dying and ways to say good-bye at a memorial service and funeral home are also included.

Chapter 6 recognizes the grief and loss issues associated with pet death and loss. "The Story of Thatcher: A Celebration of Life" shares a family's journey in saying good-bye to their beloved dog Thatcher. Resources on pet death are included.

Chapter 7 highlights issues of technology for children that have emerged so quickly onto the horizon of daily life. The digital age has created losses as well as gains that challenge young people.

Chapter 8 addresses special loss issues involved with diversity in families. Chapter 9 continues highlighting loss involving family separation involved with divorce, adoption, deployment, and imprisonment with accompanying resources to provide words to use with children on these issues.

Chapter 10 is especially for educators. It describes the challenges they and their students face daily. Guidelines for educational referrals and a children's loss inventory are included. Practical ways to use teachable moments in the classroom are described, as are helpful resources for educators.

The idea of a *global grief community* is developed in Chapter 11. Parent education, advocacy in the school system, child education, professional training, and multicultural considerations are explained, and a model of a grief team is presented. Children's grief support group programs are highlighted as well as national resources that can be helpful to adults working with children. Children's grief camps and hotlines are included as important supports.

An exploration of materials is provided in Chapter 12, where annotations are included for books for adults and children, videos, manuals, CDs and DVDs, guides, and curricula, and valuable websites for families and professionals about loss and grief. Children's literature is divided into specific loss issues with age recommendations.

Life and Loss, Third Edition, lays the foundation for working with children's grief and loss and sets the stage for acknowledging complex grief issues such as suicide, homicide, AIDS, and violence, which were addressed in my book *Breaking the Silence* 2nd Edition. It also discusses traumatic grief (terrorism, school violence, and shootings) and supporting children in natural attributes of resilience—issues that were highlighted in my book *Raising Our Children to Be Resilient.*

Life and Loss, Third Edition, creates a framework for children's grief work with today's universal child. Importantly, vast amounts of current resources, information, and research have been updated. Grief resolution techniques have been added, demonstrating children's written work and artwork. The inclusion of three timely childhood losses—the loss of the protection of the adult world, the loss of a future, and the loss of privacy—highlights issues emerging in terms of grief and loss for present and future generations.

Denial, fear, shame, and lack of appropriate role models have shaped the lives of many adults. This often makes it difficult for us to relate to children with innocence, simplicity, and openness, especially in the sensitive areas of loss and grief. Yet children are constantly immersed in this ever-changing environment, and they need grown-ups to provide mentorship. Parents, educators, and other caring professionals have the responsibility of helping these young people with their grief process.

Life and Loss, Third Edition, has been written to serve as a guide and model. Through the use of photographs, children's work, anecdotes, simple techniques, and resources, we can tune in to the world of children. Hopefully, this book will unlock the door of respect for the child's inner universe and allow us to enter it with integrity.

There appear to be so many grieving young people with so many difficult and diverse problems that we who live and work with them may often feel overwhelmed with the possible futility of impacting their lives. With the enormous amount of hurting children in our society, we may wonder if whatever strides we make actually create a difference for the endless sea of grieving children.

It is my hope and prayer that we all begin today—bound together as co-creators of a global grief community—by going back to our homes, our neighborhoods, our schools, our offices, our communities, our countries, and our world—with a shared vision and a renewed commitment to help each and every child float through their ocean of grief on the unified minds and caring hearts of the adults and children who surround them.

LINDA GOLDMAN

1

CHILDREN'S
LOSS AND GRIEF

Adoption Illness Deployment
Terrorism Natural Disasters
School Shootings Deportation
Homelessness Bullying
Suicide Violence Poverty Divorce
Imprisonment Drugs Death Abuse
AIDS Social Media
Murder Cyberbullying

There are two things we can hope to give our children
One of these is roots; the other, wings.

—Hodding Carter III

WHAT'S THE MATTER WITH KIDS TODAY?

We may ask ourselves, "What's the matter with kids today?" and realize the very fact that we are asking this question is in itself an answer. We adults have created this grieving world, and our children are left with its fear, its chaos, and its denial.

Donna O'Toole, children's grief educator and author of *Growing Through Grief* (1989), warns that so often the children "are the forgotten ones, lacking role models and assurances for a safe journey, they accumulate losses—attaching themselves to their memories," and can be left "frozen in time and buried alive in inner space" if they don't have the opportunity to work through their feelings.

We ask ourselves, "What's the matter with kids today?" The answer is that the world is very different from the one in which we grew up.

Today's children witness violence daily. A little boy asked his teacher who George Washington was. "He was our first president" was the reply. "Who shot him?" he asked, automatically assuming all presidents get shot. In the movie, "Grand Canyon," a teenager involved in gang violence was asked by his uncle, "Why are you doing this? What will you do when you're 20?" "Are you kidding me?" The teenager responded, "I'll be dead by 20."

FACTS ABOUT THE GRIEVING CHILD

Today's children live in a world of experiences and memories inundated with children's loss and death issues. The following statistics illustrate the picture of the grieving child as the norm in the present millennium.

Each Day in America

2 mothers die in childbirth.
4 children are killed by abuse or neglect.
5 children or teens (die by) suicide.
7 children or teens are killed by firearms.
24 children or teens die from accidents.
67 babies die before their first birthdays.
208 children are arrested for violent crimes.
467 children are arrested for drug crimes.
892 babies are born at low birth weight.
1,208 babies are born to teen mothers.
838 public school students are corporally punished.
1,825 children are confirmed as abused or neglected.
1,208 babies are born without health insurance.
2,712 babies are born into poverty.
2,857 high school students drop out.
4,500 children are arrested.
4,475 babies are born to unmarried mothers.
16,244 public school students are suspended.

—Children's Defense Fund (2013)

THE NORM IS THE GRIEVING CHILD

Death

The death of a parent, which is experienced by 4% of children in Western countries, is consistently rated as one of the most stressful life events that a child can experience.

Bereaved children had a threefold increased risk of depression.

—Melhem, Walker, Moritz, and Brent (2008)

More than 1.25 million children receive benefits as the result of their parent's death.

—Paventi (2010)

Children's Deaths by Guns

In 2007, 3,042 children and teens died from gunfire in the United States—8 every day—as a result of homicide, suicide, or accidental or undetermined shootings.

—Children's Defense Fund (2010)

Attention Deficit Hyperactivity Disorder and Learning Disability

In 2006, NCHS (National Center for Health Statistics) estimated that 4.5 million school-aged children (5–17 years of age) had been diagnosed with ADHD and 4.6 million children with LD.

—Pastor and Rueben (2008, p. 5)

Children who lived in a mother-only family were more likely than those in a two-parent family to have each of the three diagnoses (ADHD without LD, LD without ADHD, and both conditions (children 6–17 years of age until 2006).

—Pastor and Rueben (2008, p. 3)

Divorce

Half of all divorces involve minor children, with 1 million children a year joining the ranks.

—Portnoy (2008)

Half of all marriages are expected to fail before a child reaches 18.

—Fagan, Fitzgerald, and Rector (2009)

Adoption

Approximately 120,000 children are adopted each year in the United States.

—American Academy of Child & Adolescent Psychiatry (2011)

Grandparents Raising Children

Almost 7.8 million children under age 18 live in homes where the householders are grandparents or other relatives (10.5% of all children under 18).

—AARP et al., citing 2010 U.S. Census

Single Parents

An estimated 13.7 million parents had custody of 22.0 million children under 21 yeas of age while the other parent lived somewhere else.

—Grall, 2011

Blended Family

Seventeen percent of all children under age 18 (12.2 million) live in blended families.

Forty-six percent of the children in blended families, or 5.5 million, live with at least one stepparent.

One in 10 children living with two parents lives with a stepparent or adoptive parent.

2.9 million children live with no parents (308,000 children live with one or more foster parents).

—Kreider (2007)

Economic Loss

Child poverty increased by almost 10% between 2008 and 2009.

A total of 15.5 million children, or 1 in every 5 children in America, lived in poverty in 2009, an increase of nearly 4 million children since 2000.

Almost 60% of all children in poverty lived in single-parent families.

In 2009, more than 1 in 3 Black children and 1 in 3 Hispanic children lived in poverty, compared to more than 1 in 10 White non-Hispanic children.

The number of homeless preschool-age children increased by 43% in the past two school years. The number of homeless children and youth enrolled in public schools increased 41% between the 2006–2007 and the 2008–2009 school years.

Millions of children and families fell into poverty in 2008 from the economic downturn.

—Children's Defense Fund (2011, p. B2)

A record 46 million Americans were living in poverty in 2010.

Children under 18 suffered the highest poverty rate, 22%, compared with adults and the elderly.

—Morgan (2011)

Children With Imprisoned Parents

Fifty-three percent of the 1.5 million people held in U.S. prisons in 2007 were the parents of one or more minor children. This percentage translates into more than 1.7 million minor children with an incarcerated parent.

African American children are 7 and Latino children 2.5 times more likely to have a parent in prison than White children. The estimated risk of parental imprisonment for White children by the age of 14 is 1 in 25, while for Black children it is 1 in 4 by the same age.

—Justice Strategies (2011)

Deportation

Of the nearly 2.2 million immigrants deported in the decade ending 2007, more than 100,000 were the parents of children who, having been born in the United States, were American citizens.

—Falcone (2009)

More than 5 million children live in the United States with at least one undocumented parent. Close to 75% of those children are U.S. citizens. When one or both parents are deported, children often have to choose between living with their immediate family—in another country—or living without them in the United States.

—Reitmayer (2010)

TV Viewing

Preschoolers, aged 2 to 5, spend 32.5 hours a week in front of the television. Children aged 6 to 11 spend 28 hours a week.

—McDonough (2009)

Social Media Use

From 2005 to 2010, there has been a huge increase in ownership among 8- to 18-year-olds 18% to 76% for iPods and other MP3 players: from 39% to 66% for cell phones.

During an average day, 8- to 18-year-olds devote an average of 7 hours and 38 minutes to using entertainment media (more than 53 hours a week).

The proportion of young people who read a newspaper in a typical day dropped from 42% in 1999 to 23% in 2009.

Children in grades 7 through 12 report spending an average of about 1.5 hours a day sending or receiving texts.

—Kaiser Family Foundation (2010)

Twenty-two percent of teenagers log on their favorite social media site more than 10 times a day.

More than half of adolescents log on to a social media site more than once a day.

Seventy-five percent of teenagers now own cell phones.

Twenty-five percent use them for social media.

Fifty-four percent use them for texting.

Twenty-four percent use them for instant messaging.

— O'Keefe, Clarke-Pearson and Council on Communicators and Media, American Academy of Pediatrics (2011)

Bullying and Academic Achievement

Schools with high levels of reported bullying had lower passing rates—by an average of 3% to 6% across tests.

—St. George (2011)

Cyberbullying

One third to one half of young people have been targeted by cyberbullying.

Cyberbullying victims were nearly twice as likely to attempt suicide compared to students not targeted with online abuse.

—Holladay (2010, p. 44)

Fifty-six percent of young people say they have been the target of some type of online taunting, harassment, or bullying.

—Cass and Anderson (2011)

CREATE A SAFE GRIEF ENVIRONMENT

We can help the children by first helping ourselves. Our honesty in seeing and relaying loss and grief issues that run through our lives will indeed be the role model for our young people. By networking with other caring adults and using the many resources available, we can minimize our fear and denial of loss. This allows us to create an environment in which children know their own strength and power and can face and work through their pain.

Developing your psychological strength is just like developing physical abilities.

The more you exercise, the stronger you become.

—Bloomfield and Felder (1986)

CHILDHOOD LOSS

I have come to believe that there is not a hurt or a pain that is not based on a tangible or intangible loss. From the loss of a tooth to the death of a parent to the crumbling of a building, children grieve what they miss and cannot have back—whether it's a mom, a pet, a toy, or their dignity and self-respect. Childhood losses can fall into the following categories (Goldman, 2000; O'Toole, 1989):

Relationships	External objects
Environment	Privacy
Skills/abilities	Self
Future and adult protection	Habits and routines

Loss of Relationships

- Death of a parent, grandparent, sibling, friend, classmate, pet
- Absence of teacher, parent, sibling, friend, pet
- Unavailability of parent due to alcoholism, drugs, imprisonment, divorce, deployment, deportation

The death of a pet can be a significant loss in a child's life. Consider the following two anecdotes:

Ellen, age 9, loved her dog very much. Buffy was her friend and companion. She fed him, brushed him, walked with him, and talked with him. One day while she was at school, Buffy was hit by a car and killed. A neighbor, out of kindness, took Buffy's body to the vet so that Ellen wouldn't have to see it. Ellen never got to say good-bye. She cried inconsolably. "It's only a dog," her parents said. "We'll get you another one."

There was no other dog for Ellen. She loved Buffy and he was gone. Deeply mourning his loss for years to come, Ellen continued to carry this grief because she had no environment in which to mourn openly.

Sam loved his dog Charlie, too. He played ball with him every day after school. Charlie was a problem pet. Because Charlie was never completely housetrained or disciplined, Sam's parents made several unsuccessful attempts to sell Charlie or give him away. One day, Sam came home from school and his dog was gone. Sam's parents said they gave Charlie to a good home.

Sam questioned the truth of that explanation—no one had ever wanted to take Charlie before. The facts of Charlie's disappearance haunted Sam through his teenage years.

Was Charlie killed?
Was he abandoned?
Was he hurt?
Where did he go?
Why didn't I stay home? I could have
*   saved Charlie.*

What We Can Do for the Child

These two scenarios on pet death or loss create the following generic model of what we can do for the grieving child:

1. Tell children the truth about the pet's death or other events surrounding the pet's leaving.
2. Allow children to see the pet after it dies, if the body is relatively intact. It helps make death real.
3. Have a funeral and burial for the pet when possible. If pets are too large to bury, or a backyard is too small, a memorial service is an appropriate ritual. Let the children have a part in creating it.

4. Acknowledge children's memories and encourage them to talk about their pet.
5. Encourage children to express their feelings. Express your own.
6. Be aware of the child's guilty feelings that in some way the death or disappearance of the pet was his or her fault. (Why didn't I stay home from school that day? Why did I let my dog go outside?) Discuss ways the child was good to his or her pet. Discuss regrets, too.
7. Use rituals to work through grief. Look at photos. Write down feelings and memories. Draw a picture for or of the pet. Save a special object (collar or ball) in a special place.
8. Have parents inform the child's school. Have educators let the child know they care. Use discussions as a teachable moment in school.
9. Network: Use a support system of people who understand the depth of grief involving pet loss (e.g., family, friends, veterinarians).
10. Maintain a resource library for prevention, intervention, and postvention so that we have at our fingertips words to use for the myriad of loss and grief issues our children will experience.

Resources

A Season for Mangoes by Regina Hanson (2005)
Children Also Grieve: Talking About Death and Healing by Linda Goldman (2005)
Forever Friend: Activities for Kids Who Have Lost a Pet by Susan B. Weaver (2011)
Goodbye Mousie by Robie Harris (2004)
Saying Goodbye to Your Pet: Children Can Learn to Cope with Pet Loss by Marge Heegaard (2001)
Zach and His Dog: A Story of Bonding, Love, and Loss for Children and Adults to Share Together by David Meagher (2009)

Loss of External Objects

• Loss of a favorite toy or object (blanket, pacifier, teddy bear)
• Loss through robbery or being misplaced (diary, special gift)

Losing things of value can be very difficult for children. Consider the following anecdote. Olivia always traveled with Lizzie, her favorite stuffed animal. When Olivia visited Grandma, slept over at friends' houses, or traveled with her family, Lizzie was the first thing she packed.

Olivia's family's trip to San Francisco proved traumatic. After the first night in a fine hotel, Olivia and her parents went out to explore the city. Returning at bedtime they discovered Lizzie was gone. They searched and searched. Olivia cried and cried. "How can I sleep without Lizzie?" she wept. "I want to go home."

The family awoke to a phone call the next morning. It was the hotel staff announcing Lizzie had been found. She was in the hotel laundry. They promised to return her a little cleaner, a little shrunken, and a little more ready to be loved again.

Thirteen-year-old James relayed a poignant story of the loss of a meaningful object. He explained his mom died just after his sixth birthday. She had given him the gift of the perfect soccer ball, just the one he wanted.

Soon after his mom's death, the family moved. James confided it took three months to unpack all of the boxes. Every night he prayed to God that he would find his wonderful soccer ball. When the last box was unpacked and there was no ball, James cried out, "Where is God when I need him? That's the last time I'll believe in God." The loss of his special object created another loss, the loss of his belief in God.

What We Can Do for the Child

1. Validate children's deep feelings for their personal property as a truly important companion.
2. Actively share in the search for the missing object.
3. Actively employ a self-help group (for example, the hotel staff searched for Lizzie).

Resources

I Know I Made It Happen by Lynn Blackburn (1991)
Mending Lucille by J. R. Poulter and Sarah Davis (2008)
The Invisible String by Patrice Karst (2000)
The Memory Box by Kirsten McLaughlin (2001)

Loss in the Environment

*   Fire, floods, hurricanes, tornadoes, and other natural disasters
*   Moving, changing school, changing family structure
*   Family separation

Family separation can be a painful grieving process for a young child. Whether it is leaving Mom to stay with a babysitter, a parent going on a trip, or a grandmother dying, the loss is real and important.

When my little boy Jonathan was five, I went away for a few days. When I came back I asked him how it was for him when I was gone. He said, "Well, I got a little angry when people kept asking where you were, and, Mom, what does 'unbearable' mean?" I answered, "Something really hard to take." He replied, "It was unbearable!"

What We Can Do for the Child

1. Prepare children for the parent's departure. Whether a parent leaves for an hour, a day, a week, indefinitely, or forever, the child needs to know the facts. Open discussion decreases anxiety.
2. If the separation has an end date, make a calendar with the child that shows how long the parent will be away. Leave it in his or her room. The child can mark off the days.
3. Leave a picture of the parent by the child's bed.
4. Use a tape recorder for the child to talk to the parent or work out feelings about the parent leaving.
5. Leave the phone number of a caring adult who can support the child.
6. Inform the teacher about what has happened or will be happening at home.

Resources

The Good Bye Book by Judith Viorst (1992)
Saying Good-bye, Saying Hello by Michaelene Munday and R.W. Alley (2005)
Families Change: A Book for Children Experiencing Termination of Parental Rights by Julie Nelson (2006)
What About Me by U.S. Department of Justice (2005)
Murphy's Three Homes by Jan Levinson Gilman (2008)
Finding the Right Spot by Janice Levy (2004)

Loss of Self

- Loss of a physical part of the body: tooth, arm, eye
- Loss of self-esteem: physical, sexual, emotional, or deprivation abuse

Behavioral symptoms of grief are not always fighting, crying, or other outward expressions. Children can withdraw, detach, or depersonalize life to escape issues of grief so painful that not feeling and not talking are the only ways to survive. Consider the following case study of Mary.

Mary's dad had died of suicide when she was 5. Never told the facts, she was informed that he died in an accident. Taken from her biological mother and not told why (although Mary later discovered that Mom was an alcoholic), Mary went to live with an aunt and uncle. Mary was extremely withdrawn in school. No one asked why. Her uncle had been sexually abusing her from age 5 through age 9. She became more and more withdrawn. Still no one asked why—not at school, not at church, not her friends' parents, not the community. At age 9, Mary began begging not to be left alone with her uncle. She was punished inappropriately and told that she was unappreciative.

Mary quietly withdrew, becoming shy and unapproachable. She seemed to internalize her problems of dealing with adults. When she bravely attempted to talk about her problems, they were denied by her adult world.

Fifteen-month-old Mark acted out his hurt in a different way to secure attention. Mark's mom asked what she could do for her son, who was showing visible signs of distress after returning from visiting his dad. The couple had divorced, partially due to the husband's abusive nature. The child clung to his mom, cried a lot, had temper tantrums, and didn't want to be left alone. The court ruling had given the father two-day visitation rights, even though his abuse of his wife was on record. Mark's mom also said she noticed a bruise on the child and was angry about it. "I know my husband hits Mark but I don't know what to do about it."

Where were the adults, the advocates, and the voices for the withdrawn children who carry the emotional pain of loss and grief that is heavy and filled with fear and abandonment? These children's silent cries scream to be heard by someone who can help. We need to open our ears add inner ears to the sound of the voiceless children. Let's hear their pain with our hearts.

Knowing the signs of abuse is the first step in confronting abusive situations for adults trying to help children like Mary and Mark, whether the abuse is physical, sexual, or by neglect.

What We Can Do for the Child

There is no place so potentially violent as home. It is sometimes a place of special betrayal because the child's guard is down. If you are abusing a child, please accept help. If you are being abused, tell someone and keep telling until you get the help you need.

—Sanford (1986)

Know Signs of Abuse in Children

To help children who are being abused, we must first know and understand the signs of abused children and abusive parents. It is essential for parents, teachers, counselors, clergy, and pediatricians to watch for internal (verbal) or external (physical) signs. If more than one of the following signs is present, you need to report the suspected findings to the proper authorities. The following signals indicate suspected abuse.

If a child:

* Habitually is away from school and constantly late
* Arrives at school very early and leaves very late because he or she does not want to go home
* Is compliant, shy, withdrawn, passive, or uncommunicative
* Is nervous, hyperactive, aggressive, disruptive, or destructive
* Has an unexplained injury—a patch of hair missing, a burn, a limp, or bruises
* Has an inappropriate number of unexplained injuries, such as bruises on his or her arms or legs over a period of time
* Exhibits an injury that is not adequately explained
* Complains about numerous beatings
* Complains about a parent's paramour "doing things" when the parent is not home
* Has difficulty going to the bathroom
* Is inadequately dressed for inclement weather
* Wears a long-sleeved blouse or shirt during the summer (may cover bruises on the arms)
* Wears clothing that is soiled, tattered, or too small
* Is dirty, smells, or has bad teeth, hair falling out, or lice
* Is thin, emaciated, and constantly tired, showing evidence of malnutrition and dehydration
* Is usually fearful of other children and adults or even parents
* Has been given inappropriate food, drink, or drugs
* Talks about someone touching his or her private parts

> —Adapted from Nancy Eike, past director, 1992, of North West Child Protective Network of the Omni Youth Service and Charlene Blackmore, (2013), MSW, Omni Youth Service Family Preservation Clinical Supervisor (http://www.omniyouth.org)

Know Signs of Abusive Parents

Child abuse should be suspected and reported by any caring adult if the parents exhibit more than one of the following behaviors:

* Show little concern for their child's problems
* No responses to the teacher's inquiries and absences from parents' night or private teacher conferences
* Spend an unusual amount of time seeking health care for the child
* Offer inadequate explanations for their child's injury
* Give different explanations for the same injury
* Attribute the cause of an injury to the child or a third party
* Are reluctant to share information about the child
* Respond inappropriately to the seriousness of the problem
* Have a tendency to disappear
* Have current alcohol or drug use issues
* Do not have friends, relatives, or neighbors to turn to in times of crisis
* Have unrealistic expectations for the child
* Employ very strict discipline practices
* Have abuse, neglect, or deprivation in their past

- Take the child to different doctors, clinics, or hospitals for past injuries (possibly trying to cover up repeated injuries)
- Show signs of loss of control or a fear of losing control
- Display antagonistic and hostile behaviors when talking about the child's health problems
- When a child has been sexual abused or molested by the parent's new spouse or paramour, and the parent denies this.

Report Abuse

Nancy Eike, 1992, and Charlene Blackmore, 2013, emphasise that "these clues can help adults make an informed decision about reporting." Educators in particular are only required to report *suspected* abuse and/or neglect to the proper authorities. Investigating is the responsibility of the authorities. Parents can obtain supporting documentation from other official caregiving settings. No one needs to disclose his or her name when reporting suspected abuse to their state's children's protective services. These agencies must act within 24 to 48 hours. They may decide not to separate the child from the family. However, each report will add strength to the next one made about the same abuse case.

Meet Primary Needs

The primary needs of children under age 3 are met by physical comforting, such as hugging, holding, and permitting appropriate regression. Caregiving adults who abuse their children need guidance in working with their anger so that they become freer to love their children. Sanford (1986) stresses the following guidelines in working with abuse.

1. Encourage *no* self-blame.
2. Support repetition of telling the story.
3. Assure total belief of the abuse.
4. Maintain privacy.
5. Control your anger about the abuse.
6. Offer protection.
7. Remember that sometimes there are no visible signs of abuse.
8. Acknowledge you feel bad about the abuse.

Resources

I Said No! A Kid-to-Kid Guide to Keeping Your Private Parts Private by K. King (2008)
Talking About Domestic Abuse: A Photo Activity Workbook to Develop Communication Between Mothers and Young People by C. Humphreys et al. (2006)
I Can't Talk About It by Doris Sanford (1986)
Mommy's Black Eye: Children Dealing with Domestic Violence by William George Bentrim (2009)

Loss of Skills and Abilities

- Held back in school
- Not chosen for team sports
- Overweight, injured, ill, physically disabled
- Dyslexia, attention deficit hyperactivity disorder (ADHD), other developmental differences

In my first year of teaching, I was given a second-grade class of 22 repeaters. We were placed in a trailer away from the school. Some of the children were labeled slow learners, others were on medication for ADHD, and still others seemed to be neglected at home. The children began school with the shame and stigma of failing second grade individually and as a group. The humiliation extended to their physical isolation in the trailer. I looked at their faces the first day of class and saw a lack of joy and an aura of poor self-esteem. They knew they were different and felt the despair of their perceived lack of achievement.

What We Can Do for the Child

1. Recognize the facts about the child's school placement.
2. Allow children opportunities to discuss their retention or loss openly.
3. Incorporate the children's thoughts and feelings into creative writing and language experience.
4. Accept the children for where they are academically, athletically, or physically by using projects and tasks geared to their level of ability and comfort. See growth as individually progressing and not just as standardized grade-level comparisons of where children should be.
5. Create a project where the children can shine. For example, since the repeating second-graders are a year older than the other second-grade class, use the maturity in a creative way (plays, murals, school service projects).
6. Use every opportunity to encourage self-esteem. The following poem is a creative way (with a little humor) to bring home the point for adults and children that, despite outward differences, we're all alike inside.

No Difference

Small as a peanut,
Big as a giant,
We're all the same size
When we turn off the light.
Rich as a sultan,
Poor as a mite,
We're all worth the same
When we turn off the light.
Red, black, or orange,
Yellow or white,
We all look the same
When we turn off the light.
So maybe the way
To make everything right
Is for someone to just reach out
And turn off the light!

—Shel Silverstein, *Where The Sidewalk Ends* (1974)
HarperCollins Publishers. Reprinted by permission.

Resources

Drawing Together to Accept and Respect Difference by Marge Heegaard (2003)
Putting on the Brakes Activity Book for Kids With ADD or ADHD by Patricia Quinn, Judith Stern, and Joe Lee (2009)
Don't Call Me Special: A First Look at Disability by Pat Thomas and L. Harker (2005)
Some Kids Use Wheelchairs by Lola Schaefer (2008)
My Friend Has Down Syndrome by J. Moore-Mallinos and M. Fabrega (2008)

Loss of Privacy

- Internet, blogs, secret disclosure, cyberbullying, texting, e-mails
- Social media: YouTube, Facebook, Twitter
- Cell phones: recorders and videos

At age 3, about one-quarter of children go online daily, increasing to about half by age 5.

For children ages 8 to 10, personal ownership rates (of cell phones) rise to 31%.

—Gutnick, Robb, Takeuchi, and Kotler (2010, pp. 16, 32)

The digital age enveloping our children offers transformation and change, information and misinformation, and connectivity and loss of privacy. This world of technology presents a challenge for parents and professionals, as preschoolers learn to navigate a system too sophisticated for many adults. Chat rooms, video sharing, blogs, YouTube, and the Internet offer their stimulated minds a second home in cyberspace. As savvy as our young people are in terms of mastering this advanced scientific world, they are often stymied by the loss of privacy it creates in their lives.

No longer restricted to the playground, the social combat zone rages on through the Internet, camera phones, and more. Our kids live in a paradoxical world, caught between an Orwellian Big Brother watching and the reality that there are no secrets. Their freedom is enhanced by *immediate communication* and inhibited by *immediate exposure* of privacy.

Dillon was in the locker room after gym class. He didn't know his friend Sam was recording his conversation about Miss Hammond, Dillon's teacher that he was angry with because of a bad grade. Sam sent the recording anonymously to Miss Hammond. He thought it was a funny joke.

Grace was shopping for clothes when two classmates, the popular girls who never really spoke to her, came into the dressing room. They took camera phone pictures of her in the clothes she was trying on, told her she looked great, then instantly posted the pictures on the Internet with nasty remarks and put-downs. They thought this was funny, too.

Mattie was on the playground with friends. She naively confided in them that her parents were getting divorced. By the next day, an e-mail broadcast that information to all of Mattie's classmates. Now everyone knew, and there was nothing she could do.

Many young people feel it is deadly serious when their privacy is invaded and shared with peers, an entire school body, or the whole planet on YouTube.

It seems that nothing they do is hidden, nothing they can say is sacred, and no one they know can absolutely be trusted.

Cyberbullying, a term for online bullying, is a word that didn't exist when the second edition of *Life and Loss* was going to press. But it now represents the digital extreme of the loss of privacy and safety our children face through the skyrocketing strides in their technological world (see Chapter 7, "The Child's World of Technology"). The uniqueness of this form of bullying is its efficient and far-reaching ability to harass others and embarrass and humiliate by posting private issues and moments for all to see and hear.

Twenty years ago, kids could pass a note about a secret in their schoolroom and a few children would read it. Modern times make it easy for the same note to be posted online or tweeted for thousands to see, not just once, but for a sustained period of time.

Gray (2006) explains, "In the blink of an eye, your best friend can become your worst enemy." Often, the very relationship of *best friends* can lead to secret disclosure if that friendship turns sour or someone has a momentary impulse that results in a lasting humiliation. Then everything said in confidentiality and intimacy can explode into betrayal, shock, and exposure, leaving children vulnerable and without recourse.

Effortless access to tape recording, easily downloaded images, lax monitoring of cyberspace, and advanced photographic technology are part of our children's world. Accompanying the advantages of modern communication are the challenges of secret disclosure, life exposure, unanticipated accountability, and compromising replays of unwarranted personal scenarios that can generate painful issues of loss for our girls and boys.

What We Can Do for the Child

Safe Internet use includes parent's involvement, structure, and guidelines. Parents can:

*   Educate children about the Internet.
*   Agree on family rules for Internet use.
*   Locate the family computer in a central, open part of the house.
*   Monitor the sites children visit.
*   Block offensive sites and topics.
*   Encourage children not to enter chat rooms.

Privacy Suggestions for Children

*   Never give identification information.
*   Be trustworthy. Don't disclose secrets.
*   Tell an adult if someone asks for information.
*   Realize strangers on the Internet are just like strangers outside.
*   Check the facts on any Internet story.
*   Tell an adult if something someone does online feels uncomfortable.
*   Report online harassment.
*   Be careful about what you post online. It can't be taken away.

—Adapted from Burnaby (2011)

Resources

The Safe Side—Stranger Safety: Hot Tips To Keep Cool Kids Safe With People They Don't Know and Kinda Know by Angela Shelton and Jon Walsh, DVD (2005)
Faux Paw's Adventures in the Internet: Keeping Children Safe Online by Jacalyn Leavitt and Sally Linford (2006)
What Would My Cell Phone Do? by Micoi Ostow (2011)

Loss of Habits and Routines

- Sucking thumb, biting fingernails, twirling hair
- Change in eating patterns or daily routines
- Beginning or ending school

A bus accident on the way to school can certainly change the routine of the day for the children involved. This happened to a group of 25 elementary schoolchildren.

Chase was the only first-grader among them. The bus swerved to avoid a truck and was thrown over on its side. Miraculously, no one was severely hurt. The children waited for the police, they were taken to the hospital in ambulances, and the parents were notified. The accident was a disturbing disruption to the school routine. Some kids were emotionally shaken. One child fainted. Other kids were bruised and cut. Chase had a few scrapes on his face. He raced to his mom when she entered the hospital, hugged her tightly, and insisted in a frightened voice, "I'm never riding the bus again, and you can't make me!"

My son Jonathan, at age 8, greeted me at the door the first evening I began seeing therapy clients. "Mom, I have been waiting for you. I really need to talk with you. I have something to tell you," he explained. "I have a real grief and loss issue. I really miss you when you are gone." This was a huge change in Jonathan's daily routine.

Alyssa, age 13, described an after-school incident. She had come home from school and automatically opened the refrigerator door to retrieve the noodles her mom used to leave for her. Alyssa's mom had died recently. Alyssa burst into tears. "The noodles weren't there like always, and my mom wasn't there like always, too!" The missing snack in Alyssa's everyday life triggered the deeper loss of the absence of her mother.

Seven-year-old Rosie said she missed her mom the most after school. All the neighborhood kids played outside until dinner, and then their mothers called them to come in. "No one called me. It makes me miss my mom."

Evan was a young father left to be a single dad after his wife Margie suddenly died. His son Brian was 4 years old. Both friends and professionals advised Evan to maintain the daily routine with his son. Soon after Margie's death, Evan found her special recipe book. He began making the "super-duper" pancakes she always made on Sundays. By the fourth Sunday, little Brian looked up at his father with sad eyes. "Daddy, I just don't like pancakes anymore." Sometimes, no matter how hard we try, we can't maintain the daily routine.

What We Can Do for the Child

The following suggestions are specific to a sudden bus accident. They can be modified to help children for any traumatic change in their daily routine.

1. Bring children together to discuss feelings about their bus accident experience. Listen and echo back feelings.
2. Allow each child the time and space to retell his or her version of the story. This helps to see where support or clarification is needed.

3. Let each child mark on a diagram of the bus where he or she was and tell what he or she did.
4. Recognize any injuries that the children sustained.
5. Discuss guilt that some children may feel if they were one of the children not injured.
6. Identify the fears for future bus rides. Reassure that everything has been done to ensure safety.
7. Bring the entire school together for an assembly. Discuss what an accident is and the facts surrounding the bus accident. Allow all children time for questions. This will respond to the needs of the schoolchildren who were not on the bus.
8. Inform parents of all the children in the school. Send home the facts of the accident and how it has been handled with their children.
9. Listen, and respond with care, because children often refer to their scary experience in their talk or play for many months after the accident. To do so is normal and healthy.
10. Have parents and teachers reassure children: It was an accident, no one was seriously hurt, and we are all OK.
11. Set up a telephone network for the kids who were on the bus to call each other and share their feelings.
12. Set up a time during school where the kids who were in the accident can continue to share their feelings.

Human beings and especially children can survive very frightening experiences.

Resources

Alexander and the Terrible Horrible No Good Very Bad Day by Judith Viorst (2009)
Don't Fall Apart on Saturdays! The Children's Divorce-Survival Book by Adolph Moser (2000)
The Moving Book: A Kids' Survival Guide by Gabriel Davis (2008)
Moving With Kids by Lori Collins Burga (2007)
Two Homes by Kady Macdonald Denton (2003)
When I Miss You by Cornelia Maude Spelman (2004)

Loss of the Future and Adult Protection

- Loss of role models
- Fears of school as a dangerous place
- Lack of motivation for schoolwork
- Choice of violence as a way of solving problems

Jason was an 11th-grade student in an inner-city school system. His dad was murdered outside of his home, his mom was addicted to crack cocaine, and his brother had died of suicide. Jason was often sent to the office for using bad language, cutting school, and fighting. His English teacher sent him once again to the vice principal, Mr. Holston, because he refused to complete his assignment "What I want to do when I grow up."

Mr. Holston began questioning Jason:

"Why do you refuse to do your homework?" he
    asked.
"Why should I?" Jason shouted, banging his fist on
    the table. "I won't live to be in twelfth grade!"
Mr. Holston asked him to write his theme about that.

Jason is one of millions of children that live
every day surrounded by violence and abuse with no
outlet to share it or voice to speak of it. Too many of
today's traumatized, grief-stricken children see no
future and are unable to visualize themselves growing into adulthood. Seeing no future, it is unlikely
that the Jasons of today's world will be motivated to
do assignments for tomorrow when tomorrow may
not exist for them.

Young people who are not directly exposed to these issues may be inundated with
them through media sounds and images. The news coverage and sometimes sensational-
ism involving school shootings and terrorism can create worry and fear among children
anywhere watching TV and bombarded with constant information about traumatic events.
This can heighten the realization for kids that traumatic events can happen, and perhaps
escalate unwarranted fears of lack of protection and future safety.

What We Can Do for the Child

1. Encourage police, coaches, teachers, big brothers, big sisters, and senior citizens to
    volunteer as mentors and role models for the grieving child.
2. Create awareness of neighborhood watch programs and buddy systems to provide
    protection for children before and after school.
3. Maintain programs, assemblies, and school policies on bullying, cyberbullying, vio-
    lence, and weapons in school.
4. Parents and school personnel can create a time each day for children to voice their
    fears and concerns about the violence and trauma in their lives or their vicarious
    fears through media input.
5. Provide class meetings that allow kids to safely discuss fears.
6. Use life issues social studies and guidance curricula in the school system that are
    geared to working with children who have experienced violence, abuse, death, and
    other trauma.

Resources

Is There Really a Human Race? by Jamie Lee
    Curtis (2006)
Courage by Bernard Waber (2002)
*Teaspoon of Courage for Kids: A Little Book of
    Encouragement for Whenever You Need It*
    by Bradley Trevor Greive (2007)
*Don't Be a Menace on Sundays! The Children's
    Anti-Violence Book* by Adoph Moser
    (2001)
The Juice Box Bully by Bob Sornson and Ma-
    ria Dismondy (2011)
Confessions of a Former Bully by Trudy
    Ludwig (2010)
Nice and Mean by Jessica Leader (2011)

2/ MYTHS OF GRIEF

You'll get over it.
It's time to move on.
Crying won't help.
Be strong for your mom.
You are too young to understand.

A person is a person
No matter how small.

—Dr. Seuss, *Horton Hears a Who*

MYTHS ABOUT LOSS AND GRIEF

We ask ourselves, "What's the matter with kids today?" and we might answer, "They are being raised on the same myths of grief on which we were raised when we were young." This chapter discusses the following myths.

- Grief and mourning are the same experience.
- Adults can instantly give explanations to children about death and spirituality.
- The experience of grief and mourning has orderly stages.
- The grief of adults does not impact on the bereaved child.
- Adults should avoid topics that cause a child to cry.
- An active, playing child is not a grieving child.
- Infants and toddlers are too young to grieve.
- Parents and professionals are always prepared and qualified to explain loss and grief.
- There is closure to grief.
- Children need to get over their grief and move on.
- Children are better off not attending funerals.

Myth: Grief, Bereavement, and Mourning Are the Same

Grief . . . is an emotional response.

It is a normal, internalized reaction to the loss of a person, thing, or idea. It is our emotional response to loss.

Bereavement . . . is a state of being.

It is the state of having lost something, whether it be significant others, significant things, or our sense of self. This state can range from the death of a parent to the destruction of a home, to the loss of dreams, dignity, and self-respect.

Mourning . . . is what we do.

It is taking the internal experience of grief and expressing it outside of ourselves. It is the cultural expression of grief, as seen in traditional or creative rituals. Traditional rituals refer to ones that are sanctioned culturally, such as funerals. Creative rituals can be writing a letter to the deceased and then destroying it. Rituals are the behaviors we use to do grief work.

The story of Nicholas illustrates how a child's grief and mourning greatly affects his life. His mourning became a burden to the school. He began acting out in school, fighting with friends, using bad language, writing graffiti wherever he could, failing schoolwork, and complaining of stomachaches. The private school that Nicholas attended had little tolerance for his behaviors and asked him to leave, even though he had been there from kindergarten until eighth grade.

Often bereaved children mourn through actions rather than words. Nicholas's parents were getting divorced, and his school abandoning him further compounded the situation. Nicholas clearly exhibited behaviors to watch for in grieving children. These include anxiety, hostility toward others, and bodily distress. Had the educators in his school looked at his behaviors in a different way, the system may not have failed. Nicholas was an unrecognized mourner. He was grieving but was not given the appropriate conditions to mourn in order to work through his feelings of loss.

In yesterday's world, Nicholas's acting out in school might have been the worst that could have happened. In today's world, another Nicholas may have just as easily brought a loaded pistol and shot a teacher or classmate, or turned to escapism through drugs or even suicide.

Myth: Adults Can Instantly Give Explanations to Children About Death and Spirituality

It's okay to admit we don't know all the answers—and not feel guilty that we can't always define God or heaven or what happens after death. Life and death can be mysteries. A good example to illustrate to young children that sometimes things are part of a larger picture than we can see and understand is the book *Look Again* by Tana Hoban (1971). Using smaller parts of a larger photograph, children see there is a much larger picture than they possibly could have imagined.

Myth: Grief and Mourning Have Orderly Stages

The concept of stages of grief often is misunderstood to be progressive and linear for everyone in every way. Grief work is unique to every adult and every child. Each person approaches it in his or her own way and at his or her own pace.

No Two People Are Alike, and Neither Is Their Grief

An attitude that allows the child to be the true expert on his or her feelings is one that says "Teach me about your grief and I will be with you." We must remind ourselves not to prescribe how children should grieve and mourn, but allow them to teach us where they are in their process.

Two sons had very different reactions to their mother's cancer, chemotherapy, and loss of hair. The oldest, a preadolescent, was very embarrassed and refused to share his feelings. When he first saw his mom in a wig, he threw a towel over his head and ran out of the room. The youngest boy, a 6-year-old, talked about his feelings a great deal. Yet he still had many nightmares. His teacher later shared that he had been writing a story in an ongoing journal every month about his babysitter who was very sick and eventually died. Two siblings raised by the same parents with very unique styles of grieving.

Having a developmental understanding of children at different ages and a sense of the distinctive personality of each child opens a window to working with the hearts and minds of children.

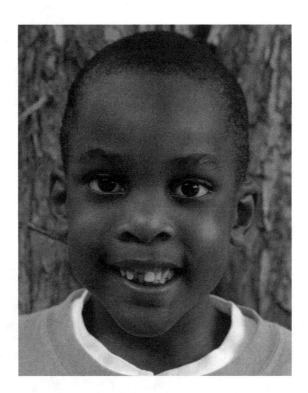

Myth: The Grief of Adults Does Not Impact the Bereaved Child

By allowing ourselves to mourn, we help the bereaved child. Parents, teachers, and adult friends are significant models for children. How adults mourn sets an example for surrounding children. If adults deny their grief, the children probably will do the same. If adults allow themselves to be sad or angry, it gives permission for the children to be sad or angry.

Often adults try to hide their feelings from kids, falsely believing it is in the children's best interest. The guilt, shame, or confusion that a child may feel after someone he or she loves has left (as in divorce or moving) or died (due to an accident or illness) can be acknowledged and released if adult modeling allows for expression of feelings.

Another aspect of adult mourning affecting children is the absence of the grieving parent, emotionally and perhaps physically as well. This is a secondary loss for kids. Many times, the caregiving parent is so distraught that he or she, too, is missing for the child for a period of time. It's a helpful idea to provide children with a caring adult who can be a support system until the grieving parent has worked out some of his or her pain.

Rosie's dad died when she was 5. It was a sudden and fatal accident at the workplace. Rosie's mother explained she was so tired from grieving she could barely get out of bed for the first year. When Rosie began first grade at age 6, she could not tie her shoelaces. This was not due to a developmental lag but a mother's grief process.

Mom explained, "I did not have the energy to teach Rosie how to tie her shoelaces. I just did it for her myself. I was so tired and overwhelmed with *my own* grief. I could barely take care of myself."

Myth: Adults Should Avoid Topics That Cause a Child to Cry

Jesse, a first-grader, began acting out in school. She became very demanding of her friends, requiring extreme loyalty from them, needing to be the boss at all times, and ultimately rejecting their friendship. Her teacher talked to her several times about friendship and what she needed to do to be a good friend.

After many conversations, Jesse burst into tears. "Well, all my friends have left me," she sobbed. Crying was Jesse's way of relieving her tension and communicating her hurt and need to be comforted. It turned out that her four best friends had left her school at the end of kindergarten. She was mourning their loss and working out her feelings of abandonment.

Her teacher did many good things to help Jesse heal. She trusted her instincts and initiated a discussion with Jesse, even though Jesse had not brought it up herself. The teacher saw Jesse's behaviors as a possible sign of grief rather than a threat. She validated Jesse's loss and encouraged classmates to be a new support system for her.

Jesse's teacher led Jesse to realize she had a lot of good memories with her old friends and still could be with them even though they weren't at school. Jesse called her old friends and reestablished their relationships. She began to be less demanding of school friends. Jesse's teacher did not continue the myth that children need to be brave. Rather, she consciously did not avoid the painful topic that caused Jesse to cry and helped Jesse get in touch with and ultimately overcome her pain.

Jimmy was another student in the class. He was sad, too. His dad was in intensive care after a heart attack, and his mom was extremely upset. His older cousin warned him "to be strong, be brave, and be the man of the house for now. Your dad wouldn't want you to cry. He would want you to take care of your mom." Jimmy burst into tears in school and told the story. He needed to cry and release his sadness and worry.

Unfortunately, many adults associate tears of grief with personal weakness, especially for males. Crying children can make adults feel helpless. Out of a wish to protect children (and themselves), well-meaning adults often directly inhibit tears.

We, as caring adults, can acknowledge the sadness a child feels if he or she fails a test, repeats a school year, or strikes out in a baseball game. We, as caring adults, can also acknowledge the sadness if the class is doing a Father's Day project and a child's dad is in the hospital, out of work, in jail, or has died. In this way, the child learns it is okay to feel his or her feelings.

Myth: An Active, Playing Child Is Not a Grieving Child

Don't expect children to mourn in the same way you do. Some may cry or say they are sad, some may appear not to be feeling anything, and others may show anger and hurt. All of these reactions need to be accepted. Remember, a child can often work out feelings best through play. What may appear to be a frivolous play activity to adults may well be an important part of the child's mourning process.

Allison's best friend had moved away. She was missing her. A sensitive teacher gave Allison a toy telephone and suggested she call her friend. Allison began speaking to her on the play phone at school, telling her how much she missed her and asking when she was coming back. She was given an opportunity through play to work out her feelings.

Myth: Infants and Toddlers Are Too Young to Grieve

If a child is old enough to love, he or she is old enough to grieve.

—Adapted from Wolfelt (1983)

One father told his boss at work, after the death of his oldest son, that he wouldn't explain anything to his two-year-old daughter because she was too young to understand. Certainly toddlers and infants are capable of giving and receiving love, yet we often hear they are too young to understand. Any child capable of loving is capable of grieving, whether they intellectually understand the loss or not.

Seth was dying. Diagnosed with a terminal pulmonary disease, he and his young wife bravely and determinedly decided to have a child and to live to see him or her be born. With love and conviction, they accomplished their goals. Their daughter, Olivia, was the joy of each of the precious days Seth had left on earth. When Olivia was two and a half months old, her dad died. A light went out in Olivia's new life.

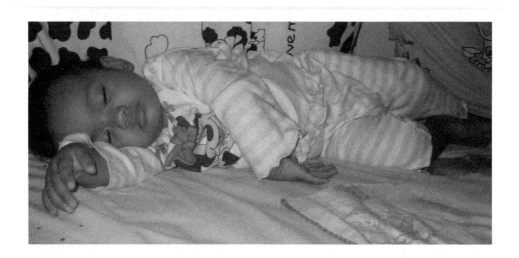

Fourteen months later Olivia and her mother were taking a walk and spotted a man that remarkably resembled her dad. Racing to the stranger, Olivia wrapped her arms and legs around the man, clung to him with every ounce of her little being, and refused to let go. Mom had to drag her away sobbing.

At 16 months, Olivia was mourning the death and the memories of her dad. Becoming noticeably sad after this experience, she began having difficulty sleeping and eating.

Mother decided to be open with her in talking and sharing feelings. Intuitively, she knew a toddler was old enough to mourn, for she had certainly been old enough to love. She invited Olivia to help create a photo album of Dad and times shared together.

This album became one of the great treasures of Olivia's childhood. She carried her book of photos constantly, literally holding her dad's love in her arms. A tangible bridge of memories had been created between Olivia and her father—a bridge of memories to last a lifetime.

Myth: Parents and Professionals Are Always Prepared and Qualified to Explain Loss and Grief

No One Has All the Answers, Not Even Parents, Teachers, Counselors, or Clergy

When our baby Jennifer died, my husband and I knew no guidelines to help us through such a tragedy. We turned to a clergyman for help. "Do we have a funeral?" "How do we bury her?" "What can we do for her?" "Don't worry," he said. "In this religion, stillborn babies are not considered a life." We had just seen her, held her, gone through two days of labor with her, and nine months of pregnancy. We knew she was a life. We sought counsel within ourselves and found the right answers for us.

When attending a meeting with professionals on ways to dialogue with children about death, a counselor remarked she was worried about a mother who insisted she had four children although one had died. The counselor wondered how she could help the mother to see she was going too far by insisting she had four children. From the counselor's point of view, the mother clearly had three children. The counselor felt that this mother's child was dead and that she needed to cope with reality.

But whose reality was it—the mother's or the counselor's? Clearly this mother, after experiencing the death of her child, felt, "Once a mom, always a mom through all time and space."

Creating language that grieving children and adults can use is helpful, especially if it allows for choices. "I have three living children and one who died" is an example. A friend and colleague gave me a precious gift by referring to Jennifer as "your daughter." It was the first time that anyone had verbally acknowledged that I indeed had had a real daughter who died. Children need this validation, too, if a sibling dies—whether it is a preschooler, toddler, stillborn, or miscarriage. By referring to this death as "your sister" or "your brother" or by name, the child can more easily become in touch with all the powerful feelings that those words evoke.

Myth: There Is Closure to Grief

Anderson Cooper interviewed his mother, Gloria Vanderbilt, on the death of his brother by suicide (Anderson Cooper Live, 2011). A discussion on closure pertaining to grief followed. Cooper asked if Vanderbilt felt a sense of closure surrounding her son's death. "Closure is a TV word." She explained. Cooper agreed.

While lecturing at a university in Taiwan, a participant posed a universal question, "When does the grieving period end?" Unable to give a specific timetable, I responded that the acute feelings and thoughts around grief might subside after the first or second year. Sometimes it might be shorter, and sometimes much longer.

Often waves of grief can suddenly inundate a bereaved child years after a mom has died. It might occur at graduation, a baseball game, or a dance recital. It may extend to a marriage, a first child, and even a first grandchild. Unexpected events can trigger a long, silent emotion.

As long as we love a person, we miss that person.
It is a part of life.

Myth: Children Need to Get Over Their Grief and Move On

Children and adults are often told that they "should be over it by now—it's been almost a year." Adults who believe this myth deny children the patience to live with and to work with their grief.

Danny's teacher responded to the death of Danny's mom by telling him, "You have to forget about this and go on." Danny said he felt like killing his teacher! The last thing Danny wanted to do was to forget his mom. He needs to remember her in a positive way to take her with him on his journey through life.

Mike woke up one morning and decided to bring in a picture of his pet cat, Iris, for show-and-tell. She had died a year ago. When he came home from school that day, he asked if he could see where she was buried. This was a healthy request, moving him toward healing. Both examples illustrate that coping with loss is ongoing.

Adults and kids often equate getting over grief with forgetting the person, without realizing that their pain is what connects them to their loss. We need to find alternative ways that connect grieving children to the lost person or event, diffuse the pain, and transform it into a positive experience.

Myth: Children Are Better Off Not Attending Funerals

Not allowing children to attend funerals creates an environment of denial that does not allow them to actively participate in the grieving process. The funeral provides a structure for the child to see how people comfort each other openly, mourn a loved one, and honor his or her life. Children learn the ways we say good-bye to the remains of the person who died and how we show respect for the deceased.

Chad's father, Ray, drowned at age 31. Chad was 7. Chad's grandfather told Chad of his dad's death, and they cried together for a very long time. Ray's body was found after several days of being in the water, necessitating a closed-casket funeral. The family, including Chad, worked together to select meaningful items to be placed in the casket. A picture of Chad, a letter from Ray's mom, and some other items were chosen. Chad was made an important part of the funeral process, and so the funeral process became an important part of him.

During the ceremony, Chad leaned over to his grandfather and whispered, "Granddad, I'm using my imagination right now and pretending I'm reaching inside the coffin and hugging Dad." He needed to say good-bye and created a way to do so.

Children assuredly follow their hearts to find their own unique ways to work through grief. Being present at the funeral, placing personal mementos in the coffin, and participating in the ceremony are very concrete ways children can contribute to the process of saying good-bye.

My son Jonathan, at age 6, attended his first funeral when my sister's mother-in-law died. Jonathan said he wanted to go to the funeral, and he did. When the family was viewing the body, he wanted to look, too. A slight panic ran through me as all of my training and knowledge said yes while I heard my mother's voice say, "no, go sit in the other room, Jonathan." The funeral director walked over to me and quietly said, "I didn't want to interfere, but I feel kids imagine far more and far worse if they aren't allowed to look at the body." Gratefully, I agreed. Jonathan walked over, viewed the body, and was quite satisfied. Surprisingly, my mother easily adjusted to the change of circumstance. Relaying the story to a friend, I was told that her son had chosen not to see the body of his grandmother and continually asks questions like, "Was Grandma's body bleeding or bruised or broken?"

We often shield children from the funeral experience because we think it is too difficult. It is difficult, but by being allowed to choose to participate in a funeral of someone to whom he was not deeply emotionally attached, Jonathan was freer to incorporate the event and become prepared for future funerals of more closely connected loved ones that could be much more difficult. Jonathan came to see death as an open part of life.

These myths are barriers to the grieving process. They disguise our own vulnerability and feelings of helplessness and perpetuate a world of denial.

We need a new way of looking at the universal issue of grief. We need to educate everyone in our global community to distinguish between fact and fiction so that our children can, too.

CHAPTER 3

**FOUR
PSYCHOLOGICAL
TASKS OF GRIEF
WORK**

Understanding
Going on Grieving
Commemorating

There are two choices when a loved one dies—to live in grief, remorse, and guilt covered thinly by a facade; or to face those feelings, work them through, and emerge with an acceptance of death and a commitment to living.

Edith Mize, quoted in Kübler-Ross (1975)

CHILDREN WORK THROUGH GRIEF: FOUR PSYCHOLOGICAL TASKS

Sandra Fox, past director of the Boston Good Grief program, cites four tasks children need to work through in order to grow. These tasks occur at every age level and for every type of loss. The four tasks are:

Understanding
Grieving
Commemorating
Going on

Understanding

Understanding is the first psychological task. Children need to make sense out of death. We define death as when the body stops working. Then each family can explain death in its own way. Fox suggests these possibilities: "In our family, we believe that when a person's body stops working, he dies, but we believe his soul or spirit lives on in heaven with God" or some people "believe he lives on in some form of plant or animal life."

We can say to children that usually people die when they are very, very old, or very, very sick. We can explain unexpected deaths by reminding young people, "Most people live to be very, very old, but once in a while an accident, illness, or injury is so bad that doctors and hospitals can't help, and a person's body stops working."

We need to remember that children's understanding of death changes as they develop. Kids perceive death differently at various childhood stages, and that their perceptions are a predictable influence of grief.

Understanding Affected by Magical Thinking

Magical thinking is a predictable interference with children's grief. Girls and boys feel responsible for what happens in the world around them. When a 6-year-old screams at her brother, "I hate you! I wish you were dead!" and these become the last words spoken to her brother who died in a drowning accident the following morning, magical thinking can assuredly make her feel she caused this death. She may live with overwhelming guilt for many years to come.

Five-year-old Kate announced, "I killed my mother." Her mother died of cancer. Yet Kate had always heard that "junk food could kill you," and she had given her mom soda the day before she died. The family did not talk to Kate about cancer, believing it was too terrible to talk about. As an adult, Kate still believes at some deep emotional level that she is in some way responsible for killing her mother.

The movie *Home Alone* is a wonderful fantasy illustrating how powerful children's magical thinking is. The boy in the film is angry and frustrated with his family and goes to bed wishing they would all disappear. He wakes up in an empty house and is sure he orchestrated their disappearance, even though they really had forgotten to take him on the family vacation.

Understanding Blocked by Common Clichés

Common clichés can hurt the grief process. Mandy's grandfather died. Her mom thinks, "I'll just tell her he's gone to heaven and that will take care of it." Mandy wonders, "If Grandpa is in heaven, why did they put him in the ground?" or "Can I go to heaven, too?"

We need to give honest answers to questions about death, using simple and direct language. Facts need to be presented accurately. Children will find them out in time. Telling children the truth will create an atmosphere of trust and confidence. Remember, children often take and believe what we say literally.

"ALBERT LOST HIS MOTHER."

"He did? Where? How? Did he look for her? How could he lose her? She was so tall!" replied a panicked little voice.

Children may fear the literal loss of their parents.

It is better to say, "Albert's mother died. He will miss her a lot."

"DAD WENT ON A LONG TRIP."

"Why didn't he say good-bye? Where did he go?" his little daughter asked.

Children may become afraid of anyone or themselves going on a trip.

They may fear their parents leaving for work or generalize to just feeling abandoned. It is better to say, "Dad died in a drowning accident. We all feel so sad, but we will get through it together."

"IT IS GOD'S WILL" (OR "GOD TOOK HIM BECAUSE HE IS SO GOOD" OR "HE'S IN HEAVEN WITH THE ANGELS.")

"Why doesn't God take me? I'm good, or I'll have to be bad so that God won't take me," thinks a little boy.

A child may develop a fear of God or a fear of love.

It is better to say, "Grandpa died last night. We will think about him a lot. We can remember all of the wonderful things we did with him."

"GRANDMA IS WATCHING YOU IN HEAVEN (SO YOU BETTER BE GOOD)."

The child thinks, "What happens if I'm bad?"

Children can have paranoid feelings, become afraid of making mistakes, and feel guilty and stuck in any "bad" behaviors.

It is better to say, "Grandma was very, very old and died. Her love for us will live on in our memories."

"MAX (THE CAT) WENT TO SLEEP LAST NIGHT (HE'S IN KITTY HEAVEN)."

"Will I die when I go to sleep tonight?" the child wonders.

Children may develop a fear of sleep or darkness that could result in sleeplessness and nightmares.

It is better to say, "MAX WAS VERY, VERY SICK AND THE SICK-NESS MADE HIM DIE. NO ONE REALLY KNOWS IF HE WENT TO HEAVEN. SOME PEOPLE BELIEVE THAT HE DOES, AND SOME PEOPLE DON'T."

Understanding Children's Developmental Stages

A child's understanding of death changes as he or she develops. Knowing how children perceive death at different developmental stages of childhood is important so that we can then work with predictable and appropriate responses.

Approximate Ages 0 to 2

Piaget's Stage of Development: Sensorimotor

Child's Concept of Death: "All Gone"

- "Out of sight, out of mind" appears to be the infant's perception. If the young infant cannot see something, it does not exist.
- Peek-a-boo or hide-and-seek are games that after six months help develop the concept that things and people exist even if we can't see them.

Approximate Ages 2 to 7

Piaget's Stage of Development: Preoperational

Child's Concept of Death: Magical, Egocentric, and Causal

- Child thinks death is temporary and partial.
- Preschoolers see death as reversible, a journey from which there is a return.
- A child conceives the possibility of reviving the dead person by giving hot food or keeping the body warm.
- The child believes some functions continue, like feeling and thinking.
- Children may see dead people as living in a box underground, connected to other boxes by tunnels, or on a cloud in a place called heaven. Timothy, a 6-year-old, explained, "Heaven is a place way deep underground, deeper than anyone has ever gone, deeper than bulldozers go. Your body disintegrates and goes there."
- The child thinks his or her own thoughts or actions could cause death. The child feels guilt and fear of retribution for perceived bad things done or angry thoughts. A child tells mom she hates her and wishes she were dead. Mom is killed in an accident the next day. The child's magical thinking convinces the child that she caused her mother's death.
- The child thinks death is like sleep. This creates a fear of sleep and darkness, and the child needs to be reassured.
- The child gives inaccurate estimates of an average life span. The child thinks that "people live for 150 years."

Approximate Ages 7 to 12

Piaget's Stage of Development: Concrete Operations

Child's Concept of Death: Curious and Realistic

- Children are curious and inquisitive about birth, death, and sex differences. They are very interested in details of death.
- Children begin to internalize the universality and permanence of death. They can conceptualize that all body functions stop.
- Dead people can't breathe, move, hear, or see. Children are aware of a death vocabulary. They can express logical thoughts and fears about death.
- Children can comprehend thoughts of a belief in an afterlife.
- Children can accurately estimate how long people live.
- Children think of death's occurrence in specific observable concrete terms. They may ask, "What are the reasons people die?" (war, poison, floods, car accidents, plane crashes, murders, etc.).
- Children still basically believe that the very old, the severely handicapped, and the extremely awkward people are the ones who die.

Approximate Ages 13 and Older

Piaget's Stage of Development: Formal Operations, Implications, and logic

Adolescent's Concept of Death: Self-Absorbed

- Adolescents understand mortality and death as a natural process.
- They often have a difficult time with death because they are absorbed with shaping their own lives. Death seems remote and something they can't control.
- The denial of their own death is strong. They usually feel death is caused by old age or serious illness.
- Adolescents are more comfortable talking about death with peers than with adults.

Julie and Lila are two young girls who chose to use writing as a way to work out their feelings. Julie, a 5-year-old, had a cousin Mary who had died. Julie kept dictating letters to her cousin and asking her mother to mail them. She didn't understand that death was not reversible.

Ten-year-old Lila, mourning her Uncle Bryan's death, had a different issue. Rather that writing to Bryan, she wrote about Bryan in private poetry she kept hidden in her room. She understood only too well how final death was but felt ashamed to share it.

At age 5, Julie had no problem being open about her feelings, but she didn't really understand the nature of death. By age 10, Lila did understand what death was about, but she was uncomfortable being open about her feelings.

Uncle Bryan Is a Flower Blooming

by Lila Feikin

When he comes light-jogging
into my arms . . . he delights me.
Like a child getting his own pet,
And I still love him.
He always was playing sports
And he puts a smile on my face.

When he comes light walking
into my heart
He opens his arms to me
Like vines wrapping around a tree
. . . and I love him.

Even though he is gone
Uncle Bryan is a flower
Blooming
. . . that fills me with joy.

Grieving

Grieving is the second psychological task for bereaved children and adolescents. Anger as well as death must be dealt with, and many times anger is less acceptable to parents, schools, and communities. Children's grief is an ongoing process, often continuing through adolescence.

"When someone you love dies, you have a feeling of numbness; a yearning; and a protest. You have lost part of yourself; you feel disorganized; and you do much crying. You're restless, and you may feel guilty.

Perhaps you could have helped the one who died but you did not know how. You are angry because the person died, and you are angry at the world. You feel so alone, and loneliness is one of the biggest problems of grief."

—Edith Mize, quoted in Kübler-Ross (1975)

Phases of Grief

These are not rigid stages but interchangeable and continuous processes.

Phases of grief can resurface at any time. A number of grief educators have suggested that grief can be seen as occurring in four phases. They are:

Shock and disbelief
Searching and yearning
Disorganization and despair
Rebuilding and healing

—Eberling and Eberling (1991)

We can see how these phases change through Bobby's story. Bobby's brother died when he was 8 years old. His *shock and disbelief* began. He was very confused. He couldn't understand how his brother could be in the hospital, in the ground, in the funeral home, in heaven, and living in his memory all within the same week. He then began to *search* for meaning in a world that made no sense. Years later, at age 12, he began acting out at middle school, concerning his teachers and parents. He had been looking back on his brother's death with *despair*, believing his parents had let his brother die and would probably let Bobby die, too.

A new phase of grief work began—*rebuilding and healing*. Bobby was reassured that everything had been done for his brother and would be done for Bobby, if needed. He discovered he had done much for his brother by holding him and sharing toys. Bobby's giving had really made a difference that no one could take away.

Bobby had learned to feel pain, be out of control, and gain mastery over his feelings. He began using a punching bag to work out some of his anger and choosing times to be alone when he was frustrated. Bobby's family had communicated clearly when his brother died, yet still misconceptions arose at a different stage of grief.

We Cannot Expect to Explain the Loss Instantly, and a Child Cannot Learn It Instantly

The grieving process is ongoing and ever changing. As caring adults, we need to create an understanding of the grieving child for parents, teachers, counselors, and other school personnel.

Symptoms of Normal Grief

Behavior

sleeplessness	loss of appetite	poor grades
crying	nightmares	dreams of deceased
sighing	listlessness	absentmindedness
clinging	overactiveness	social withdrawal
verbal attacks	fighting	extreme quiet
bed-wetting	excessive touching	excessive hugging

Thought Patterns

inability to concentrate	difficulty making a decision
self-destructive thoughts	poor self-image
preoccupation	confusion disbelief

Feelings

anger	guilt	sadness	mood swings	rage
depression	hysteria	relief	helplessness	fear
intense feelings	loneliness	anxiety	feeling unreal	

Physical Symptoms

headaches	fatigue	shortness of breath
dry mouth	dizziness	pounding heart
hot or cold flashes	heaviness of body	sensitive skin
increased illness	empty feeling in body	tightness in chest
muscle weakness	tightness in throat	stomachaches

Common feelings, thoughts, and behaviors of the grieving child:

- Child *retells events* of the deceased's death and funeral.
- Child *dreams* of the deceased.
- Child *idolizes or imitates behaviors* of the deceased.
- Child *feels the deceased is with him or her* in some way.
- Child *speaks of his or her loved one in the present.*
- Child *rejects old friends and seeks new friends* with a similar loss.
- Child *wants to call home* during the school day.
- Child *can't concentrate* on homework or class work.
- Child *bursts into tears* in the middle of class.
- Child *seeks medical information* on the death of the deceased.
- Child *worries excessively* about his own health.
- Child sometimes *appears to be unfeeling* about loss.
- Child *becomes the class clown* to get attention.
- Child is *overly concerned* with caretaking needs.

Commemorating

The third task of grief is *commemoration*. Children need to establish ways to remember the person or animal that died or the object that was lost or destroyed. *Involve* kids in formal and informal ways to commemorate. Their creative ideas are an essential part of this process.

Formal Commemoration

- Schools, camps, and community groups can arrange memorial services, commemorative plaques, or tributes in a yearbook.
- Scholarship funds, donations to a particular charity, or a memorial garden can be established.

Informal Commemoration

- Children can bring seeds to school to plant flowers honoring a principal, teacher, or student who died.
- Children can choose a book to honor a child who was killed in an auto accident and donate the book to the library.
- Children can create a school play and use the proceeds to begin a memorial fund in memory of a beloved teacher or classmate.
- A class can decide what to do with the things inside the locker or desk of a student who has died. They can make a booklet of memories for his or her parents.
- Children can make a memory video of the person who died.
- Children can bake cookies to bring to a grieving friend.
- Children can blow bubbles or send off a balloon to remember a loved one.

Sandra Fox, author of *Good Grief: Helping Groups of Children When a Friend Dies* (1988), has emphasized that "the life of every person who dies needs to be commemorated if we are to teach young people that all lives have value." Many schools are afraid to acknowledge a suicide, thinking denial may prevent further occurrences. By remembering a "tragically too short life" rather than the way someone died, the school can create a teachable moment to talk to young people about how to recognize and work through feelings of pain and hopelessness.

Going On

The last psychological task for children experiencing significant loss is one that emphasizes *going on*, not *moving on*. It underscores a time when young people can again join in fun activities, revisit places previously painful, and bring their memories into life rather than avoid them. Children can begin to risk loving again and enjoying life. This does not mean forgetting the person who's gone or the object (i.e., a toy or a pet). Going on means developing a readiness to participate. Sometimes it signals a release of some of the deep guilt that is often felt.

Henry, whose best friend died in a car accident, tells his mom, "I want to go out with my friends again. We were talking about how much fun we had with Bill when he was alive, and we decided to go swimming where we used to go with him." The boys spent the day at the pool, reminiscing about old times with their friend.

Hunter loved his father very much. For the first 7 years of his life, Hunter's dad was his mentor and buddy. Their favorite pastime was to go fishing at the pier at the end of their house. They would sit for hours, talking, laughing, or waiting silently for a fish to bite. When Hunter turned 8, his father died.

Hunter said he didn't want to fish anymore. He put his fishing pole in the very back of his closet. For a year and a half Hunter never went fishing. He never looked at his fishing pole. Then one morning he woke up very early. He rushed to the closet, took out his fishing pole, and put on his fishing boots. Hunter ran in to wake up his mom. "Wake up, wake up!" he shouted. "I'm going fishing today, and I am going to catch a fish for Dad!"

Perhaps during that year and a half Hunter was able to transform his sadness and grief into a way he could live life again and bring his father into his world with him. Going fishing for his dad was a wonderful way to remember him.

Understanding, grieving, commemorating, and *going on* are important parts of the child's process of loss, change, and growth. Recognizing these tasks can create a richer picture of where the child is in his or her process. Caring adults can see if a child is stuck in one particular task and help him or her to work with and through the grief.

THE STORY OF STAR

Star was Blake's pet dog. Star was hit by a car and was severely injured with no chance of recovery, while Blake, a second-grader, was at school. He came home, and his dog was gone. He needed to understand why. His mom told him, "Star was put to sleep." Blake imagined that Star would wake up soon and would be back. Mom said, "No, he's gone forever." Blake began to worry that when he goes to sleep, he, too, might not come back.

There's a better way to help Blake grieve. It's OK for him to see his mom crying because she saw Star's favorite ball. She loved him, too. Kids need explanations of what is happening so that the missing pieces won't be filled in with their own unrealistic imagination and interpretation.

Give young children the simplest information possible while still sharing needed facts for their growth. "How did Star die? What did the vet do? Who took him to the vet? Did he cry? Where was he buried? Can I see?" All of these questions need to be answered. Finally, we need to say, "Star won't be back. We won't see him again. He died. His body has stopped working."

"It is very sad and we will miss him very much. We can give Star a funeral and say good-bye to him."

Blake needs to work through the following various feelings associated with grieving:

Understand that the loss is real.
Feel the hurt.
Learn to live life without the loss object.
Transform the emotional energy of grief into life again.

Let Kids Know

"Star won't be in your daily life, but he will be in your memory."

Let Kids Talk

"I'm sad, angry, or frightened about what happened to Star. I feel so lonely without him."

Let Kids Participate

Blake can choose what to do with Star's toys, bowl, or collar. Ask Blake, "Where should we put Star's pictures? What kind of a ceremony would you like to have? Who would you like to invite?"

Let Kids Be Unique

Each child is different, and so is his or her grief. Blake wants to build a doghouse underneath Star's favorite tree. It's Blake's own way of remembering Star.

Blake can commemorate Star's death informally or with a real ceremony. As long as Blake is involved, if he wants to be, he will be able to work through his grief. In his way, Blake can affirm the value of the life that was Star's. Blake decided to invite his family, neighborhood friends, and two pet dogs in the neighborhood. He read poetry, played music, and planted flowers as a tribute. He put a picture of Star by his bed to help remember him.

Once Blake has understood, grieved, and commemorated his dog's death, he will be ready to "go on." This readiness involves knowing it's OK to start life again—to play with other dogs or even hope to get a new one. Going on is not the same thing as forgetting. Star will live in Blake's heart. It may hurt on Star's birthday or the day that he died, yet Blake's grief experiences with Star will strengthen his ability to cope with other losses that he will assuredly have to face as life goes on.

4

TECHNIQUES
FOR GRIEF
WORK

Identify feelings Memory boxes
Role-play Drama **Clay**
Journals Letters Art Music
Puppets Questions
Sand Table Memory books

Anything that's human is mentionable, and anything that is mentionable can be more manageable.

—Mr. Rogers, *Life's Journey According to Mr. Rogers*

IDENTIFY FEELINGS

When we can talk about our feelings, they become less overwhelming, less upsetting, and less scary. The people we trust with that important talk can help us know that we are not alone.

—Mr. Rogers, *Life's Journey According to Mr. Rogers*

Children under stress tend to cut themselves off from the "now," often becoming only half present. As caring adults, we can draw upon many techniques that will enable children to become more in touch with all aspects of themselves and to directly communicate with others by being fully and completely engaged.

Anger

"How could Daddy have died and left me all alone?"

Children often feel angry about the death or illness of a loved one. Losses such as divorce, moving, or the death of a pet or people certainly provoke anger. Often feeling they have no control over what has happened, kids may project their angry feelings onto the person or thing that's gone, doctors, teachers, parents, siblings, or God. Girls and boys learn at a young age not to express anger. They push it inward to get their needs met and to avoid being rejected or abandoned. Violet Oaklander, gestalt therapist and author of *Windows to Our Children* (1969), stressed, "Anger is an expression of self."

If a child holds back and holds in his anger, he gives his personal power away by projecting his real feelings onto another person or object. Sammy had been fighting on the playground a lot. His teacher asked him why. "All the kids are mean," Sammy replied. Sammy's underlying anger was a dad who had abandoned him. He kicked and hit the kids on the playground instead.

Adults can help children by acknowledging their angry feelings and guiding them to say, "I'm angry." Let them know it's OK to feel anger and own it as theirs. "It's OK that I'm angry."

Create anger awareness through dialogue.
What is anger?
How does your body feel?
What could make you angry?
How do you show anger?
What do you do when you're angry?

Children can then use new skills to incorporate their anger. One productive expression of anger is direct communication—talking to the person with whom you are angry and telling him or her why you are angry. Another way to express anger personally is by taking the angry energy when it can't be expressed directly and using it in good ways.

Kids can work with their anger in appropriate ways. They can vent angry energy by punching a pillow, building a project, using physical activity, role-playing, drawing, writing, or talking to a friend or adult.

Panic

"Mommy, are you going to die too?"

Young children may have a huge fear of abandonment if one parent dies or leaves the house. They are afraid that if one parent has gone, the other could go, too. They may cling to the remaining parent, refusing to play with friends or do other activities. Children need to rebuild trust. It takes time.

Ben explains to Mom, "I won't go to Grandma's. You could die while I'm away . . . like Dad did!"

Guilt

Mom frowns. Ben thinks, "I must have done something wrong to make her so angry. It's my fault. I've been such a bad kid lately!"

He didn't understand Mom had just heard bad news on the telephone. Children can't separate themselves from the experience. They take in the adult messages, "swallow it" and "stuff it," sometimes carrying these messages all of their lives. Many of us live with the belief system of a 4-year-old. We carry traumatic messages from early childhood, not only as if they were true then but as if they are still true today.

Denial

"I can't believe Grandpa died. He couldn't have died. He'll be back."

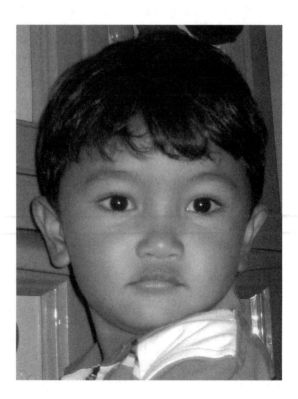

Death, illness, or other loss can come as a surprise, and children as well as adults are shocked. If these experiences are overwhelming, children may push them away as temporary relief from grief. Respect this as the child's way of saying what he or she can handle.

Withdrawal

"I won't go with the new gym teacher. I want to be alone."

Jason's mom's new boyfriend decided to stop being with Jason and his mom. Two years earlier, Jason's dad had left town. Afraid to be vulnerable again, Jason withdrew from any new men that entered his life. The new gym teacher at school is a man. Jason refuses to go with the teacher and is sent to the principal's office for disobedience. No one understands that previous abandonment may have recreated Jason's fear of being hurt. Children may withdraw from loved ones as a safeguard against them leaving, too. If kids have been traumatized too severely, they may be afraid to trust. Adults need to find creative ways to connect with children and build a relationship.

Stuffing the Feeling

Adults often urge children to stuff or deny their feelings because adults are uncomfortable with seeing those feelings in kids. *"What we resist persists!"* The more we promote denial of feelings, the greater the feelings become.

Identifying the Feeling

When children's feelings are identified and given a name, those feelings are then validated. Although adults sometimes fear naming feelings will create a larger problem, it actually reduces the hurt by bringing it out into the open.

Identify Feelings by Dialogue

Sidney's mom died of a sudden heart attack. She was 8 years old and missed her mom very much. The following three drawings allow us to understand Sidney's memories and thoughts. The first picture explains that Sidney would like people to know she has a good heart, and within the heart she writes her mom had a great heart, too!

In the second drawing, the important thing Sidney doesn't want people to know is that her mom died. In the third drawing, Sidney shares what scares her; the drawing illustrates a tombstone signifying her mother's death.

1. What is the most important thing you want people to know about you?
2. What is the most important thing you don't want people to know about you?

3. Write or draw about a scary thing that happened to you.

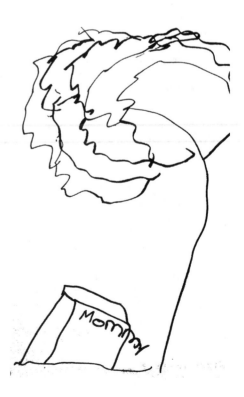

4.   What do you wish?

Amy's mother was murdered. She was distraught about the way her mother died. She had many questions to ask.

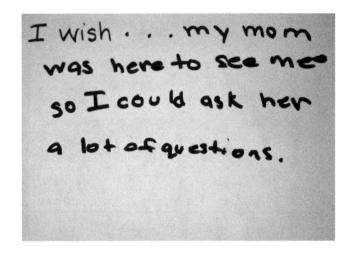

Identifying Feelings: Technology

Creative approaches to aid children's expression of grief have surfaced. Useful tools are found in tablet computers equipped with apps to engage children in the exploration of thoughts and feelings about loss with an engaging style.

Moody Monster Manor (McClam and Varga, 2011, p. 31) is an app for children ages 3 to 6 that allows kids to create a monster that portrays their immediate emotions and gives caring adults an indication of how to dialogue with the child.

The National Parenting Center gave the Moody Monster Manor app its Seal of Approval (2011, p.1) and explains, "This free app uses monsters, of all things, to teach children about the various emotions that they experience, recognizing them, and recognizing them in others. The app uses bright, happy colors and grabs children's attention quickly."

GRIEF TECHNIQUES: IDEAS FOR ALL AGES

Grief techniques create and stimulate open discussion and exploration of feeling.

Storytelling

Begin a story with *"I wish"* or *"If only"* or *"Once upon a time there was a ___ who died"* (got divorced, got sick, etc.). Each person in a small group continues the story.

Have children create this story: *Pretend you are an alien trying to find out what death is on earth.* (Possible words and phrases to use include final, stop breathing, mystery, universal, happens to everyone, out of control).

Creative Writing

Letters to loved ones	Poetry	Memory books
Feeling journals	Autobiographies	Diaries
Pictures and stuffed animals for projective story writing		Essays

Letters to Loved Ones

Letters to loved ones are a useful tool to work through held-in thoughts and feelings. Using specific headings such as "Dear Mom" or "Dear Uncle Tom" helps kids really project themselves into the letter. Be sure they understand the loved one is not really getting the letter, and give the child a choice in the decision of what they want to do with it—put it somewhere special, share it, and so on.

Lori Weiner, coordinator of the Pediatric HIV Psychosocial Support Program, American Cancer Institute, generously donated the following letter and drawing. Her work with children and AIDS has led her to feel that "the most exquisite, intense, intimate, and painful life experiences have been those where we have been given the opportunity to give to another human being and the strength to let go and say goodbye" (Weiner, 1991, p. 378).

Sara's dad died of AIDS. Her mom is infected with HIV and so is Sara. Sara has two siblings. She is 10 years old.

Dear Mom,

I miss you. Sometimes I get scared when you get sick. I worry that you will not come home. I want you to take care of yourself. If you ever got real sick will you tell us? I worry too much. I worry about you because you might get sick, not tell me and die. If you died I would really be upset and sad and cry a whole lot. I cried last night because I missed you so much. Sometimes I worry about me getting sick too, and what you would do if I got real sick. Like would you cry or would you come see me in the hospital? If you were in the hospital I want to come see you.

Sometimes I even think about heaven. It is quiet and peaceful there and I know that you and I will be there together one day.

Mommy I love you and know you love me.

Sara

Ashley's mom died at age 29 of a sudden heart attack. Ashley was 6 years old.

Dear Mom,
    I really miss you. I am doing fine in school. I think about you everyday. I am really sorry you had to go down there. I wouldn't like it there myself. I don't know yet what to give you for mother's day.
Love,
Ashley

Letter Writing

Letter writing is a wonderful grief resolution technique for people from 3 years old to 103. It allows the expression of feelings and the ability to have an ongoing, ever-present internal relationship with a loved one that can continue to grow and develop.

A well-known celebrity explained in an interview his secret for keeping his son alive in his heart. When his son died, he was inundated with grief. He began to write him letters and mail them. In 10 years, he has written hundreds of letters, and continues to mail them. *"It's the only thing that helps to keep him alive for me."*

Griffin's dad died of a sudden heart attack while he was playing baseball. Griffin was playing at another game and wasn't there when his dad died. Griffin explained, "If only I had been there, I could have saved his life." He missed his dad and wanted to write him a letter. He expressed his deep regret that he wished he could have saved him, and would spend all of his allowance if only that would bring him back.

Dear Dad,
I love you a lot! I wish you could come back and if I could see you and start all over again—I'd take you to the doctor and pay my life savings.
Love,
Griffin

Tara was a 9-year-old who had recently experienced the death of her grandmother and missed her very much. Tara worried excessively about the health of her parents, a very common sign of the grieving child. One day she came to a therapy session, very concerned and upset with her dad for not wearing his seat belt.

I suggested she write a letter to her dad telling him how she feels, and she even put a reply box on the letter for her dad to answer.

Eleven-year-old Roxanne was grieving the recent deaths of three of her grandparents. She also worried excessively about her dad's health, especially his smoking. The following is a letter she wrote to her dad explaining her feelings and concerns about his health.

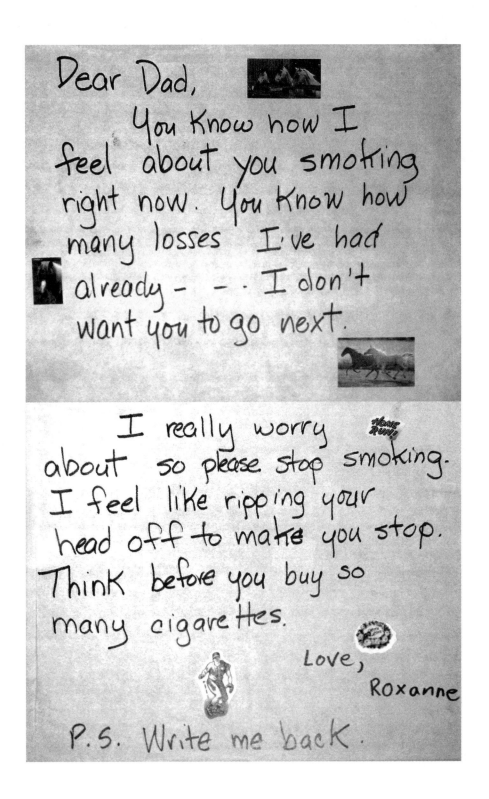

Dear Dad,

You know how I feel about you smoking right now. You know how many losses I've had already - - . I don't want you to go next.

I really worry about so please stop smoking. I feel like ripping your head off to make you stop. Think before you buy so many cigarettes.

Love,
Roxanne

P.S. Write me back.

Poetry

Kim is a 16-year-old who loves her grandfather very much. After living with his long and serious illness, she remained by his bed during his final hours. This poem is her way of expressing her deep and powerful emotions as she experienced being with him at the time of his death.

All I Could Say

by Kimberly Seff

I love you was all I could say.
He did not cry, He felt my pain.
On his bed where he lay,
I held his hand as he slipped away.
I love you was all I could say.
Have a great life.
Don't change a thing.
You're perfect in my eyes, deeply from within.
Are you all right?
Please tell me the truth.
Take care of Red for me.
She needs your love and frolicsome youth.
I want to go home now where I can be free.
From this wretched moroseness and fervent agony.

Don't miss me too much,
I will never really leave.
My soul and spirit will live on in your memory.
Looking down at him with a congenial smile,
Attempting to hide my tears and my sadness.

It was emphatic as to what the future foretold . . . and still
I love you was all I could say.
His spirit flutters around me like an elegant butterfly.
Soaring like a sparrow through the winter sky
Overlooking and protecting the life and love he left behind.

The missing and all the memories are running through my mind.
The tears flow like rivers in the darkness where no one can see.
How I sulk in my own misery.
A saint in my eyes due to gallantry ways, but I told him "I love you" and "Ditto" was all he could say.

—In loving memory of Bill Seff

Essays

Essays can be used as a grief resolution technique. Not only do essays allow students to express their feelings, but teachers and college personnel can know and understand how profoundly these loss and grief experiences affect the lives of these kids and shape who they are.

Eric, a 15-year-old, wrote the following article in his school newspaper after his mom's death. He hoped to reach out to other teens who had also experienced the death of someone close to them.

Help With Tough Times

by Eric Dreisen '95

As some of you might be aware, my mother passed away from cancer this school year. In experiencing this loss, there have been some positive things that have come from it. I have learned to take care of myself, my family and friends have become more important, and I have learned to help other people who are going through tough times.

The purpose of this article is to invite any student who is suffering from a loss or who is going through tough times, to meet on a regular basis as a group to talk about the problem. I will organize this group by having speakers come or get information to help with this long, hard process. Please contact me at ____ _____ .

Allison, a 17-year-old junior in high school, wrote the following essay. She was asked to write, as a college entrance requirement, about an important experience that greatly affected her life. She wrote the following warm and sensitive tribute to her dad, Alan, who died when she was 7.

Ten years ago, my father, Alan Lee Rothenberg, died. He was my best friend when I was seven years old. He became sick and had to go into the hospital. I asked my mom, "Is he going to die?" She said, "Of course not," and told me not to think like that again.

His death shocked me, and no one in my family expected something so tragic to happen. After all, my dad died at the early age of thirty-nine. When my mother told my brother and me, we were stunned. My brother, Andy, was only four and didn't understand but knew something bad had happened. I thought it was a nightmare. I couldn't comprehend it. The thought of his death scared me. I didn't even know what to say, but when I realized it was true I cried my eyes out. I remember my mom and I cried so much that we went through a whole box of Kleenex.

I kept my feelings inside me for a long time, but as I got older and began to understand "why" it became easier to express how I felt. I'm so grateful that we spent special moments together. Things like driving his car while I was sitting on his lap in an empty parking lot or trying on his shoes and acting like a clown. We'd always end up laughing and spending unforgettable times together.

I remember my dad told me to strive for the best, and if I really put my mind to it, my wishes would come true. Well, two birthdays had gone by and the only thing that I wished for on my candles was to have my dad come back. This was one of the only wishes that never came true and the most important.

I miss him a lot, but I know he's out there somewhere looking out for me and guiding me in the right direction. I still feel there is a part of him with me—after all, we both have the same middle name, and my family and friends always tell me and my brother how much we resemble my dad.

Thanks to my dad's saying, "Strive for the best," I never settle for anything but that.

His words keep me moving. Even though he's gone, I always have the memories. Those will never die.

Pictures for Projective Play Techniques

Using Imagination

Pictures, storytelling, and props can be used as a projective technique. They allow children to safely express feelings. Consider the following examples.

Jerry's brother Greg was killed in a plane crash. He put Greg's favorite sunglasses on his dog, Casper, and then began to talk about his brother to Casper.

Chase and Sarah went up to their tree house after their dog, Rex, was hit by a car and killed. Their favorite puppets were there. They began to tell the puppets what happened.

What do you think they talked about?

Geneograms

Seth's sister Donna died of leukemia when Seth was 7. Donna was 18. Now Seth is 10 and exploring Donna's death as well as other losses in his family. The geneogram, a pictorial family history, helped him to see which family members have died, which ones are still living, and which family members are those he can and cannot depend on. When Seth circled his Grandma Rose as someone he couldn't depend on, I questioned him about it. "What is it you can't depend on?" I asked. "Her memory," he replied. "She has Alzheimer's."

This geneogram helped to create a teachable moment with the use of a wonderful resource, Vacinda Nelson's *Always Grandma* (1988), a book for children about a grandmother with Alzheimer's disease. Seth loved the book and asked if he could borrow it to share with his mom. His mother called a few days later to say the book was a true gift. Because it explained in simple words many of the losses she was feeling constantly living with her mom's disease, she asked if she could share this resource with her adult siblings.

Sometimes children's literature provides a useful tool for all members of the family to begin a dialogue about their common loss issues.

CHILDREN'S QUESTIONS AND TECHNIQUES FOR ANSWERING THEM

Questions for God

Why Did You Have To Kill My Father?

Four years after Ryan's dad died in an airplane crash, he asked this question for the first time. "You must be pretty angry at God," I commented. "I am!" he declared. Then we began to talk about his anger. I handed Ryan some clay, and he began to form figures of God and an airplane. "Why did you do this?" he cried, and the tears began to release his anger. He smashed both figures, screaming, "I hate you, why did you kill my father?" Then he slumped, whispering, "It's not God's fault, and it's nobody's fault." This was the beginning of the meltdown process.

Questions for a Mom That Died

What Did It Feel Like To Die? (And Did You Think About Me?)

Gina feels lonely after her mom died and wonders if Mom thought about her when she died. We can talk about her feelings of abandonment and rejection caused by death and her worry that her mom may have suffered. "What do you imagine?" I asked. "I imagine she was bleeding and in a lot of pain," Gina responded. "Let's write down some questions, and ask Dad to write the answers. Then you will know." Sometimes children imagine far worse than if they know the truth. Some of Gina's questions were:

What did mom look like?   What did the doctor say?

Did the doctor say Mom was in pain?   Did you see her die?

Questions About Forgetting

Will I Forget My Dad?

Gabby is afraid she will forget her dad. She thinks about him a lot at school. She tries to remember his voice, but sometimes she gets scared because she can't hear it in her mind.

At night before Gabby goes to bed, she wants to picture his face. Sometimes she can't. Gabby often replays the home video of Dad, and it helps her remember.

Looking at family photos or drawing a picture of Daddy helps too. Gabby can ask friends and relatives to send a picture of her father. Seeing a new picture creates a new memory.

Questions About Clichés

Why Do People Always Say Only the Good Die Young?

"Even though my mom was 30 when she died, my grandmother is good and now she's 78. I'm only 8. Does that mean that God will take me? That makes me scared." Sally then began to explain her terror that she might die young like her mom. Only then could we begin to examine this magical thinking by exploring the facts about her mom's death.

Questions About Connection

Can I Visit the Place Where My Brother Was Killed?

Mary's brother, Adam, was murdered randomly by a neighborhood gang while walking home from work late one night. Mary needed to go back to the scene of the crime and see where the murder took place. She asked her boyfriend to bring her there, retracing every step of the murder account that she had read in a newspaper until she felt she had relived it. "Suddenly I felt Adam was with me, and I was glad I was there."

Questions About Secrecy

Why Doesn't Anyone Talk About Dad?

Peggy's dad died when she was 10 years old, and no one in her family ever talks about him. She, her brother, and Mom never say a word about his death. He had died of suicide. Now Peggy is 15. "I miss my dad so much, but even more I miss being able to talk about him. I feel so alone." I suggested she might like to join a support group for suicide as a way to feel less alone and to be with people who can understand her experience.

Questions About Facts

What Exactly Happened When My Dad Died?

JoAnne heard lots of different stories about her dad's fatal car crash when she was 6 years old. At age 13, she asked the question above for the first time. She explained she wanted to know the facts and asked if she could look up the account of the accident in the newspaper so that she could really know what happened.

We examined the newspaper article together and recorded a list of facts and misconceptions and discussed the similarities and differences. Now, at a different developmental stage, she was ready to regrieve the death in a new and age-appropriate way—discovering concrete facts about her dad's death.

Questions About the Inability to Grieve Openly

Why Don't I Cry Anymore?

Donna explained that she used to cry and complain a lot before her dad died. She was 9. Now she is 15, and she says she never cries. "I wonder why?" she asked me one day. I asked Donna if anyone had ever given her the message that crying wasn't good. She relayed a powerful story. After the funeral, her sister, Beverly, told her, "You need to be strong and take care of Mom now because you are the only one home with her." "I guess strong meant not to cry. I never realized that before," Donna told me in astonishment. This was her first step toward releasing her hidden tears. She began to bring in pictures of her life with her father. In this safe environment, we explored her repressed sadness of her dad's death and how much she missed him.

Questions About Dying

Will You Die, Too?

Sara worried excessively about her parents' health after the death of her grandmothers. She feared her mom and dad would die, too. We made a "worry box" with magazine pictures showing her worries.

Sara wrote them and put them in the box. Both of her parents also got medical checkups, and each doctor wrote a note to Sara confirming their good health. Sara felt happy and reassured when she read the following letter.

Dear Sara,

I am pleased to report to you that after doing a complete medical exam, with lots of tests and examinations, your dad is very healthy and seems to be in great shape. If you have any questions, please let me know.

Love,
Dr. Brenner

Questions About Magical Thinking

Is It My Fault My Dad Died?

Henry's dad took him to the park when he was 4. He and Dad sat down on the park bench. Henry's dad shot himself in the head in front of Henry. Henry's mom continually told him it was his fault, because he did not stop his dad. As a teenager, Henry was obsessed with wanting to murder someone, so "he could know what it feels like" to cause a death as his mom accused him of doing.

Savannah's mom was killed at the Pentagon on 9/11. A few weeks later she whispered in my ear, "I killed my mommy." "How did you do that?" I asked. "My mommy was sick and I didn't make her stay home that day."

Questions About Heaven

What Is Heaven?

Michelle wondered what heaven was like. She decided to write a story about it and draw the picture below to explain what she feels heaven is like. It helped her express a lot of ideas about where her mom was, and how she felt heaven was a safe and wonderful place. She also got to share more about her mom with me that I didn't know.

What Is Heaven?

This is what heaven is to me. It's a beautiful place. Everyone is waiting for a new person, so they can be friends. They are also waiting for their family. They are still having fun. They get to meet all the people they always wanted to meet (like Elvis). There are lots of castles where only the great live, like my mom. There's all the food you want and all the stuff to do—There's also dancing places, disco. My mom loved to dance. I think she's dancing in heaven.

Animals are always welcome. (My mom loved animals.) Ask her how Trixie is. That's her dog that died.

Tell her I love her.

Michelle, Age 11

Drawing a picture about heaven "helps children feel comforted and safe if they can hold a positive image of where their person is" (Goldman, 2009, p. 42).

Questions About Safety

What Can You Do So That I Will Feel You Are Safe?

Susie came to a grief therapy session very angry. "I won't let my dad go away with Tammy (his new girlfriend) for the weekend." She slammed the door and began to cry. "Why not?" I questioned. "I'm afraid he'll die, too, just the way my mom did." Susie's mom had been killed in a sudden car crash. She was not wearing her seat belt. "What could dad do in order for you to feel safe?" I asked. We brainstormed about it, and Susie came up with several ideas. She was afraid to tell Dad how she felt, so she decided to write a letter.

Dear Dad,
I am afraid you will get killed like mom did if you take the car away for the weekend. Please borrow Uncle Tom's Jeep. It's new and it has airbags. Don't speed, and wear your seatbelt.
Love,
Susie
P.S. Will you call me when you get there?

Susie gave me permission to share the letter with her father. He first thought it didn't make sense, but soon realized that Susie's fears stemmed from her mom's death. He agreed to borrow Uncle Tom's Jeep, wear his seat belt, and call at a designated time. Susie felt more in control now that her feelings were validated and she had a plan.

MEMORY WORK

Memory Boxes

Memory boxes are an excellent craft project for grieving children.

Children can collect special items that belonged to or remind them of the person who died. These objects can be put in a shoebox and decorated as a valuable treasure of memories. It also can serve as a tool for stimulating conversation. *The Memory Box* by Kirsten McLauglin and Adrienne Rudolph (2001) is a good resource to introduce a memory box.

Nathan's favorite uncle died of cancer when Nathan was 9. He decided to make a memory box and decorate it with stickers and pictures that reminded him of Uncle George. He placed a very precious object inside, Uncle George's black belt karate certificate. It served as an inspiration as well as an ongoing place to be with his uncle's memory.

Picture Albums

Often I have found that creating "My Life" picture albums with children is an extremely useful tool in creating dialogue and sharing feelings. Veronica's dad died of cancer when she was 10. I invited her to choose pictures she loved and make an album about her life before and after her dad died. She chose each picture, and we wrote a sentence about it.

Memory boxes and picture albums *are important tools* that enable children to share feelings and ideas. A memory table also allows kids to share meaningful objects that link them to loved ones.

Memory Table

Memory tables can be used at home, in a counseling office, or a bereavement support group. Children can place special objects or pictures on the table that remind them of their person who died. They are tools that allow the child to share about what is on the table, or the child may choose to display something without talking about it.

Memory Mural or Collage

Children love to express memories through artwork. They can draw a memory mural or create a collage from magazine pictures that remind them of the person or pet that died. Eight-year-old Carol experienced the death of her cat, Samantha, when Samantha was hit by a car and killed. Carol felt a tremendous loss in her life and grieved her sweet pet for many months to come.

Carol made a memory collage using magazine pictures. She shared a lot about Samantha and how much she missed her.

Memory Work and the Internet

Memory e-mails are a creative example of memory work and computer use.

After Chelsea's classmate Ronald was killed in a car crash, she and her classmates decided to create e-mail memories. Each child began writing and sharing e-mails with the rest of the class about time spent and experiences with Ronald.

Memory Pillow and Photographs

Murray was a beloved dog and friend to 12-year-old Ross and his 16-year-old sister, JoJo. Murray's dying process was slow and difficult. The family surrounded the dog with love and cared for his needs until he died. Murray spent much of his last time on earth on his dog bed. Ross took the following picture of this bed and made copies to share with family and friends.

After Murray's death, JoJo's mom made a pillow from Murray's bed and put his name on it. She gave it to JoJo to take with her to college so that she would feel Murray was always with her.

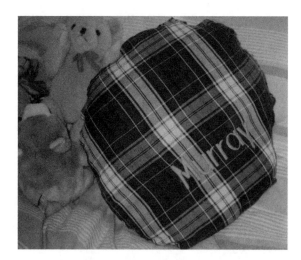 

Memory Projects

Even the youngest of children can take part in a memory project. Making a simple heart, a decorated box or picture frame, or even a holiday decoration allows for expression of memories.

Memory Books

Memory books are extremely useful tools to allow children to express feelings and share unfinished business (what they didn't get a chance to say). Children can express themselves through writing and drawing in age-appropriate ways. Inside the memory book, kids can use stars, stickers, photographs, and other decorations. There are many different kinds of pages kids can make. Here are a few suggestions.

The most important thing I learned from the person is . . .
Write a letter (Dear ___, Love ___)
What is the funniest memory you have?
My most special memory is . . .
If you could tell your loved one just one more thing, what would you say? What do you think he or she would tell you?
If there were one thing you are sorry for it would be . . .

The following images are five memory book pages donated by Allyson Nuggent, bereavement counselor. A 13-year-old boy drew the first picture showing his dad's funeral in great detail. The next picture shows a young girl's perception of life before and after her dad's suicide and the troubled relationship with her mother after her dad's death.

Melissa is a 13-year-old whose father died of lung cancer. Her love for him shines through her warm memory of her dad.

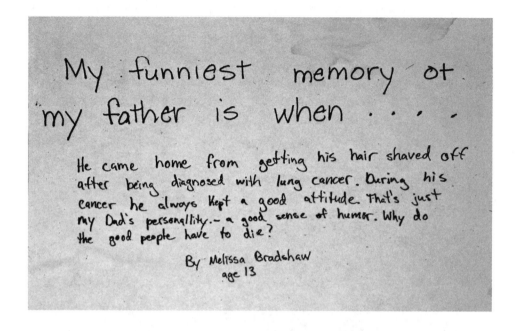

> My funniest memory of my father is when . . . .
>
> He came home from getting his hair shaved off after being diagnosed with lung cancer. During his cancer he always kept a good attitude. That's just my Dad's personallity — a good sense of humor. Why do the good people have to die?
>
> By Melissa Bradshaw
> age 13

In these last two pictures, a 6-year-old girl explored her feelings about her dad's death. She shares her anger, sadness, and worry in her memory book.

I Get Angry About they DiD not do anything to him since the death of my Person

I show my Anger by telling someone

This is me when I Am ! Angry!

The thing that worries me ā the most since the death of my person is...
becaues my family is sad.

This is a picture of what I am worried about

Interactive Story and Memory Book

Children Also Grieve: Talking About Death and Healing (Goldman 2005) is an interactive storybook about death shown in the following two pictures. It includes a memory book for children, vocabulary, and a message for adults.

Tamica, age 8, was reading this page in the memory book. Her grandfather recently died. Henry shares his physical signs of grief and invites the children to share theirs as well.

Tamika exclaimed. "I get headaches at school too, just like Henry. I know how he feels!"

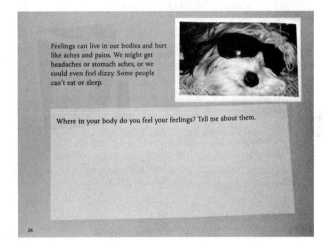

Feelings can live in our bodies and hurt like aches and pains. We might get headaches or stomach aches, or we could even feel dizzy. Some people can't eat or sleep.

Where in your body do you feel your feelings? Tell me about them.

Memory Book Resources

Bart Speaks Out on Suicide by Linda Goldman (1998)
Changing Faces by Donna O'Toole (1995)
Children Also Grieve: Talking About Death and Healing by Linda Goldman (2005)
Fire in My Heart, Ice in My Veins by Enid Traisman (1992)
The Memory Box by Kristen McLaughlin (2001)
Kids Can Cope: An Activity Book From Children for Children Who Are Living With Change and Loss by Emilio Parga (2009)
Lucy Let's Go: Helping Children Love a Pet Through Death and Dying by Linda Goldman (in-press 2014)

Ongoing Memory Work

Zacky was 6 years old when his friend Andrew died. At age 9, Zacky drew the following picture for the cover of Andrew's memorial booklet, *On the Occasion of Andrew's Third Anniversary.*

This drawing allowed Zacky to continue to actively remember his friend and participate in ongoing memory work. This drawing was called "Andrew Shooting Baskets in Heaven."

DRAMA AND IMAGINATION

Children use drama and imagination with props, costumes, and puppets to help them act out and identify feelings and thoughts. The young child can use a toy telephone to call someone who has died and create a dialogue. Using costumes with young children is another technique enabling them to immerse themselves in role-playing, becoming the loved one or another member of the family. Children also can role-play with toy figures or figures in a sand table to show how they feel.

Fantasy is a powerful tool for projection.

Stimulating Open Discussion

Photographs are a safe and natural way to communicate about the person who died. We can sometimes ask the children to help make scrapbooks about their loved one. This not only stimulates conversation but creates a memory to keep for years to come. Personal items specially chosen by the child that belonged to the deceased also are a wonderful remembrance and a way to keep getting to know what that person was like as the child gets older.

Locked diaries are a tool to create a space to write thoughts and feelings privately, with the availability to be shared at another time.

Polaroid pictures are good encouragement for open dialogue. By taking a Polaroid picture of the child and placing it within one of his or her drawings, the child can project him or herself into the drawing and begin to role-play.

Punching bags and stuffed animals allow children to express anger and frustration in a safe way.

The use of stuffed animals, puppets, and grief dolls is a child-oriented projective technique to allow discussion and expression of feelings.

Tape recording thoughts and feelings allow children to safely store or erase anything. It also gives them the choice to share if and when they are ready.

Projective Play

Toys and objects facilitating projective play are useful for the young child. Girls and boys can act out their grief, dialogue with their person who died, and recreate the traumatic event.

Props such as a firefighter's helmet and clothes helped children reenact a fire that took place at their school. "Now I am the fireman," Tommy said. "I can help other people."

A magic wand can serve as a useful object for projective play. Eight-year-old Isabel waved the magic wand. Her father had recently died of cancer.

"If I had one wish, it would be I could bring my dad back from the dead."

Nurturing props allow children to symbolically give and receive the nurturance they can no longer give to or get from their person who died. A girl or boy doll, a baby bottle, and a blanket are a few props that can be very comforting.

A "safe" or "peaceful box" can be used in a child's bedroom or classroom to reduce anxiety and stress often accompanying grief work for children. Comforting objects and pictures can be placed inside the box, and the box can be put in a convenient place with easy access for the girls and boys.

Puppets

Puppets help children role-play, dialogue, and express feelings in safe ways. Children can process their grief through play. Puppets are a wonderful tool to create an imaginary dialogue between a child and someone who has died.

Art

Through art therapy children and adults have an avenue of expression that may reduce anxiety, increase memory retrieval, and share narratives. Often expression through art creates that safe space to communicate enormous reservoirs of grief in ways direct conversation may not permit. A simple drawing speaks volumes. Nancy Boyd Webb (2002, p. 299), quoting Robin Goodman, explains, "Therapeutic communication can be easier or more direct through the use of symbols or images rather than the complex world of spoken language."

The media of art also can promote open discussion and enhance open feelings. Children can:

• Draw the loss (death, divorce, moving, etc.).
• Draw how they would like it to be.
• Draw their house and who's inside.
• Draw "What drives me nuts?" Kids write feeling words as they talk about what bothers them.
• Draw a mural of a common loss.
• Make a class booklet with words, pictures, poems, and photos.
• Draw scribbles on a large piece of paper. Let the child choose a section, create a drawing, and talk about it. Give the drawing a title. If it could talk, what would it say? The scribble becomes a story for discussion.

Children can choose from art materials, such as size and color of paper, and what kind of crayons, pens, or markers they want to use. As children draw, we can ask:

"Do you mind if I watch you draw? Can you tell me about your picture?"

Begin a dialogue that will create a story. The parent, teacher, or counselor can come closer to the picture to see if there is something in it the child can identify with and ask, "Tell me more about it." The child may realize then that the dog he or she drew in the picture is connected to him or her: "I'm like that dog. I bark at my sister all day."

Interpretation has limited value to children. Even if it's correct, it may not help the child express his or her feelings. In grief work, the most important aspect of artwork is freedom of expression without judgment.

Twelve-year-old Steve decided to take his father's T-shirt and make a memory to keep forever. He wrote the name of every family member on the shirt and now wears it to bed. Steve said it helps him to feel his dad is with him. Steve's mom made one, too, in memory of her husband Jim. Steve and Mom loved to wear these T-shirts together.

Five-year-old Caroline was asked to answer the question "What is death?" She simply responded that death was her grandma in a coffin. She drew a picture that illustrates how she views death—Grandma lying inside of her coffin.

Caroline also remembers Grandma in happy ways. "Grandma gave me a happy book before she died. My happy book has pictures of Grandma and me."

Children can draw themselves as large figures and show how they feel. Caroline created sock puppets and used these puppets as a tool to dialogue with her loved one.

Clay

Clay is a very versatile medium to use with children. It is reusable and easy to work with. Kids can mold their family, friends, or animals, and create dialogues between themselves and others. "Clay has a very calming effect for children (and adults) and they can gain a feeling of mastery by . . . pounding, squeezing, pinching, ripping, smoothing, and poking it" (Goldman, 2001, p. 97). Feelings can be expressed in a safe way.

Blake made a figure of his deceased brother out of clay. When asked, "What would you like to say to him?" Blake began to say good-bye. "You were a good brother; sorry you had to die." Then he kissed the figure. Blake also made the doctors that took care of his brother. "I hate you!" he shouted, "You wouldn't let me scream." He began pounding the clay and smashing it to bits. He was using his clay as a good projective tool to express anger.

Five-year-old Kyle had twin baby brothers. One of the baby twins, Andrew, died. Kyle's mom encouraged Kyle to use clay to work with his feelings. He created a clay angel and gave his mom the following note:

This is My brother Andrew. He died after He was born. He was a twin.

Music

Music is the voice of the human spirit. . . . It expresses better than our mere words the passions and emotions that inexorably accompany human life.

—J. Frohnmayer, "Music and Spirituality: Defining the Human Condition"

Music is an expressive tool that enables children to go beyond their cognitive mind and feel deeply. Sometimes kids may not be able to access the perfect words to share tender feelings about a loved one. Music helps children create words and feelings that can be difficult to articulate.

"Songs are an important vehicle for expression of thoughts, feelings, and emotions" (Rogers, 2007, p. 103). Rogers develops several creative exercises involving music that include life reviews through song, writing a song, or modifying the original words to an existing melody.

Kids can share music that reminds them of a person who died. Andrew, age 14, loved music. After 9/11, his teacher asked his class to bring in music to describe their emotions. His friend Joey played "God Bless America" and explained how much America meant to him. Melanie shared the song "From a Distance" and her vision of world peace. Andrew loved the song "My Hero." He explained that the song captured his feelings about the firefighters and police officers who were injured or killed helping others. "I wish I could be like that!"

Sally's kindergarten class used music to express feelings after their classmate Wayne died suddenly. Mrs. Jones, the music teacher, asked the children to choose an instrument that tells how they feel. Joey started beating the drums loudly and said, "I feel angry!" Sally blew into the flute. "This makes me sad." Lila shook the tambourine. "It's scary when someone dies!" "These bells make me feel happy!" Maria exclaimed.

Music can be used as a resource to explore feelings.

Kids can listen to sounds that different instruments make to create feelings.

Some feelings representative through different instruments might be . . .

drums–anger	bells–sadness
tuba–awkwardness	flute–sad
harp–angel-like	cymbals–shock
harmonica–loneliness	bells–happy

Feelings can be projected into the music through body movement and dance. Doing so is very freeing to children. Many of Hap Palmer's albums create wonderful music to use with young children. They include *Sea Gulls: Music for Rest and Relaxation* (2006), *Educational Activities: The Feel of Music* (2003), *Movin'* (2008), and *Getting to Know Myself* (1972).

Nicole's baby sister Alicia died of sudden infant death syndrome. Her grief ran very deep. Sometimes she was unable to find words to use to express the pain she was experiencing of never seeing Alicia again and never watching her grow up. Nicole asked if she could share a song that honored her innermost feelings, Eric Clapton's "Tears in Heaven."

"I just couldn't talk about it," she explained, "but the song understood my silent thoughts." Songs like Eric Clapton's "Tears in Heaven" and Elton John's "Goodbye England's Rose" can provide music to help create discussion and sharing.

Computers and the Internet

Computers can serve young people with processes helpful for their grief. E-mailing a friend about someone who died, creating a memory chat room, or building a file of memories is useful. Thirteen-year-old Savannah explained, "I made a journal of all of my feelings after my brother died. Then I created a secret file that I hid. It was like having a diary with a key."

The Internet can also serve as a useful tool for children and teens to discover information to help with their grief process as well as allowing them to connect with national and global grief support (See Chapter 7, "The Child's World of Technology" and Chapter 11, "The Global Grief Team").

CREATING A RESOURCE LIBRARY

A resource shelf at home or in school is important for kids. Be sure to include age-appropriate children's literature on the grief and loss issue they are experiencing. Chapter 12, "Let's Explore Resources," provides an extensive annotated bibliography on children's grief and loss issues.

IDENTIFYING FEELINGS

Kids Can Identify Feelings By

- Painting a picture of the feeling. "How does anger look when mom yells?"
- Keeping an ongoing notebook of feelings with writing and drawings.
- Doing feeling homework. Make a list of what makes you angry, sad, afraid, frustrated, and so on.
- Creating the feeling out of sand, clay, or puppets.

Parents Can Identify Feelings By

- Allowing kids to identify and express dislikes openly. Make up a game with them where they say what they don't like.
- Having a "Mad Session." During the routine bedtime ritual, parents can ask "Is there anything that made you mad today?" Be sure not to make any judgments or comments on answers.
- Practicing yelling "no!" or pounding on a pillow.
- Reading books that open discussion about feelings.
- Talking about things. "What was your nightmare about last night? Let's see if you can draw what frightened you."

An important part of all these techniques is their *projective value*. Children can't easily integrate emotions and intellect. We can help them access thoughts and feelings by creating an environment that supports their grief process.

CHAPTER 5

PREPARING FOR A GOOD-BYE VISIT

You know Grandpa is very sick. He's going to die soon. He probably won't talk much. He looks terrible.

Some people come into our lives and quickly go.
Some stay for a while, leave footprints on our hearts, and we are never, ever the same.

—Flavia Weedn, *Flavia and The Dream Maker: The Musical*

LET'S PREPARE KIDS TO SAY GOOD-BYE

Preparing a child for a good-bye visit to a dying loved one is a topic that is usually avoided or denied in our culture. A visit to an aging, sickly grandparent can be approached in a sensitive way.

To include children in the decision making is important. Does the child want to visit the ill person? If he or she answers no, find out what the fears are. If discussed openly, these fears could be eliminated. If the child decides to go, talk about the hospital and the room where the sick person will be. Explain how he or she will look and his or her physical appearance may have changed with the illness. Suggest bringing a gift to the loved one. It's another way of saying good-bye. Make visits brief and provide space, both in time and location, for kids to discuss, write, or draw how they feel after their visit.

To prepare young people for the visit, we need to be honest in language and feelings. Kids can, and often do, model themselves after the adults around them. "Grandpa had a heart attack last night. He is very sick." Mom explains. Ben asked a very common and direct question, "Will Grandpa die?" "He may," his mom answered, adding hopefully, "but the doctors are working very hard to make him well again! I was scared when I heard about Grandpa, and very sad," Mom confided. "Is that how you feel? What can I do to help you?" Because adults are often not sure what to say, it is necessary to have comfortable language to use.

Preparing Children for a Good-bye: A Family's Story

The following is a wonderful account of how a family approached their good-bye visit. "Preparing a Child for a Goodbye Visit" is an article written by Judith Rubenstein (1982) that illustrates a farewell to a grandfather dying of cancer. The children, ages 4 and 6, were prepared by the parents. Their mother tells the story.

The Situation

There was no denying Grandpa was dying. My husband, who rarely travels, was suddenly making frequent short trips to Chicago to visit him. The children overheard the anxious, daily, long-distance telephone calls to or from my mother-in-law, and afterwards the anxious conversations between my husband and me.

The children had a loving relationship with their Grandpa, built on pleasant visits several times a year when Grandma and Grandpa would come to Boston from Chicago. I remember in particular tireless sessions teaching toddlers to walk, and then later, long intimate walks, sometimes including "rest stops" at the candy or toy store.

Because of this warm relationship, we felt that the older children were entitled to say good-bye to him . . . We decided I would take our 6-year-old daughter to Chicago on one trip, and my husband would take our 4-year-old son on a separate trip.

Many people, friends, and family, strongly objected. They said, "Let them remember him the way he was." "He has deteriorated, and his changed appearance will frighten them." We rejected this well-meaning counsel in the belief that children have to learn that, however sad, sickness ending in death is part of life and that human beings have a need to say good-bye when time shared is over, whether it is a short, social visit or life itself.

Our Words

My husband and I together spoke to each child alone. We chose the time after breakfast one morning, since our children were most refreshed and alert at that time of day. Also, they had the rest of the day to think and ask questions. (Speaking of such an emotional concept in the evening would only have upset bedtime.) Our presentation to each child took only five or ten minutes, including questions from the child and repetitions by us. We began something like this:

"We have something important to talk to you about. Come and sit on my lap. I'm going to Chicago in a few days to see Grandpa, and I'd like to take you with me, if you want to go. Before you decide, listen to what we have to say."

The children wanted to go. They responded to our statements as we made them, and my husband and I backtracked and repeated, and our presentation was not a smooth monologue, but we did speak the following phrases in more or less the following order:

You know Grandpa is very sick. He's going to die soon.
This is probably the last time you are going to see him.
He's changed a lot since you saw him last.
He looks terrible.
He's very thin. He's very pale. He's very weak.
He probably won't talk much. He may cry.
But you don't have to be afraid.
He's still your same Grandpa.
He's unhappy because he knows he's going to be dying soon, and he doesn't want to
    leave us.
You may give him a big hug and kiss.
It will make him feel better.
You don't have to be afraid to kiss him.
You can't catch his sickness. It's not a kind of sickness you can catch.
You love your Grandpa and he loves you.
You may tell him you love him if you want to.
That will make him feel good, too.

Following our explanation, each child asked more questions. Both children wanted to be reassured that they wouldn't catch any "germs" from Grandpa, and we repeated that his illness didn't have germs one could catch. Then the conversation turned to details of travel in the airplane, who else we would see in Chicago, and more questions about "germs." Then, before the questions and repetitions became too great, and the emotional tension turned to annoyance, we ended the conversation with: "We have talked enough for now. If you have any more questions or if you want to talk about it again, you can ask us later. You can go play now."

Throughout the day and the following ones, the children asked questions from time to time, while I was preparing a meal or folding laundry, or doing some quiet task not focused on the child, and we discussed the idea again, but in a more casual way.

The Visit

A few days later, when my 6-year-old daughter and I visited my father-in-law, he was in pajamas in a wheelchair in the hospital waiting room. A compassionate physician and a humane hospital policy made this possible. My daughter approached him with poised self-confidence and affection, without fear, lugubriousness, or false cheerfulness.

She said, "Hi, Grandpa." She reached up and put her arms around his neck and kissed his cheek.

She smiled coyly and handed him a slip of paper on which she had drawn a picture and written, "I love you."

Grandpa and granddaughter hugged each other and smiled. The old man started to cry, and the little girl slipped down and sat on a chair. The adults talked a little while longer, and then we left. As I pushed open the heavy glass doors to leave, my daughter turned and waved good-bye to Grandpa and followed me, skipping and smiling. The next week my husband told me that he and our 4-year-old son had a similar experience at their visit.

In the years following my father-in-law's death, our children have mentioned that last visit from time to time. Although their remembrance of specific details, including their conversation, has blurred, they speak of the visit with a certain wistful pleasure that makes us happy that we did not deny it to them.

Rubenstein, Judith. (May 14, 1982). Preparing a Child for a Good-bye Visit to a Dying Loved One. *Journal of the American Medical Association* (JAMA), *247*, 2571–2572.

Good-bye Visit Memories

Lindsey had visited with her grandpa as he was dying when she was 7 years old. At age 9, she expressed her memories of her good-bye visit with her grandfather and her experience of his death through the poem *Grandpa*.

Grandpa

by Lindsey Reynolds, Age 9

There he lays sick
He was sick for a long time.
But this time the sickest
My mom's sisters, cousins, aunts, uncles
Everyone was there, quiet hoping
praying his heartbeat will quicken

Silence no one talks, just watching
my Grandpa laying on his white
silky sheets wanting to reassure
everyone he was going to be okay
but he couldn't cancer the horrible
demon wouldn't let him get off
that easy. He should've been in the
hospital everybody said no he has to
be in his own bed, his own house when
angels blow their holy trumpets and
sweep him off to heaven suddenly
Aunt Judy talks she says "This is a time
for dad, he needs us" that might have
not been what she said but I
sort of felt her saying it in my
heart. At the time I was
at home with my dad and sister watching TV.

But back at Grandpa's house no happiness
through the room just love and worriedness
It was strange Grandpa knew everyone
knew he was going to die tonight but
everyone knew he wasn't worried or
was he. We could see a twinkle in his
eyes his eyes weren't open but you could feel it
was his last moments
alive he wanted to
spend it all with his daughters.

Suddenly his heart stopped
his heart was so tired too old to stay alive
it needed its eternal sleep and
so did Grandpa. Suddenly his silky
white sheets turned into angels that
put him on their back and carried
him off. Then one of the people said
that he was gone. Everyone cried a little.

After the crying the phone call to my
Dad when my dad picked up he talked
then he said his apologies then I knew

I took the phone and said Grandpa died
didn't he when mom said yes
I wanted to cry but I knew
I had to be strong.

Saying Good-bye at the Funeral Home

The funeral home can be a place where girls and boys are allowed to say good-bye in a very child-oriented way. An innovative funeral home asked me to help it create a children's room, where boys and girls could play, write good-bye letters to loved ones, and make good-bye items out of clay to place in the casket.

The funeral director spoke of the enormous appreciation of parents for having a safe haven within the funeral home. Children could stay in this special room with supervision if they chose to leave the service. The children's room was equipped with materials for children to express feelings, whether through play, writing, or drawing. Many puppets were available as well as blocks and trucks. Books on death and loss issues were placed throughout the room for kids at different developmental stages; resources for parents were also available.

Children expressed their grief in different ways. Alex used the dog puppet to talk about her sadness. Kyle and Melanie watched a video. It was about a cat named Barney that died.

Tom wrote a letter to Mom and placed it in the casket. Susan made a heart out of clay.

The children's room at the funeral home was a safe place to creatively say good-bye.

Saying Good-bye at the Memorial Service

Sometimes children can't have the opportunity to say good-bye. The loved one dies unexpectedly. Bobby died suddenly, leaving his four children no opportunity for a good-bye visit. They actively participated in saying good-bye at the memorial service by writing the following note to their dad that was a special part of the funeral service booklet that day.

> *Good Daddy,*
>
> *We thought you would be with us for years to come,*
> *But we know that you are happy wherever you are.*
> *We love you from all of our hearts.*

Pat, Jackie, Bobby, and Tiffany

Children Participate in Memorializing

Andrew died suddenly on a family vacation. His kindergarten classmates were invited to join in a very child-oriented memorial service.

Each year for several years there was a memorial remembrance for Andrew. It included a memorial booklet. Andrew's cousin Christina created the cover with stars, a heart, and a flying unicorn to remember Andrew.

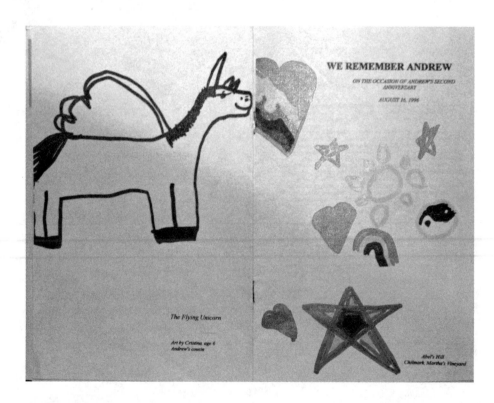

REMEMBERING A YEAR LATER

Aria's great-grandfather, Stanley, had died when she was not even 2. At age 3, her parents invited her to participate in the Jewish custom of commemorating at the cemetery a year after his death, called an unveiling. She had talked about Great-Grandpa Stanley a lot and how much she missed him.

At the unveiling, the family gathered together to say a prayer or share a memory. Many left a stone or note by the graveside. Aria did, too, placing her special stone near the headstone. She wanted Great-Grandpa to know she had visited.

Aria also wanted to leave a note. Although she couldn't write yet, she "wrote" in her way a message for her great-grandfather. Later, Mom asked her what it said. Aria responded, "I love you Great-Grandpa. I miss you."

A DYING CHILD SAYS GOOD-BYE

Cory was dying and wanted to talk about it. He shared with his mom his many thoughts and feelings about his critical illness. He also drew comforting drawings and explained his vision of his journey after death.

Cory's drawing was made into the following poster. It was done a year and a half before his death. The poem was written by his mom, Shirley, as described by Cory and at his request.

Summerland

By Cory

*Where the sun always shines
and they never see rain.*

It's all beauty, light, and love.

No one can remember pain.

*Where friends and loved ones await
the glorious days.*

*Where the spirit leaves its earth body
to find its way.*

*To the crystal castle in the sky, over
the rainbow bridge to dwell on high.*

*In God's presence forevermore he
will be waiting patiently for you and
me—*

*To join him in the presence of God's
love in that beautiful kingdom up
above.*

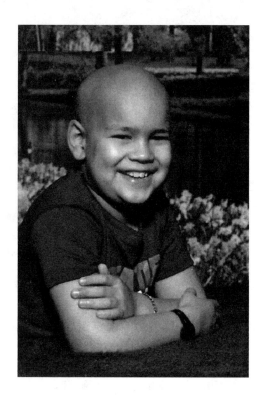

Cory's mom stated best in her own words her son's bravery and resilience while living with a life-threatening illness. "Cory taught me that living with a terminal illness doesn't have to get in the way of being happy and enjoying the time you are given." The following quote is Shirley's tribute to her beloved son.

I am the proud mother of Cory, the wonderful little boy for whom the book *Over the Rainbow Bridge* was written. He taught me how to live my life with joy, purpose and integrity.

His short life and the lessons he shared were a gift to thousands of people worldwide thanks to his loving relationship with Dr. Elisabeth Kübler-Ross. He asked me to write this book to help Elisabeth teach people that death is not the end and that we should not be afraid.

Cory loved the message in the song *The Rose*. Especially the part about 'those afraid of dying cannot learn to live . . .' His courage was astounding. His lessons were and are still profound. Not about dying . . . about living the life you have been gifted by God.

Shirley Enebrad, *Over the Rainbow Bridge*

www.overtherainbowbridge.info

I, too, am grateful to my friend and colleague Elisabeth Kübler Ross. After attending several of her trainings in the 1990's, I purchased Cory's poster, lovingly framed it, and kept it in my grief therapy office for all the children and parents to see. Cory's words served as an inspiration and testament to life and living it fully in the face of adversity.

DO TALK WITH CHILDREN ABOUT DEATH

Realize that grief is an ongoing process with no easy answers.
Allow new loss to be the first priority with a child's classmates.
Trust your instincts.
Initiate discussions of loss issues if the child does not.
Encourage children to attend the funeral, if they would like.
Consider ways to commemorate loss (bulletin board displays, letters to family, letters to the person who died, photographs, a memory book, tree planting).
Realize that not talking about the loss doesn't make it go away.
Remember, what we resist, persists!
Encourage classmates to be a support system.
Recognize that laughter and play are a part of grieving.
Understand that separation is the underlying pain of a grieving child.
Acknowledge that children often believe they have magical powers and need to create a reason for what has happened.

COMMUNICATE WITH CHILDREN BY

Using children's own language.
Realizing children can talk about their experiences.
Allowing children to ask their own questions.
Creating honest discussion.
Listening, watching, and waiting for the child to process his or her experience.
Explaining to children the facts surrounding the loss.

Resources for Children on Dying

Beyond the Rainbow: A Workbook for Children in the Advanced Stages of a Very Serious Illness by Marge Heegaard (2003)
Gentle Willow: A Story for Children About Dying by Joyce Mills (2004)
Scarlet Says Goodbye: An Activity Book for Kids When Someone Enters Hospice Care by Christine L. Thompson (2012)
Water Bugs and Dragonflies: Explaining Death to Young Children by Doris Stickney (2009)
And Still They Bloom: A Family's Journey of Loss and Healing by Amy Rovere (2012)

Resources for Adults

Great Answers to Difficult Questions About Death: What Children Need to Know by Linda Goldman (2009)
The Private Worlds of Dying Children by Myra Blubond-Langner (1980)

CHAPTER

6 /

SAYING GOOD-BYE TO A PET

Decorations **Balloons** Memories **Hugs** Good-byes Dressing up Songs **Rituals** Pictures **Thank-you** **Friends** Ceremony **Poetry Cookies**

While we try to teach our children all about life,
Our children teach us what life is all about.
—Angela Schwindt Quotes, *Quotes.net*

THE LOVE FOR A PET

My husband Michael and I went to a teacher's meeting for my son Jonathan when he was in first grade. It was right before Thanksgiving. We happily listened to the report on Jon, and then the teacher, Mrs. James, ended with this caveat. "Jonathan is so happy about the puppy he is getting for Thanksgiving." "What puppy?" I asked, trying to understand. She responded, "I asked the children what they were thankful for in celebrating Thanksgiving, and Jon said the new puppy he was going to get."

Jon got his Thanksgiving wish, the wish to love a dog before he had ever met him. The dog turned out to be a rescue puppy, Bart, which our family cherished as a dear friend throughout the rest of Jon's growing up until college. And our family owes Jonathan a great thank-you for bringing Bart into our lives as a loyal and dear companion.

When Bart died, we deeply grieved. He was "our heartbeat," with us and by our side day and night for 11 years. Bart's death was a profound loss.

All too often, pet death is discounted as not important, and those undermining words "we'll get you another one" are offered as a hollow consolation. They diminish the love the child has for the pet, whether it is a goldfish, a hamster, a dog, a cat, or a horse.

Sophia came home from school and her mother was very distraught. She began to explain, "Sophia, something terrible has happened." Sophia later disclosed she panicked. She didn't know if it was about her sick grandfather or the family dog, Oscar. She wasn't sure which one she wanted it to be. Her mom continued, "Oscar was hit by a car and got killed." Sophia was devastated.

Spencer had a similar experience. He came to grief therapy with so many feelings. "My grandfather died this week, and so did my four-year-old goldfish, Goldie. I will miss them both so much." I invited Spencer to make a memory book for his grandfather and Goldie.

In Goldie's book, he drew the goldfish having a Viking funeral under the sea. Spencer was 14 years old and needed to express the love for his pet with honor.

THE STORY OF THATCHER: A CELEBRATION OF LIFE

The Story

Thatcher was a 12-year-old dog. She was the beloved pet of the family and was dying of cancer. Although Thatcher was a brave and proud dog, no one could deny how seriously ill she was. Thatcher's eyes were tired, her energy was low, and her favorite walks and ball-catching escapades had long since stopped. All of the children, Nate, Ben, and Norah, saw the difference in their pet; the only thing that remained forever the same was Thatcher's ongoing love for them—and, of course, their love for Thatcher.

Nate was the oldest. He was 11. Thatcher had been with the family since before he was born. When his mom was pregnant, Thatcher as a pup would lie down on her stomach and feel Nate kicking inside.

When Nate was being born, Thatcher sat patiently with Nate's grandmother, paws on her stomach, waiting for Nate to come home.

Saying Good-bye to Thatcher

Thatcher was dying. She had cancer. The vet said it was an inoperable tumor and it was only a matter of time before Thatcher died. Everyone in the family was very sad as they saw their beloved dog get weaker and weaker and watched her loving, weary eyes stay eternally focused on them.

Grandmother came for a visit and felt the unhappiness about Thatcher's critical illness. "Let's give Thatcher a party. Let's celebrate her life," she proposed. And that is just what they did!

The Preparation

Grandmother, Nate, Ben, and Norah went shopping. They bought Thatcher presents and dog biscuits.

They got doggy party balloons, animal crayons, plates and napkins, doggy party hats, dog bone pens, and doggy wrapping paper.

They drew pictures of special times with Thatcher with animal crayons. Then they began to write a play for Thatcher, with stories about her life and songs to sing to her. They set the table for a true dog party.

The Party: A Wonderful Tribute

Everyone came together to have a party for Thatcher. The table was set for a festive dinner. Thatcher stayed in the seat of honor, her dog bed, as each person paid tribute to his or her wonderful friendship.

Norah, Ben, and Nate saved a special treat of food for Thatcher and gave her that gift after their presentation. The children's friends sent dog cookies for the people, too!

Ben made a story with pictures to read to Thatcher. It made him feel good to let Thatcher know what she meant to him. He read his story for Thatcher, telling her how cute she was and how much he liked to play with her—and that dogs are by far the best pets.

Norah decided to dress up for Thatcher. She put on her special dress-up gown, her tiara and pearls, got her microphone, and beginning singing, "I love you" to Thatcher. She thought she saw Thatcher smile. Then she read Thatcher her story.

By Norah
I love you
thatcher You're
the sweatest
dog in the hole
wide world. And
that dog is name
thatche oohhh
to; the Dog thatcher

Nate greeted people at the door with doggy balloons and a welcome. He invited everyone to sit down and listen to the stories. Brothers and sisters, parents and grandparents joined together for the tribute to Thatcher.

Nate and Norah talked to Thatcher. They shared good times with her. One was Thatcher at the beach with the family. Norah said, "I love you so much, Thatcher," and gave her a hug.

Saying Good-bye

After Thatcher died, the family gathered in the backyard for a service. They placed a memorial plaque with Thatcher's name in the ground. Each person found a special stone and flower to place by Thatcher's name as a memorial ceremony.

Ben said he needed to write Thatcher one more time. It was his way of saying good-bye. Ben read his good-bye at the ceremony.

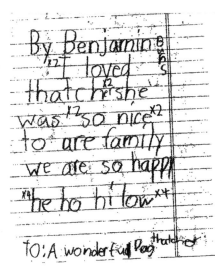

By Benjamin
I loved
thatcher she
was so nice
to are family
we are so happy
he ho hi low
TO: A wonderful Dog thatcher

Nate wanted to say good-bye, too. He read next. He told Thatcher she was amazing and that she will live in everyone's heart. He knew how much fun Thatcher had watching all of the children grow up and how loved Thatcher knew she was. He was grateful she had a long and happy life.

NATE

Thatcher was a very special dog. All the things she did, if it was silly or just plain amazing. The best thing about all that stuf is it will awalys be remembered in our heartsand that is what im proud of the most. Thatcher lived a very long life too and one of the most fun thing for her was to watch us grow upOne other thing I was proud of was Thatcher knew we loved her with all of our hearts.So we shouldn't be sad we should be glad that Thatcher lived such a long happy life.

Norah was last. She wanted Thatcher to know the whole family was grateful for her protection. And she got one more opportunity to say, "I love you."

'I love you thatcher for being with me and protecting me and my family

INCLUDING CHILDREN IN PET DEATH: WHAT WE CAN DO

Truly these children were recognized mourners by parents and grandparents, and made to feel an integral part of a tribute to a dying pet. Their love and grief for their lifelong companion was honored and respected. The spontaneous party to remember Thatcher's life served as a teachable moment to include children in commemoration. Nate, Ben, and Norah were active participants in creating a celebration of life, an environment to share special feelings, and an avenue to say good-bye to their friend Thatcher.

Ways That Work

Children Can

- Celebrate a life.
- Talk about the dying pet.
- Create a ritual or ceremony.
- Express feelings.
- Say good-bye.
- Share resources.

RESOURCES

For Children About Pet Loss and Death

Children Also Grieve: Talking About Death and Healing by Linda Goldman (2005)
Lucy Let's Go: Helping Children Love a Pet Through Death and Dying by Linda Goldman (In-press 2014).
Goodbye Mousie by Robie Harris (2001)
The Forever Dog by Bill Cochran (2007)
Zach and His Dog: A Story of Bonding, Love, and Loss for Children and Adults to Share Together by David Meagher (2009)
Forever Friends: Activities for Kids Who Have Lost a Pet by Susan Weaver (2010)

For Adults on Pet Loss and Death

Pet Loss and Children: Establishing a Healthy Foundation by Cheri Barton Ross (2005)
Pet Loss and Human Emotion, 2nd Edition: A Guide to Recovery by Cheri Barton Ross and Jane Baron-Sorenson (2007)
When a Family Pet Dies: A Guide to Dealing With Children's Loss by JoAnn Tuzeo-Jarolmen (2007)

A Special Good-bye to Henry

A handsome rascal,
A comic trickster,
A great and loyal friend

We love you Henry
2001–2012

CHAPTER **7** /

THE CHILD'S WORLD OF TECHNOLOGY

Internet Facebook E-mail
iTunes Video texting Twitter
Sexting iPhone Privacy invasion Friending Cyberbullying Smartphones
Skype MP3 player iPod
Texting Computer YouTube

Technology gives (children) tremendous freedom and power to reach out and touch in nearly every moment, for good or evil.

—Mike Donovan (quoted in Holladay, 2010)

TECHNOLOGY: A BLESSING OR A CURSE

The Internet and its social media, cell phones, and even iTunes allow children of this new electronic age entry into instant communication, companionship, and information. Kids have fresh ways to combat isolation and loneliness with the new social media technology as their constant buddy. Its value is unquestionable in a global community in accessing immediate data, news, and intimacy.

> Our students are digital natives, a term that means that teens look at the Internet, cell phones, instant messaging, and text messaging as a part of their normal social lives. [In contrast,] adults are digital immigrants who use technology as a tool to supplement our lives. (Trim, 2009)

Children have access to technology that didn't exist at the last printing of this book. Now "It's where they live, what they do, how they're connected" (Donlin, quoted in Trim, 2009). Young people have become so comfortable with these digital tools that face-to-face contact and online interaction seem to blend as one and the same.

The Blessing

One mom explained the value of her son's constant Facebook interactions:

> I was home with my boys, Brandon and Jack, and the ground began to shake beneath me. The earth itself trembled, the noise was loud and eerie, and I had no idea what was happening. I ran outside and called for my sons to do the same. I tried my cell phone but the line was dead. Within seconds my oldest, Brandon began to explain, "Mom, there's an earthquake. It is all over Facebook. The same thing is happening to my friends in New York, and DC. Flynn and Benjamin said they felt the same thing we did!"

A natural disaster was confirmed, normalized, documented, and impetus to generate a support group was created in the blink of an eye.

Another mother shared with me the new challenges of raising her children with this advanced technology.

They don't talk to each other. They go to Facebook.

Facebook allows the children born into its time of creation to iChat, multi-chat, and video-chat so constantly that the computer has become a best friend. Twelve-year-old Violet told her sister, "The only punishment that works on me is taking away my computer." Zachary was in fifth grade when he got his first cell phone. The next month his dad got the phone bill, which had an added charge for 6,000 texts. "How could you possibly text this much in one month? You are in school all day, come home, eat dinner, do homework, and sleep for eight hours. How did you find time to do all that texting?" Dad questioned. "I don't know, I just did." Zachary's mom watched him get ready to go on the computer. He combed his hair, put on a favorite T-shirt, and turned his baseball cap in just the right way because he didn't know who might enter his video chat that day.

There is nowhere to hide. Is it a blessing or a curse? Perhaps it is both for today's young people. Levi was a fourth-grader with a nervous tic and sensitivity to his environment. "I love iTunes," he told his friend. "It calms me down. I can get all the music I like and listen to it when I am upset." The computer and its virtues helped to soothe an unnerved child. Willow loved her computer, too. Her fifth-grade homework was so much easier for her because she could look up her homework online and even include pictures of the subject matter.

The Curse

Computers and cell phones broaden the range of old-fashioned bullying.

Three-fourths of the young people in an Associated Press–MTV poll said they "consider the darker aspects of the online world, sometimes called 'digital abuse' a serious problem" (Cass and Anderson, 2011). This poll is part of the Associated Press–MTV campaign, "A Thin Line," geared to prevent the increase of digital harassment.

The Seattle School District created a curriculum to help middle school children understand the misery technology can generate by exposing humiliating pictures, mean-spirited online comments, and hate groups on social networking sites. This digital abuse manifests most frequently as online behavior that:

1.   Spreads false rumors on Internet pages or by text message;
2.   Shares a victim's online messages without permission;
3.   Impersonates someone by logging onto their social network page;
4.   Spies by logging onto the victims' electronic account. (Cass and Anderson, 2011)

Cyberbullying is defined as "the repeated use of technology to harass, humiliate or threaten" (Holladay, 2010, p. 43). Holladay explains that the extreme repercussions of loss of privacy and harassment can culminate in "bullicide"—suicide by bullying. Holladay shares the story of Phoebe Prince, an Irish immigrant who hung herself after viciously and constantly being harassed in person and on Facebook. She was maligned over the Internet as "a whore" and "a bitch." This exposure of insults impacted her so greatly that she took her life.

Seattle Public School's senior project consultant, Mike Donlin, explains, "Cyberbullying occurs under the table. It's digital natives bullying one another in the land of the natives—even high-tech adults don't go there" (quoted in Trim, 2009).

Young people don't feel as compelled to take responsibility for their actions with Internet bullying. When youngsters can easily target peers online, they are able to so without feeling emotion or seeing the response of that targeting. In the past, bullying was limited to face-to-face torment. Today with 24/7 access to technology, there is no escape.

Trim (2009) explains that "cyberbullying researchers Sameer Hinduja and Justin Patchin (*Bullying Beyond the Schoolyard*) found that between sixth and seventh grades, incidences of cyberbullyng make a significant increase." Middle school is the time when young people experiment, and cyberbullying is an increasing form of that experimentation.

And yet one of the biggest fears among Internet-savvy girls and boys is that if they tell an adult about a cyberbullying incident, their computers, cell phones, and MP3 players will be taken away and that adults can't really help anyway. Trim (2009) states that 90% to 95% of secondary schools students carry a cell phone.

The simple yet powerful message is: Don't say or do things online that you wouldn't say or do in person.

The Challenge

Children need to learn the lesson of respect, online and off.

Children need to learn the lesson of respect on the playground, on the bus, in the lavatory, and on the Internet. Technological communication is constant for young people in a world that most adults can't possibly understand.

After a physical altercation stemming from a Facebook post in a middle school, the principal asked every parent to support a two-day moratorium on Facebook activity in their home. Parents were asked to discuss the appropriate use of social networking sites with their children during the moratorium. Parents were called if their children engaged in the online conversations. Another middle school suspended more than 20 students who friended or became fans of a Facebook page maligning another peer. Taking immediate action, setting strong boundaries, and enforcing consequences against harassment are key in promoting safety and protection for girls and boys.

Glee, a popular TV show, aired an episode (February 21, 2012) involving a teenage boy, Dave Karofsky, who attempted suicide after being bullied and harassed over his sexual orientation. This violence occurred after Dave was outed by peers at school for being gay. An anonymous messenger posted this private information on a chat room and sent texts to most of the student body. With no way to stop the avalanche of ridicule that followed, Dave felt his only recourse was to take his life. Thankfully, his dad found him and he recovered. *Glee* exhibited great courage in creating an emotional environment with the strong message "It gets better." Each student shared the vision of their future in 10 years, with people and hopes and ambitions to strive for. A clear message was sent that one day high school would end and no one would have to be with "these jerks ever again." Friends reached out, apologized for insensitivity, and pledged to be his friend and love him for who he is. The challenge to fight cyberbullying was fought well through this media example viewed by millions of young people who watch this show.

Sexting has also become a new phenomenon. O'Keefe and Clarke-Pearson (2011) reports a recent survey that indicates 20% of teens have sent or posted nude or seminude photographs or videos of themselves. Sexting is defined as "sending, receiving, or forwarding sexually explicit messages, photographs, or images via cell phone, computer, or other digital devices (O'Keeffe and Clarke-Pearson, 2011, p. 802). Adolescents engaging in sexting have been threatened or legally charged, expelled from school, or become victims with accompanying mental distress.

Dating abuse is another outgrowth of the digital age. Three in 10 young people say their partner has checked up on them electronically multiple times per day or read their text messages without permission. Fourteen percent say they've experienced more abusive behavior from their partners, such as name-calling and mean messages via the Internet or cell phone (Cass and Anderson, 2011).

The American Academy of Pediatrics defines a new paradigm called "Facebook depression" as "depression that develops when preteens and teens spend a great deal of time on social media sites, and then exhibit classic symptoms of depression" (O'Keefe and Clarke-Pearson, 2011, p. 802). Thirteen-year-old Isabelle explained, "Facebook is a popularity contest. Whoever gets the most friend requests or the most pictures is the winner." Peer contact and acceptance is extremely important to vulnerable young people, and the intensity of social activity online can trigger depression in youngsters. Some feel isolated and seek out blogs and risky Internet sites for companionship.

The 2011 Associated Press–MTV (Cass and Anderson) poll of young people ages 14 to 24 indicates the increase of mean behavior online. This poll found that young people who frequently see others being mean to each other on social networking sites rose from 45% in 2009 to 55% in 2011.

Many parents say they have no idea what their child is doing online. A 2009 study from Common Sense Media found that parents nationally underestimated children's use of social networking sites and often are unaware of how they are used. Thirty-seven percent of students admitted they'd made fun of a peer online, but only 18 percent of parents thought their child would engage in such conduct" (Holladay, 2010, p. 45).

Adults Taking Action

The Internet is not written in pencil. It is written in ink.

—Aaron Sorkin, *The Social Network*, 2010

One mom and dad took action against online bullying. Their 12-year-old son, Cameron, was a top athlete on the lacrosse team. Cameron loved his teammates and looked forward to online chats with them. The team had played a big game and lost the game with great disappointment. Many of the players blamed the goalie, Taylor, for his poor performance. One team member, Seth, posted malicious slurs in the daily team chat. "Taylor sucks. He is the worst goalie. He cost us the game."

Cameron told his parents about the post. "That's terrible. It's humiliating!" his mother told him. "This has to stop, and we need to do something about it." Cameron's father called the coach and told him about the online harassment. The coach contacted all parents involved, and the slanderous words were soon removed.

Then Cameron's dad sat down with him and had a talk. He explained to his son the following: "Don't be so hard on Taylor. Lacrosse is a team sport, and we are all in it together. Your teammates can blame Taylor, but everyone is responsible for losing the game. You can't point the finger at just one person."

A few days later, Cameron's parents received an e-mail from Taylor's mother. "Thank you for raising such a wonderful son." She had overheard Cameron defending Taylor at a game, almost saying to teammates verbatim what his father had said to him—"We are a team and we all need to take responsibility for losing a game. Don't be so hard on Taylor—we all deserve the blame."

Cameron told his father that he had posted the message on the team chat. This scenario illustrates the effectiveness of diminishing online bullying through parental involvement and action. It underscores the strength of the bystander to change the balance of power inherent in bullying. By becoming an advocate for his teammate, Cameron and his parents created strong action to distinguish verbal harassment online.

WHAT WE CAN DO TO HELP THE CHILD

Promote Safety on the Internet

Use simple interventions to eliminate cyberbullying. Listen to the child if an incident of harassment has taken place, create a conversation, ask questions, and request that the child *shows* as well as tells. Create awareness of the importance of the bystander in changing the balance of power inherent in bullying, whether on the playground or in a chat room. Remain calm as you listen and talk and allow the young person to tell his or her story and be heard. Also provide an anonymous procedure for sharing cyberbullying to guard against fear of reprisal. The following are suggestions for intervention.

Dispel the myth for children that Internet communication is anonymous. Help them with the impulse to respond as the bully did. Holladay (2010) shares that the Library of Congress is archiving all Twitter messages sent from March 2006 forward, immortalizing "mean tweets" for posterity. Educate children that their online communication will echo throughout their future. One mom warned her 13-year-old, Olivia, "Whatever you post on Facebook, write it as if your mom and dad are watching over your shoulder. It can hurt you for the rest of your life."

Create a respect for privacy. Privacy is at risk for preadolescent and teens online as misinformation, slanderous information, and false information about themselves and others creates a digital footprint for the future. Naïveté regarding these issues among youngsters can influence future jobs and college acceptance. All caring adults must help young people understand that what goes online stays online.

Mrs. Jarvis, a seventh-grade teacher, gave examples of postings that can hurt reputations. She cited an example of a student who posted gossip about a classmate on the Internet for all to read. This student was angry at her friend and impulsively tried to hurt her. Once done, the malicious rumors couldn't be erased. This example supports the following goals of the Cyberbullying Prevention Program shared by Mike Donlin: "We want to give teachers practical tools to help them help their students consider consequences, stay safe and make good choices" (quoted in Riley, 2008).

Interventions to Stop Cyberbullying in Schools

Donlin makes the following recommendations (from Trim, 2009):

- Provide a safe place in school for the victim to go.
- Take screenshots of the cyberbully's work and save them.
- Make sure parents get involved. Make sure adults get the message to the abuser to stop.
- Bring evidence to school officials' attention—the school needs to be actively involved in stopping the cyberbully.
- Get the police involved, if need be.
- Save the evidence, save the URLs, download copies to give to the police.

Parent Involvement

It is essential that parents understand the inherent issues of bullying, social acceptance, risk taking, and the potential development of depression and social anxiety that can be by-products of the digital age. Only then can they develop strategies to create healthy and productive ways to use computers, the Internet, and social media with guidelines and supervision. The new American Academy of Pediatrics (O'Keefe and Clarke-Pearson, 2011) guidelines include recommendations for pediatricians to help families navigate the social media landscape. They include:

1. Advise parents to talk to children and adolescents about their online use and the specific issues that today's online kids face, such as cyberbullying, sexting, and difficulty managing their time.
2. Advise parents to work on their own "participation gap" in their homes by becoming better educated about the many technologies their children are using.
3. Discuss with families the need for a family online-use plan, with an emphasis on citizenship and healthy behavior.
4. Discuss with parents the importance of supervising online activities via active participation and communication, not just via monitoring software.

RESOURCES

It is important to present resources for children and adults on this newly evolving subject in the technological age.

For Children

What Would My Cell Phone Do? by Micol Ostow (2011)
When Charlie McButton Lost Power by Suzanne Collins and Mike Lester (2005)

For Adults

Bullying Beyond the Schoolyard: Prevention and Responding to Cyberbullying by Sameer Hindjuda and Justin Patchin (2008)
Teen Cyberbullying Investigated by Thomas Jacobs (2010)

CONCLUSION

The wave of the future is coming and there is no fighting it.

—Anne Morrow Lindbergh, *The Wave of the Future*, 1940

How do grief and loss and the world of technology intersect in the lives of our children? Not only are bereavement and the computer age intertwined, they cannot be separated. Young people use sophisticated communication to blog their feelings about intimate personal issues, find websites that support challenges, create chat rooms with friends, and instantly message 24/7.

The death of Steve Jobs, the creator of Apple, had a great impact. Memorials spontaneously appeared at Apple stores throughout the world, with many with tributes by children. Girls and boys needed a forum of expression to a man they never met but whom they identified with for the many gifts he gave them. The following two notes are examples of children's outpouring of grief and love for this hero of the computer age. The first note was caringly placed with other messages and flowers in front of an Apple store.

The death of Steve Jobs served as a teachable moment for countless young people. They were able to express grief and became recognized mourners, often through e-mails to Apple about this death and a tribute to this life. The children's memorial letters speak to many of this generation born into the digital age. "Thank you for making computers. You changed my life."

CHAPTER 8

FAMILY DIVERSITY— THE NEW NORM: CHALLENGES FOR CHILDREN

Immigration Community
Cultural outreach Connection
Same-sex parents **Shades of people**
Family Multicultural families

Let us put our minds together and see what life we can make for our children.
—Sitting Bull

E PLURIBUS UNUM: OUT OF MANY, ONE

E pluribus unum—out of many, one—are the words on the Great Seal of the United States. Its underlying meaning values the aspects of unity, harmony, kindness, and compassion so intrinsic to the growth of humanity. It seeks to eradicate the outdated paradigms connected with being separate, or feeling prejudice and hatred for oneself or others. Our goal as gatekeepers to tomorrow's world is to help young people understand and incorporate its core concept: out of many cultures, ethnic groups, races, religions, and gender issues, we are all one people.

Issues in family systems ranging from divorce, adoption, deployment, immigration, imprisonment, multiculturalism, and same-sex parenting present today's young people with challenges socially, legally, politically, and spiritually. The rainbow of sizes, shapes, colors, and languages of our diverse population of global citizens is complex and fluid. More and more, our children observe in schools, homes, communities, and real time through the technology of the Internet and media the vista of pluralism so representative of the world population.

Young people and their families from every aspect of society are portrayed in more human and approachable ways. While outdated stereotypes and cultural biases about family systems and structures still exist, a new concept embedded in our history and leading us forward is emerging . . .

E pluribus unum—*Out of many, one.*

DIVERSITY IS THE NORM, NOT THE EXCEPTION

Racial and ethnic minorities surpass whites in U.S. births for the first time.

—Yen (2012)

"New 2011 census estimates highlight sweeping changes in the nation's racial makeup (Yen, 2012)." "This generation is growing up much more accustomed to diversity than its elders," states Roderick Harrison, former chief of racial statistics at the Census Bureau (quoted in Yen, 2012).

"Racial and ethnic minorities make up more than half the children born in the United States . . . Minorities made up 2.02 million, or 50.4 percent of U.S. births in the 12-month period ending July 2011" (Yen, 2012). This paradigm shift, diversity as a majority, is still subjected to negativity and prejudice that result in a groundswell of disenfranchised young people. It is essential that parents, professionals, and other caring adults talk with children and teens about diverse family issues.

Marginalizing, bullying, social stigma, and harassment of others due to race, culture, family makeup, and gender results in bias and loss often leads to low self-esteem, poor school performance, internalization of teasing, isolation, and depression for young people.

Creating a clear and nonbiased language for dialogue and providing adequate community resources and mentorship and guidance are essential steps in eliminating some of these challenges.

GRACIE'S STORY: A CHILD OF FIRST-GENERATION PARENTS

Gracie found herself caught between two worlds. One world was America and the language and customs she grew to accept as her own. The other world was one filled with her parents' resistance to change and tenacity to keep customs and language familiar to the Vietnamese people but not Americans.

Gracie was a 10-year-old girl whose Vietnamese parents barely spoke English. She was teased at school about her immigrant mom and dad. Kids would make fun and belittle them. "It makes me so angry! Katie says my parents are stupid. Nobody understands how smart they are. They just don't know English well."

The scenario is familiar to children with foreign-born parents who don't or scarcely speak English. Gracie's mother and father were well educated in Vietnam. Her mom was a nurse, and her dad was an engineer. When they arrived in America, they couldn't find work and fought hard to save money to open their own restaurant business. However, unfamiliar with language and customs, they remained insolated in a closed Vietnamese community that maintained their native culture.

Caught Between Two Worlds

Gracie explained that she felt a lot of "shame" for feeling "less than" with her peers at school, because her parents couldn't help with schoolwork, attend PTA meetings, or create ways to have friends visit. Her life was scheduled in ways that many American children couldn't imagine. Her parents held the Vietnamese work ethic very seriously. They also adhered to the tradition that children should support their elders and sent much of their earned income back to their family in Vietnam. Mom and Dad worked day and night and had little time for the children. The grandparents became the caretakers.

A Role Reversal

Yet the grandparents didn't speak English, and Gracie became the translator. At age 4, she felt responsible for answering the phone and deciphering which calls were important and then translating the messages. By age 8, she was managing all the bills to be paid as well as taking care of her younger brother, Michael, supervising his schoolwork and living skills. Gracie's older sister was responsible for driving the family everywhere, translating doctor's appointment information, and so on. While her grandparents sometimes stayed with the children, they were much older and sickly. Often, Gracie became the caretaker, making them dinner, cleaning the house, and remembering their medicines.

What Do I Do at School?

Gracie's parents never went to PTA meetings or parent–teacher discussions. They could not speak the language, and their work ethic placed earning a living above school attendance. Gracie and Michael had no guidance or support about homework issues, tests, and assignments. Their parents did not understand the language or practices and had no one to guide them in helping their children.

No One's Home

When her grandparents were unavailable, Gracie became a latchkey child. Many times she couldn't find the key. Often not able to get in the house, she and her brother would sit on the steps and wait for a neighbor or relative to help. Sometimes they would cry because they were so hungry, unable to get into their kitchen for food.

Mom and Dad rarely were home. They left for work before Gracie woke up, and she was sleeping when they got home. At 9 years old, Gracie realized how frustrated she was. "I had a major temper tantrum while my mom was packing to go to work. I pleaded with my mother. 'PLEASE DON'T GO TO WORK! We don't need the money. I miss you too much. Stay home. I never get to be with you.'" She put her head in her hands and sobbed. Yet her parents remained determined and left for their jobs. Feeling abandoned, Gracie threw her fist through a glass window. She showed me the scar it left.

Confined and Lonely

Summers were difficult. "They were so boring." While other friends went to camp or had scheduled activities, Gracie and her little brother stayed home almost every day, alone. She read, and Michael watched TV . . . all day, every day. She complained bitterly and begged to be allowed to walk to the park or go to the library. The answer was always no. Mom finally brought the children to work with her. They had to sit in a chair and found it very restrictive. When they went with their parents to the family restaurant in the evenings, they had one book or one toy to occupy them. That was the traditional way things were done, and, again, Gracie was caught between two worlds.

Respecting Both Worlds

Gracie had also learned to adhere to and respect many of the Vietnamese ways. Some of the social customs created difficulties for her. "Vietnamese kids are supposed to be quiet and not bother adults," she explained. "When they are around adults they are to be obedient and have good behavior." She called this attitude "the young Vietnamese girl syndrome." Gracie was put in a special program for children with speech delays. It took quite some time for the teacher to realize that Gracie could speak very well but didn't know she was allowed to talk to adults. Her teacher assured her, "This is an American class. We love to hear you talk."

Gracie loves and respects her parents. She values their hard work ethic and has tried to emulate them in her work in school and responsibilities at home. She understands the culture they were brought up in, enjoys communicating with them in their native language, and knows she is loved. Yet the following are issues she assuredly experienced as a second-generation child in America.

Issues Involving Second-Generation Children

- Isolation
- Low self-esteem
- Overresponsibility
- Difficulty in communication
- Shame
- Peer rejection and stereotyping
- Abandonment
- Child care
- Caretaker
- Lack of guidance
- Conflict of two cultural norms

IMMIGRATION

Naomi was a first grader, barely in the United States for three months before the teasing and bullying began. She told her mom that the bus was the hardest place of all. "There is a third-grader, Quinn, who picks on me all the time for my English." Naomi started to cry. "I'm learning English as fast as I can. But Quinn screams at me in front of all the kids. 'I can't understand what you are saying. Talk louder. Talk louder.'" Naomi then told her mom that this older girl pushes her off the seat over and over again and tells Naomi she is too stupid to understand the rules about switching seats on the bus.

Naomi's mother explained to the teacher and eventually to the school principal the way her daughter was being treated. Quinn had told authorities what happened with *a different slant*, that Naomi was upset because she was a foreigner and couldn't understand. The principal said it was a cultural issue.

Too many children from other countries are forced into situations involving ridicule, stigma, and lack of safety. Because of learning a new language, a new culture, and a new way of life, many young people feel low self-esteem and unprotected.

Despite these challenges, many are remarkable. They are capable of learning the language, adapting, assimilating, and rising to the top of their class as students and mentors. Naomi was one of these children. By second grade, she was earning all As and reading on a fourth-grade level.

Children's Voices

The following passages are expressions from children's literature and from children themselves who have immigrated to America. Their insights help to create a broader understanding of the challenges they face as outsiders in a foreign system.

> *I didn't want to say my name from another country. I was afraid the kids wouldn't like me. I was ashamed of my parents. My friends thought they were stupid because they didn't speak English.*
> *Mostly I wish I were still smart.*
>
> —Lai (2013)

> *I don't want to go to school, where the English word tastes like metal in my mouth.*
>
> —Mak (2001)

> *I did not want to learn the new way. I wanted to go back home to Korea. I did not like America. Everything was different here.*
>
> —Recorvits and Swiatkowska (2003)

CULTURAL CONNECTION THROUGH OUTREACH AND SERVICES

Boat People SOS (BPSOS)

Boat People SOS is a national Vietnamese American community organization with the mission to "empower, organize, and equip Vietnamese individuals and communities in their pursuit of liberty and dignity" (BPSOS, 2011). It empowers individuals, strengthens families, and builds communities through direct services, advocacy, community development, leadership development, grassroots media, research, and international initiatives.

Three following examples are innovative initiatives by the BPSOS-Delaware Valley Asian Youth Empowerment Program's New Jersey projects, which enable Asian youth to be successful with challenging issues involving culture and immigration as they balance cultures in America. *The Basement Breakers* are young people who are passionate about raising awareness on community social issues. They participate in their own school activities as well as inspire youth to take action.

After School Power Hours helps students ages 6 to 12 with academics, providing exercises for practice and supervision by high school volunteers. The goal is to help younger students improve academic and social skills as high school students build leadership skills and serve as role models. *The Southeast Asian Roots Gardens* project is a multigenerational education opportunity for low-income children to learn about nutrition and science, discover their parents' and grandparents' cultural vegetables from Vietnam, and practice sustainable community gardening. This project meets the needs of the Vietnamese community by providing access to nutritional foods and academic assistance for youth.

Latin American Youth Center (LAYC)

The Latin American Youth Center is a multiservice youth development organization that offers multicultural, multilingual services to youth of all backgrounds in the Washington, DC, area.

LAYC works to support academic achievement, promote healthy behaviors, and guide youth toward successful adulthood by conducting advocacy and policy work to broaden opportunities for young people. Youth and their families are helped to live, work, and study with dignity, hope, and joy. Programs include educational enhancement, counseling, community wellness, workforce readiness, residential placement, art and media, healthy recreation, and advocacy.

Education, Interconnection, and Community

LAYC's Art + Media House partnered with the Art Museum of the Americas of the Organization of American States and the Museo de Arte de El Salvador (MARTE) to display a year's worth of artwork. Participants from El Salvador who have migrated to the Washington, DC, area have maintained a community with an active, involved Salvadoran population since the 1960s. The program in El Salvador took place in Casas de la Cultura, government-administered centers that promote cultural and artistic activities and a strong sense of local heritage. MARTE connected with youth of the Casas de la Cultura, welcoming those who are interested to take part in *Two Museums, Two Nations, One Identity*. In Washington, DC, youth participants, while learning painting, photography, and video art, engaged in a series of workshops on the themes of self, family, tradition, school, neighborhood, community, migration and bilingualism.

Art Museum of the Americas: Reaching Out to Community

The Art Museum of the Americas also reaches out to the community. Its mission is to interconnect, promote, and create positive impact on the people and cultures of the Western Hemisphere. This photo is a self-portrait in which a girl chooses to represent herself by wearing her Quinceañera dress.

Hazel Serrano Photograph

The museum provides a range of educational and outreach activities, providing an engaging, educational, and fun service for community families and children. Workshops for children ages 5 to 15 offer projects to create a piñata, a cornhusk doll, a carnival mask, a friendship bracelet, or cast of a child's hand. This photo is from a family workshop at the museum in which families create art projects to solidify art concepts in the galleries.

Courtesy OAS I Art Museum of the Americas

What We Can Do

The LAYC created a project for children whose families had fled as refugees to America. Girls and boys created the following murals the size of several city blocks in Washington, DC. Its artwork and colors are exquisite, as is the storytelling of their loss and grief issues coming to a new country as well as the sharing of their culture and hopes and dreams. The following photographs document their visions. The project began in 1991, when families were forced to leave El Salvador, and it was updated in 2005 by Salvadoran youth from the center. It allowed children creative expression and ongoing sharing.

Life in Home Country

A deep sense of culture and a rich heritage are expressed in this piece of the mural.

What Happened That Caused You To Leave?

This pictorial account of escape from El Salvador graphically identifies reasons for fleeing a country. We see from young people's accounts invasion, war, death, destruction, and great suffering, which are perhaps easier to share through artwork than words.

Life in Washington, DC

The mural depicts life for these young people in the United States. A beautiful Statue of Liberty is shown, as well as a boy reading "No human being is illegal" on his computer screen and a nightmarish scene with a sign saying "Say NO to drugs."

Life in an Ideal Future

This section of the mural idealizes humanity holding hands as one with planet Earth while dancing under a rainbow sky. Seeing a future of harmony and happiness is apparent.

This creative project allowed young people from another country to share what life was like before they came, display visually their life experience in America, and present, in a beautiful way, their hopes and dreams for a brighter tomorrow.

Interventions

> *In America the dream is to have a home*
> *In our country, the dream is to have a business.*

—Sophie, age 12

Community and national resources can provide support for adults and children from other countries. The following interventions are helpful in assisting with language, finances, healthcare, and other services.

1. Mentor others. Children can join a volunteer program to help tutor younger children from their country.
2. Provide childcare. Childcare is provided for working parents.
3. Volunteer to help with language and customs. Families need help with paperwork, taxes, finding markets for food and products from their country, and health care.
4. Help others realize their dreams. Provide financial support for small business loans to help families create homes and businesses and help to pay for education.

5. Offer guidance. People who speak the language to provide guidance for parents for educational goals, career paths, and so on.
6. Provide translators for parents to attend school meetings and functions and translate school messages and reports.
7. Find community resources. *Boat People SOS, the LAYC, and the Art Museum of the Americas* educational program are community outreach programs providing services and childcare for the community.

Resources on Immigration for Children

Inside Out and Back Again by Thanhha Lai (2013)
Escape from Saigon: How a Vietnam War Orphan Became an American by Andrea Warren (2008)
A Look at Vietnam by Helen Frost and Gail Saunders-Smith (2000)
When You Were Born in Vietnam: A Memory Book for Children Adopted from Vietnam by Therese Bartlett and William Bartlett (2002)
Vietnam by Michael Dahl (2006)
Sing 'n Learn Vietnamese by Hop Thi Nguyen and Selina Yoon (1998)
My Chinatown by Kam Mak (2001)
My Name Is Yoon by Helen Recorvits (2003)
This Is My Story: I Come from Ukraine by Valerie Weber (2007)
Mexican Immigrants in America by Rachael Hanel (2009)
The Name Jar by Yangsook Choi (2001)

MULTIRACIAL FAMILIES

In the world, there's light and dark, and everything in between.

—Rotner and Kelly (2010)

LAYC Project

The Broadway show, *Memphis* (Frost and Adams, 2009–2012), dramatizes society in the 1950s, with strong racial boundaries and segregation. Felicia, an African American woman, and Huey Calhoun, a White man, fall in love—a relationship forbidden in Tennessee at the time. Calhoun pleads with Felicia to marry and have a family. She responds that it is impossible—that they could never have children together. Nowadays, the impossible has happened, and multicultural families have moved to the forefront of American society.

Although prejudice, ignorance, and intolerance have progressed in this modern, diverse world, they have not gone far enough to eliminate the bias and stereotyping that still exists for our children. Rachel overheard her little friends talking at the snack table in kindergarten. She wasn't sure what they were saying, but it seemed there were rules about liking people. That night at story time, she asked her dad, "Is it OK if I am friends with someone with a different color skin? Is it OK if I like them? The kids at school said it wasn't." Rachel's dad explained it was more than OK. "I have liked people of different colors. They are my friends. It is normal to be friends with and like lots of different people. It has to do with your heart, and not your skin color." In that teachable moment, Rachel received a valuable lesson from her dad—he did not see the world through prejudiced eyes.

Four-year-old Marcus drew a picture of himself and his family. His was the only face colored with brown crayon. Marcus asked his mom, "Why am I the only brown person in the family?"

Marcus's family was multiracial. His mother, Maggie, and his little sister Dominique were White, his father Joseph was African American, and Marcus was African American as well. Marcus often reflected about skin color, comparing his shade to his mother's.

"Mommy, I'm tan like you. The kids at school say I am black, but I am tan like you."

"Everyone comes in different sizes and shades," Mom said. Maggie explained that at least once a week when she came to pick him up from school a classmate would blurt out with a puzzled look on their face, "Are you Marcus's mom?" She confided that she felt they were wondering, "How could you be his mother if you are White and he is African American?" Maggie wished she could find the words to help her dialogue with her young son about differences in the color of skin.

What to Say

Shades of People by Rotner and Kelly (2010) is such a resource. The book presents beautiful photographs of children with many shades of skin color. It serves as a good introduction to racial and ethnic diversity and helps stimulate discussion of that diversity. In simple language that preschoolers can understand, it clearly explains all the different shades people can have and that "our skin is just our covering, like wrapping paper. You can't tell what someone is like from the color of their skin" (pp. 13–14).

Sometimes young children take what they hear literally. Catherine was a 5-year-old African American girl. Her dad was also African American, and her mom was White. She told her mother quite often. "I'm not Black." She pointed to her skin and explained, "Just look at my arm." After reading *Shades of People* with her parents, she realized she wasn't the color black, but her skin was a shade of brown.

Catherine realized that was OK. People come in all shapes, sizes, and colors. Children gain the concept that there are many shades of children within one family, at school, on the playground, and at the park or beach.

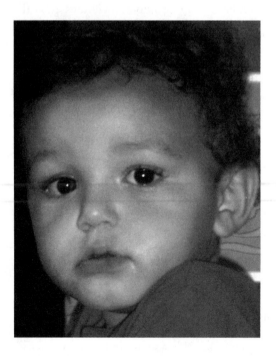

Resources for Children

Chocolate Me! By Taye Diggs (2011)
All of the Pieces That Make Me, Me by
    Kathryn Scott (2011)
Shades of People by Shelley Rotner and
    Sheila M. Kelly (2010)
The Skin I'm In: A First Look at Racism
    by Pat Thomas (2003)

SAME-SEX PARENTING

Roughly two million children are being raised in LGBT families.
Same-sex couples raising children are more racially and ethnically diverse.

—Movement Advancement Project (2011, p. iii)

Girls and boys are naturally inquisitive. Many questions center on girl–boy topics. Even the youngest of children may have questions about same-sex parents, asking, "Even though there are two moms, who is the real mommy?" It is important to emphasize to kids who have two moms or two dads can love each other just like moms and dads do. Both are the real mommies.

Rosemary was a precocious 6-year-old living in a family with two moms. She was engaging with adults and delightfully loved by teachers and classmates. Rosemary was invited to a business dinner with her moms and two of their clients, Alice and Ethan. Rosemary began to actively engage the grown-ups with enthusiasm and gusto.

"I'm so happy," she spontaneously reflected with cheer. "Why are you so happy?" Ethan asked with a smile. "I'm lucky. I have two dogs and two moms." "You are a very lucky girl to have two dogs and two moms. Wow!" Ethan responded.

But that night before bed Rosemary confided in Mommy Marge, "Janie says I don't have a real family. She says two dogs can be in a family but not two moms. Is it true that two moms and a kid aren't a real family?" Her mom responded that it wasn't true. "Families come in all different ways . . . in all sizes and with different people in them. You have two moms, two dogs and you, and that is your family. Families are people that love and care for each other" (adapted from Goldman, 2010).

Emily was 11 years old when she testified before a state senate committee for marriage equality for her two moms, advocating for her family's legal rights. She questioned vehemently to the senators, "Why won't you let my moms get married?" She explained to them that she had been a premature baby. She had learned that when she was in the hospital one of her moms was not legally allowed to hold her. She burst into tears, asking the senators, "Do you know how that makes me feel?"

Emily's story confronts the issue that children of same-sex parents feel marginalized, not only by family, peers, and society, but by the legal system as well. Although diverse families are an integral part of the American landscape, children of lesbian, gay, bisexual, and transgender (LGBT) families face social stigma and discrimination. They live in a society where many expect everyone to be heterosexual, challenging LGBT families to cope with inappropriate questions, the politicization of their families, and legally discriminatory laws. Racial and ethnic minorities often feel greater stress in LGBT families. A 2008 study of LGBT parents and school-age children found that 40% of students with LGBT parents reported being verbally harassed because of their family (Kosciw, Joseph and Elizabeth Diaz, Gay, Straight Education Network, 2008 [p. xvi]).

The Child Welfare League of America (CWLA) has affirmed, "A diversity of families is needed to help ensure that vulnerable children attain safety, find permanent families, and achieve well being. As such, lesbian, gay and bisexual parents are essential child

welfare partners because they are as well-suited to raise children as their heterosexual counterparts." (Movement Advancement Project, Family Equality Council, and Center for American Progress, 2011, Foreword by CWLA, p. i).

The Supreme Court ruling on June 26th, 2013 declaring, DOMA, The Defense of Marriage Act, to be unconstitutional was truly ground breaking. This decision creates equal rights for same sex married couples under federal law, taking a giant stride to achieve inclusion for all families.

Resources for Children on LGBT Issues

Uncle Bobby's Wedding by Sarah Brannen (2008)
King and King by Linda De Haan and Stern Nijland (2000)
Asha's Mums by Rosamund Elwin and Michele Paulse (1990)
Mother's Day on Martha's Vineyard by Ursula Ferro (2007)
In Our Mothers' House by Patricia Polacco (2009)
And Tango Makes Three by Justin Richardson and Peter Parnell (2005)
How It Feels to Have a Gay or Lesbian Parent: A Book by Kids for Kids of All Ages by Judith Snow (2004)

Resources for Adults

Coming Out, Coming In: Nurturing the Well Being and Inclusion of Gay Youth in Mainstream Society by Linda Goldman (2008).
My Two Moms: Lesson of Love, Strength, and What Makes a Family by Zach Wahls (2012).

WHAT A FAMILY IS

Families are as rich and varied as the people who make them up. They are a kaleidoscope of the diversity that encompasses human beings and can be valued for their uniqueness and special qualities.

—Goldman (2010)

Family means different things to different people. Appearance, opinions, and attitudes can create an artificial, limited perception of family for many young people. Single parenting, adoption, same-sex parents, foster care, divorce, and more have created new paradigms for the everyday family unit. Imprisonment, deployment, immigration, and more shift the ways family relate to one another. Differences of race and culture within families paint a new brushstroke of the modern family.

The vision of nonjudgment pertaining to family issues is essential in shifting to a paradigm of inclusion for our children's sake and their future. Outdated thought forms from negative imprints can be transformed to positive and expanded visions of acceptability and respect for all—regardless of gender, race, culture, skin color, or size and shape of family . . . creating a new harmony in our multifaceted world.

Dialogue About Families

We can say to children that a family is a group of people who love and care for one another. Some families have kids with a mom and dad, and some have only one dad or one mom. Still other families can have two moms or two dads, or a grandmother and her grandchild. You might be the only child in your family, or you might be one of three. Your best friend could have a brother and sister. There are lots of ways to be a family.

Families come in all sizes and have different people in them. Even your pets are part of your family. The important part of a family is respect and love (Goldman, 2010).

Core Family Concepts

Bullying and teasing impact the youngest of children through verbal slurs and even physical harassment. Feelings of isolation and shame surrounding family can lead to isolation, poor school performance, and depression among youth. An important goal is to provide girls and boys with nonjudgmental dialogue and open-ended options about family, cultural, race, and gender issues. The following core concepts pertaining to these issues for children create a powerful new paradigm to allow boys and girls and caring adults more freedom and options about issues involving societal, peer, and family stereotyping. Creating an inclusive and nonjudgmental dialogue for children on diversity enhances self-esteem and harmony for everyone. These dialogues include the following topics:

- Name-calling and teasing are never OK.
- There are no such things as "girl colors" and "boy colors" or "girl games" and "boy games" or "girl toys" and "boy toys."
- Girls and boys don't have to act, dress, or talk a certain way.
- Everyone is different, and that is OK.
- I can choose what I want to be.
- Families are different, too. They come in all shapes, sizes, and relationships.
- Loving and taking care of each other is what makes a family.

Talking to young people about family diversity issues has become a prime focus for educators, parents, mental and physical health professionals, and other caring adults. Harassment of others due to stereotypes and bias can lead to low self-esteem, internalization of teasing, and depression for children and teens. Creating clear and nonbiased language for dialogue is an essential step in eliminating this abuse.

Children can learn to respect sameness and difference with families. Creating key concepts is essential. Leaving kids out because they are girls or boys is hurtful. Name-calling, teasing, or bullying about stereotypical beliefs and attitudes about girls and boys is unacceptable at home and at school. Attitudes involving cultural, family, racial, and gender stereotyping bombard our children at very young ages. Too often society projects an outlook that diminishes divergence from stereotypical characteristics for girls and boys. Our cultural indoctrination can inhibit freedom for girls and boys to be who they are rather than whom others think they should be.

A Portrait Project

Children can create a portrait project. They can call it "These are the families in our class" and display the photos to share with others. Discussion can be created on what is the same and different about families by asking the following questions:

What Does a Family Look Like?

Mom, dad, and children

Dad and two sons

Two moms and a daughter

Father and son

Children can write or draw their own family. Next they can label everyone in their family. Finally, they can explain what makes them a family.

How Is My Family the Same as Everyone Else's Family? How Is It Different?

Same

Different

Children can make a list of the ways their family is the same as everyone else's. Then they can make a second list of ways their family is different.

Resources on Family

Many effective tools are available that allow children and adults to create conversations on issues of family diversity. Sharing words of inclusion and fact rather than outdated stereotyping enhance inclusion for all. Picture books for young children reinforce the concept that families come in many forms and that all family forms are equal.

Welcoming Schools, a project of the Human Rights Campaign Foundation, is a school climate improvement program that provides tools, lessons, and resources on embracing family diversity, avoiding gender bias, and ending bullying and name-calling in elementary schools. It offers an inclusive approach for diversity in communities.

For Children

> *Families in Many Cultures* by Heather Adamson (2008)
> *Global Babies* developed by the Global Fund for Children (2007)

For Adults

> *Growing Up Global: Raising Children to Be at Home in the World* by Homa Tavangar (2009)
> *Early Childhood Strategies for Working and Communicating With Diverse Families* by Janet Gonzolez-Mena (2006)

CONCLUSION

"What is a family?" This is a common question for boys and girls living in a culturally diverse world. Children often wonder if their family is a *real* family because it might not fit into society's prescribed norm. Many young people imagine the "average family" as a mom and dad and brothers and sisters living together. Then they might be in a different family where they feel ashamed or minimized.

Families consist of a rainbow of diversity that includes every human form on the planet. Each family needs to be valued as an integral and important part of the whole of creation. They are as unique and special as the people that make them up, and they reflect every race, color, culture, gender, and religion of humankind. Some families have divorce and adoption issues, some have same-sex parents and single parents, and others may have homes with an older sister and the pet dog. Kids may live in foster care or with grandparents.

Parents and professionals can plant the seeds of understanding for children by building a framework of tolerance and acceptance for each and every person. In this way we enlarge the daily world of our youth to one where they feel comfortable in their own skin and inclusive of those around them.

Our diverse nation is founded on immigration and integration. America has earned its description as a melting pot of all peoples. A blend of every race, color, country, culture, and gender has merged into one face and one idea . . . out of many, one.

FAMILY COMPLICATIONS AND SEPARATION: GONE BUT NOT FORGOTTEN

Divorce Deportation Imprisonment
Shame Outreach Adoption
Two homes Support groups
Termination of parental rights
Stigma Deployment

Two of the best kept secrets of the twentieth century are that everyone suffers and that suffering can be used for growth.

—Lawrence LeShan (quoted in Jackson, 1993)

CHALLENGES AND DIVISION WITHIN THE MODERN FAMILY

The Loss of the Idealized Family

Incarceration, deployment, divorce, deportation, foster care, and adoption are a few of the many issues involving some form of judgment, isolation, loss of routine, safety, and protection. So many of us were raised and continue to raise our children on the myth that a family with a mother and dad and children living in the home is the norm and the model of how life should be. Today's kids live in a different norm and model. Adjusting to change, separation, and presumed safety are commonplace in a fast, ever-changing society, where children are separated from their parents, moved from their homes, and ridiculed or judged for their complex family issues as a secondary loss.

CHILDREN OF IMPRISONED PARENTS

> *Seven million, or one in ten of the nation's children have a parent under criminal justice supervision—in jail or prison, on probation, or on parole.*

> —San Francisco Children of Incarcerated Parents Partnership (2012)

Children of imprisoned parents suffer as well as their parents. Many times they lose contact with parents or visit them rarely. They are more likely to drop out of school, engage in delinquency, and subsequently be incarcerated themselves (Dallaire, 2007). More mothers are being incarcerated, and evidence indicates that this can be more damaging to children. The increase of imprisoned parents can have a great impact on families and communities.

Schirmer, Nellis, and Mauer explain in *Incarcerated Parents and Their Children: Trends 1991-2007, The Sentencing Project (2009)* that young children " 'have been observed to suffer a variety of adverse outcomes that are consistent with the research on the effects of insecure attachment'. . . and that more than half of children with incarcerated parents have had school problems such as poor grades and instances of aggression" (citing Parke and Clarke-Stewart, 2002, p. 11).

Creating Dialogue

Sometimes children feel confused, isolated, forgotten, angry, and sad about their parent being in prison. They may feel powerless to control their lives because their mom or dad goes to prison. They have questions, feelings, worries, and changes to consider. The following are a few interventions that allow young people to have a voice, become empowered, and feel they have choices in their life. The first is a bill of rights for children of incarcerated parents created by *Friends Outside*, an organization that provides services to incarcerated and reentering people, their families, and communities.

Children of Incarcerated Parents Bill of Rights

1. I have the right to be kept safe and informed at the time of my parent's arrest.
2. I have the right to be heard when decisions are made about me.
3. I have the right to be considered when decisions are made about my parent.
4. I have the right to be well cared for in my parent's absence.
5. I have the right to speak with, see, and touch my parent.
6. I have the right to support as I face my parent's incarceration.
7. I have the right not to be judged, blamed, or labeled because my parent is incarcerated.
8. I have the right to a lifelong relationship with my parent.
(San Francisco Children of Incarcerated Parents Partnership, 2012)

courtesy of Get on the Bus

Support Groups

Often children are ashamed to speak about their parent in jail or prison and may need reassurance that they have support in sharing. Their home life may change, creating many secondary losses. They may live with the other parent, another family member, or in foster care. Sometimes children change neighborhoods, schools, towns, and states, or they may live with a brother, aunt, or grandparents for a time.

Some communities have support groups for children whose parents are incarcerated. It helps them to have peers with similar issues. They can also make a list of people they can trust to share difficult or confused emotions about their parent and prison.

Open Dialogue

The following statements are some suggestions that might help children dialogue in an open communication.

"Two of every 100 children have had a parent in jail or prison."

"You didn't do anything wrong. People should not try to make you feel guilty or ashamed."

"Sometimes, it is easier not to talk about a parent who is incarcerated, but you may learn that there are plenty of other kids in the same situation."

"It's OK to love your Mom or Dad who is in jail or prison, even if some people don't think you should." (California Department of Corrections and Friends Outside, n.d.)

Answer Questions

Young people with parents in prison often have lots of questions. Is this my fault? Will I go to prison? What will happen to me? What will happen to my dad? Can I visit? Can I talk about my father? Griffin was 5 years old when his dad was put in prison for robbery. The first question Griffin asked his mother was, "Will I go to prison, too?" The following suggestions for talking with children can be reassuring.

- Their parent's incarceration is not their fault
- The facts about why their parent went to prison
- What is happening to their parent
- How to contact their parent if they can
- What will happen to them
- What will stay the same and what will change
- They can express feelings about a parent's incarceration in a safe way
- How they can visit and maintain contact with their parent
- When will the parent be released?
- People make choices that lead to different consequences. (adapted from www.friendsoutside.org)

Create Projects and Outreach

"When my mother was sentenced, I felt that I was sentenced . . . She was sentenced to prison—to be away from her kids and her family. I was sentenced, as a child, to be without my mother." Antoinette, now an adult, was eight years old when her mother was incarcerated.

—Bernstein (2005, p. 5)

Get on the Bus is a program of the Center for Restorative Justice Works, a nonprofit organization that unites children, families, and communities separated by crime and the criminal justice system.

For the annual Father's Day event on June 8, 2012, *Get on the Bus* brought children from California to visit their fathers in prison. "Sixty percent of parents in state prison report being held over 100 miles from their children." *(Get on the bus, About Us, [2009])*

"Regular prison visits lower rates of recidivism for the parent, and make the child better emotionally adjusted and less likely to become delinquent," according to the Center for Restorative Justice Works, the nonprofit organization that runs the *Get on the Bus* program (Nicholson, 2012). Each child is provided bus transportation to prison. The children are given a travel bag, a photo with their parent, and meals for the day. On the trip home, children receive a teddy bear with a letter from their parent. Post-event counseling is also provided.

During their time together, one 12-year-old hugged her dad, who is serving a life sentence for murder. Another 10-year-old met her father for the first time. One imprisoned inmate held his 8-month-old grandson for the first time. A little girl made a Father's Day card that said, "I love you." A prison employee read letters from inmates to their children. One father shared, "Hello my handsome prince . . . I want to tell you how proud I am of you." Another dad wrote "To the Best Son on Earth."

Activities during the visit included fathers reading books to kids, holding children hands, talking to them, or painting their faces. With a backdrop of the Golden Gate Bridge, family pictures were taken for kids to keep and remember.

Resources for Children

Wish You Were Here by Autumn Spanne and Laura Longshine (2010)
An Inmate's Daughter by Jan Walker (2010)
My Daddy Is in Jail by Janet Bender (2003)
Visiting Day by Jacqueline Woodson (2002)

Resources for Parents

Parenting From Prison: A Hands-on Guide for Incarcerated Parents by James Birney (2011)
Empowering Children of Incarcerated Parents by Stacey Burgess, Tonia Casselman, and Jennifer Carsey (2009)

UNDOCUMENTED CHILDREN AND FAMILIES: DEPORTATION

About 4.5 million U.S. citizen kids have at least one undocumented parent.
There are at least 17 million people who are legally living in the U.S. but whose families
have at least one undocumented immigrant.

—Vargas (2012, p. 42)

In *Shadow Americans*, Jose Antonio Vargas (2012) describes how, as a teenager, he discovered he was in the United States illegally. Not only unable to get his driver's license, he also suddenly realized he had no rights and privileges of citizenship. His mother had sent him to live with grandparents in the United States at age 12. Applying for his driver's license at age 16, he was shocked to realize his green card, his primary legal identification, was a fraud. His naturalized grandparents, his American-born relatives, never told him.

Vargas explains that these types of families are called mixed-status families, and his new status was alarming. He boldly states, "In 21st century politics, diversity is destiny." Politicians, educators, and community leaders must incorporate a new vision of a "growing multiethnic America that adapts to the inevitable demographic and cultural shifts" (p. 44).

The fear of deportation for family, parents, and friends is one of the outcomes of the immigration issue. The 2011 film *A Better Life* (Weitz) shares the living terror of deportation for children and families, the stress of living with a secret, and the lack of protection of the legal system. The movie depicts an illegal immigrant father, Carlos, struggling to create a good life for his son, Luis. Carlos crossed the border from Mexico when his son was a newborn, hoping to give him the opportunities he never had.

While Carlos works as a gardener day and night, Luis explores gang membership as a surrogate family. When Carlos's truck is stolen, the consequences of reporting the theft outweigh legal protection. These consequences could mean deportation. Father and son align to get the truck back, only to ultimately be discovered. Carlos is sent back to his country, and Luis is left in America. Tragically this story shares the love of family and the devastation of that family system trapped in the space of an immigration status that is not working for many who seek refuge to find a better life.

The Dream Act

As many as 800,000 young people live in fear of deportation.

—Caldwell (2012)

Thousands of undocumented youth earn American high school diplomas or equivalencies, yet their illegal status prevents most from achieving educational achievement, career opportunities, and increased economic opportunity. "This facet of the U.S. immigration debate that focuses on children who are brought into the country illegally by their parents' choice is a contentious one. Should the underage illegal immigrants growing up and moving through the American educational system be punished, deported or offered a chance at citizenship?" (Conger, 2011).

The Development, Relief and Education for Alien Minors Act (the DREAM Act) was introduced in 2001, failed many attempts to be passed by Congress, and remains in limbo to be signed by 2013. Its goal is to offer incentives for educational achievement and the pursuit of legal residency in the United States for undocumented youth, allowing them higher education, military service, conditional permanent resident status, and eventual citizenship as productive Americans.

In June 2012, President Obama announced a policy change to "stop deporting younger illegal immigrants who came to the U.S. as children will make the system 'more fair, more efficient and more just'" (Caldwell, 2012). Foley (2012), describes this policy to include undocumented immigrants who came to the United States under the age of 16 and presently under age 30, living in the country at least five years, having been an honorably discharged veteran of the Coast Guard or armed forces, or a student who has graduated from high school or obtained a GED. Convicted felons or those with a "significant" misdemeanor or multiple misdemeanors are ineligible.

Foley reports the sentiments of Senator Dick Durbin, who introduced the DREAM Act in 2001. "This action will give these young immigrants their chance to come out of the shadows and be part of the only country they've ever called home." President Obama agrees: "They pledge allegiance to our flag. They are Americans in their hearts, in their minds, in every single way but one: on paper" (Foley, 2012).

Resources for Children and Teens

Gervelie's Journey by Anthony Robinson and Annemarie Young (2010)
Growing up Rita by Michael de Gusman (2011)
The Fifth Sun by Mary Helen Lagasse (2004)

CHILDREN OF DIVORCE

Sadie's Story

Sadie's mom and dad separated when she was 8 years old, and eventually divorced. After one year, the family began to feel like they could begin to live life in a different way. Sadie lived with her mom during the week and with her dad on the weekends. Her father began dating a woman named Maria, the same name as her mom's. Several weeks later Sadie burst into tears in her support group.

"Why are you so upset, Sadie?" asked her group support leader. "I don't want my father dating Maria. I hate it! I hate it!" she screamed. "Why don't you write your dad a letter about how you feel? You don't have to show it to him, but you can if you want to." She began writing the following letter.

Many children have these feelings when a surviving parent begins dating. Sadie was frightened to share her father, and feared she could lose him too.

Magical Thinking

Another common feeling for children of separation and divorce is the magical thinking they caused the divorce. "If only I had made my bed, my parents wouldn't have argued." "If only I had gotten a good report card, my dad wouldn't have left." In a situation where children feel they have little control over outside events, they may feel more powerful thinking they caused their parents to not be together. Sometimes they admit, "It just doesn't make sense."

One little girl, Gabriel, cherished the hope her parents would get back together and held on to the idea that the divorce wasn't "really real." She told her older sister many times, "You'll see . . . you'll see . . . Mommy and Daddy and you and Walker and me will all live together. I promise." She drew a picture about her idealized family together and said to her sister, "This is what it will look like. We will all be together again."

Gabriel, like so many children of divorce, finds it hard to accept her new life with two homes, two routines, two parents living apart, and the shame and stigma she feels about it. Even those children who do not experience divorce directly may begin to question their own family unit when a friend's family splits up. Shawn came home from a birthday party in tears.

"Mom," he shared, "Mitchell's mom and dad are getting divorced. He said they fight too much. You and dad had a fight last night. Does that mean you are getting divorced too? Please don't. That scares me."

What We Can Do: The National Family Resiliency Center, Inc.

The National Family Resiliency Center, Inc. (NFRC) is an exemplary organization providing services for individual, family, and group counseling for children, teens, and adults to aid in understanding, identifying, expressing, and accepting the realities of life-changing experiences in their family. Programs, workshops, support groups, and resources are offered to help navigate life changes by addressing premarriage, marriage, family transitions, separation, divorce, and remarriage.

These programs enable girls and boys to understand what is happening in their world, and *separate situations that they cannot control from those that they can*. A more realistic view of changes in their family begins to develop as productive communication and relationship-building skills are developed. Counselors keep parents informed on their child's progress, offering advice and support on reinforcing lessons and coping skills their children are learning. Parents can then participate in key sessions to better understand and support their child's needs. More information is available at http://www.divorceabc.com/.

Kyle's Story

Fifteen-year-old Kyle was deeply concerned about his dad's drinking too much alcohol, which began after his mom and dad separated. He revealed in a group session that he was often terrified when driving with his father and began to feel overwhelmed. He loved his dad and was conflicted. "If I say anything about my father's drinking," he shared, "I'm afraid I won't be allowed to see him." Kyle explained his dilemma openly with the group and through discussion began to realize this problem might be *too big* to handle alone. Options were explored. One idea was for Kyle to first speak with his father about his safety concerns and fears concerning driving and alcohol. Kyle eventually had this conversation with his father, which enabled his dad to realize the jeopardy he was placing his son in by being reckless and to eventually get help.

Support Groups

This scenario exemplifies the work done in weekly groups that the NFRC provides. Young people explore options for resolving issues surrounding separation and divorce in an atmosphere allowing their voice to be heard and change implemented. The strength of the multiple family group sessions lays in its bringing together children, teens, and parents to actualize the concept of a "community of families" in a nonjudgmental environment. Parents join their children in multifamily activities and discussion that include reading stories, looking at pictures, drawing, music, role-playing with children and adults, and putting on plays with puppets and stuffed animals. The framework of the group allows children and teens to:

- Work on labeling and expressing feelings about divorce.
- Learn an appropriate role for themselves in the family.
- Examine and address problems in their relationship with each parent.

Peer Counselors

The NFRC model also provides peer counselors. They become extraordinary role models for young people and adults and an integral part of the process, volunteering time to discuss their own experience of coping with family transitions support and providing hope for others.

Fourteen-year-old Natasha came to a group session very upset because her mother would not allow her to go to a sleepover at her friend's house. She explained her mom had insisted it was her time to be with Natasha. Infuriated by the restriction, Natasha felt that her only alternative was to threaten to not spend any time with her mom or not speak if she did. Amy, a peer counselor in the group, explained her dad had acted the same way after her parents' divorce, insisting she be with him because their time was limited. Amy helped Natasha find words to speak to her mom about how she felt. Other group members volunteered to role-play a scenario of Natasha and her mother and possible discussions about the sleepover restriction. This group support gave Natasha the necessary tools to open up dialogue and eventually come to a mutual resolution with her mom. The support group formed a framework that allowed Natasha to step back, be thoughtful about her problem, and create a new resolution.

Resources for Children

Two Homes by Claire Masurel and Kady MacDonald Denton (2003)
Mom's House, Dad's House for Kids: Feeling at Home in One Home or Two by Isolina Ricci (2006)
Was It The Chocolate Pudding? A Story for Little Kids About Divorce by Sandra Levins and Bryan Langdo (2006)
Standing on My Own Two Feet: A Child's Affirmation of Love in the Midst of Divorce by Tamar Schmitz (2008)
Divorce Is Not the End of the World: Zoe's and Evan's Coping Guide for Kids by Zoe Stern and Evan Stern (2008)

The Divorce Helpbook for Teens by Cynthia MacGregor (2004)
Dear Judge (Kid's Letters to the Judge) by Charlotte Hardwick (2008)
*I Don't Want to Choose: How Middle School Kids Can Avoid Choosing One Parent Over the
    Other* by Katherine Andre (2009)

Resources for Adults

Putting Children First: Proven Parenting Strategies for Helping Children Thrive Through Divorce
    by JoAnne L. Pedro-Carroll (2010)
Remarried With Children: Ten Secrets for Successfully Blending and Extending Your Family by
    Barbara LeBey (2005)
Creative Interventions for Children of Divorce by Liana Lowenstein (2006).
Mommy and Daddy Are Getting Divorced: Helping Children Cope With Divorce by Kristine
    Turner (2010)
Parenting Apart: How Separated and Divorced Parents Can Raise Happy and Secure Kids by
    Christina McGhee (2010)
Parents Who Cheat: How Children and Adults Are Affected When Their Parents Are Unfaithful by
    Ana Nogales and Laura Golden Bellotti (2009)

ADOPTION: I DO BELONG

Rachel came home from school and burst into tears. Her friend Quinn kept asking her "Who is your real mom?" She cried to her mother, "I didn't know what to say . . . What do I say, Mommy?"

Young people often are unsure of what to say to these kinds of questions. Many girls and boys are familiar with hearing them. It helps children to remember that "real parents" are the parents whom they have loved and who have taken care of them. Both birth parents and adoptive parents are real parents.

Every child is unique, and so are their circumstances in terms of their age at the time of placement, their experiences prior to adoption, and any issues involving their birth parents and their first homes. Birth parents are usually people who loved them but were unable to provide for them. Marge Heegaard (2007, p. 4) defines adoption as "an agreement in which the birth parents pass their parental rights and responsibilities to the adoptive parents."

Children crave truth. Feelings of being unwanted or unloved may be expressed as a question: Why didn't they want me? This question creates a teachable moment in which to explain what a hard decision it can be for parents to place a child for adoption, and how they may not have had a choice. Sometimes moms are very sick, or dads are very poor, or for many other reasons families are unable to raise their children. Knowing as many specific details as they can about their history helps children build a strong self-image as they piece together their understanding of who they are.

It helps children become comfortable with their own sense of identity if they are able to feel at ease asking questions about their birth parents, and these questions should be answered as fully and honestly as possible, in an age-appropriate way—even if the answers are difficult to give. Remember that the known reality, however upsetting, can be processed with loving help, while the unknown can never be integrated.

Children May Wonder . . .

Why couldn't I stay with my birth
    family?
Is there something wrong with
    them?
Where are they now?
What's wrong with me?
Why was I "given up"?
Is it my fault I am adopted?
Will my parents always want to
    keep me?
Why do people always say "the
    adopted child of . . . "?
Why can't they just say "the child of
    . . . "?

If children are not asking these questions, it doesn't mean they aren't thinking about them. They may be worried about their adoptive family's feelings. Parents can overcome this by demonstrating their comfort in discussing their child's first family. Simple statements such as "I wonder where you got your beautiful blue eyes from? That must have been from your birth family," or "I love listening to you sing. You know, your birth mother had a lovely voice, too" can show children that you are not threatened by talk of their first family and may help them to approach you with their questions when they are ready.

Bodhi's Story: An Open Adoption

Sometimes children have questions concerning the parents who are raising them. One common question is "Why did you want me?" Children may naturally conclude that if their first parents gave them up, their new parents might do the same. Some decide they had better be extra good, while others may feel "What's the use?" Either way, young people may experience renewed anxiety around rejection and abandonment.

One of the most welcoming adoption stories is that of Bodhi, a child whose mom, dad, and brother Skylar wished for and loved long before he ever came home to them. The level of research and preparation that was done before the adoption process, the beautiful openness and bonding that was able to take place between the adoptive family and the birth mother prior to birth, and the intimate time spent together in the hospital and before bringing the baby home all set the stage for a continued love and level of integration that could only lead to the essence of a true family.

Mani had at first wondered how she could ever go through the open adoption process or love an adopted child the way she loved her biological son, and the thought terrified her.

It seemed impossible to navigate the complex world of adoption.

Now she realizes that "Anytime you care for a child, you love that child. The caring creates the love." She is just as amazingly proud of Bodhi as she is of her older son, and she adores him just as much as she possibly could a child she had carried and given birth to.

The Process

When first considering the idea, Mom and 10-year-old Skylar made a chart on the pros and cons of adoption and presented it to Dad. Everyone decided they were in. As Skylar exclaimed, "It's a no-brainer!"

After much research, the path they chose was open domestic newborn adoption, with the entire family preparing by going to classes, reading books, and eventually bonding with the birth mother who later chose them. Everyone openly shared feelings associated with bringing this new family member home.

Skylar was included in every step of the way, and his mom and dad prepared him for the ups and downs that could occur along the way to bringing Bodhi home, including the reality that anything could happen until the baby was born and his birth mother actually signed the papers terminating her rights.

Skylar was told the age-appropriate facts. He was invited to join monthly support groups with his parents where he could ask questions and hear about the experiences of others who had adopted.

"Skylar was born to be in an adoptive family. His determined desire to adopt and his fortitude in facing the challenges of the journey catapulted the family forward. He doesn't see any difference between an adopted brother or a biological one," Mani explained.

"In fact, his biggest fear was not that I would love the new baby more, but that I wouldn't love him as much. His level of maturity, along with his security regarding his place in our hearts, made him a natural for becoming an amazing big brother."

As Skylar explained when his mom asked him about whether he thought he might become jealous of baby Bodhi, "Mom! Babies bring more love. They don't take any away."

The Birth Mother

Of course, Bodhi's birth mother was an integral part of the adoption process. Skylar and his parents attended "match meetings" with her, and they wrote her letters back and forth. One of Mani's favorite moments came at the end of a long visit, when Bodhi's birth mother broke into a huge smile and told her. "I'm so excited you are going to be my son's mommy."

In less than three months, Bodhi was born and soon in the loving arms of his mother, father, and brother. The respect they had developed for his birth mother continued. After an intimate few days at the hospital together with Bodhi, everyone shared in his birth mother's sadness when she signed the papers that terminated her parental rights. The family recognized that while they were receiving an enormous blessing, she was experiencing a profound loss.

Mani made a website for her and her family with pictures and stories about Bodhi that she updates regularly. She also writes letters of caring and appreciation for the incredible gift of Bodhi, along with anecdotes about his growing up. They are even friends on Facebook!

"Many women are petrified by the idea of their child having two mothers," Mani said. Yet through education and research, she felt able to put aside those fears to focus on what was best for her son. "It had to be handled just right for Bodhi. Intuitively I felt the best way was to love, embrace, and honor his birth mother, thereby loving, embracing, and honoring *him* and *where he comes from*."

Mani projected that as Bodhi grows up, he will certainly be aware of any negativity expressed toward his birth mom and could easily internalize that as negativity felt toward him, and she did not want that.

"Loving and respecting his birth mother can only help Bodhi love and respect himself. I am so thankful to her for giving my son life. I love her for so many reasons, including her strength and bravery. But even if I had never been able to meet her, I would love her just for creating him. How could I not?"

A Mother's Thoughts on Adoption

Mani states that one of her goals is to work through issues, fears, questions, and concerns as they arise within her son, herself, or those in their life. Creating an ongoing conversation with her son from infancy to adulthood is as an integral part of her parenting plan.

"For me," she shares, "adoption has been an amazing experience. I truly believe that Bodhi was meant to be in our family, and I could never love him less because of the way he came. Adoption is nothing to be ashamed of—it should be celebrated!"

What We Can Do

Discussing adoption with a child requires open communication. Allow children to ask questions, especially about birth parents and where they were born, and acknowledge and support their thoughts and feelings. The following are core concepts to underscore with children:

1. *Adoptive families are different and the same as other families.* Families can have differences in terms of race, culture, and physical appearance. Family members can have different places of birth, different birth parents, and so on. Yet families are the same,

too. They go to baseball games together, have family dinners, and watch TV; most importantly, they love each other.

2.   *Who is my real mom, birth or adoptive?* Children often hear negative attitudes from peers and other adults. Children need to understand that when someone is adopted, their mom is just a *mom*, and she is the one who takes care of them every day. The person who gave birth to them is called a "birth mom." Both of them are *real* moms.

3.   *Share adoption information.* Children may feel afraid to ask questions about adoption, thinking it is some kind of betrayal. Being open and encouraging questions about birth parents and places allows better understanding and extinguishes confusion. Preparing older siblings and other family members by sharing information on adoption helps create a culture of openness in the entire family, thereby making the newly adopted family member more comfortable.

4.   *Present honest birth parent information.* Discussions about the difficulties a child's birth parents may have had in making the decision to place their child for adoption can be helpful and comforting to a child who may wonder why his or first family "didn't want me." Sometimes it might be helpful for adoptive parents to seek professional help in determining the best way to share information about birth parents that might be potentially damaging to a child's sense of self, such as a birth parent in prison or who is drug addicted. It is important to tell the truth about birth parents.

5.   *Prepare for a time of adjustment for everyone in the family after placement.* It takes time for a child to attach to new people, and children may display a wide range of behaviors, including testing the boundaries of their new parents' commitment to them by acting out or becoming "the perfect child" out of fear of rejection. These are both common and should improve with time and as they become increasingly secure in their new family.

6.   *Children may project onto parents and siblings.* Older adopted children may feel a sense of loss and abandonment, with accompanying feelings of anger, sadness, guilt, or shame, and they may project these feelings onto others in the family. Keeping clear rules and firm boundaries while a child is processing these emotions and giving accurate birth information promotes an eventual sense of comfort. Adapted from *Rosove, 2001, Rosie's Family: An Adoption Story*, Notes for Parents.

Resources for Children

Rosie's Family: An Adoption Story by Lori Rosove (2001)
Every Year on Your Birthday by Rose Lewis (2007)
When You Were Born in Vietnam: A Memory Book for Children Adopted From Vietnam by Theresa Bartlett (2001)
Adopted and Wondering by Marge Heegaard (2007)
I Wished for You: An Adoption Story by Marianne Richmond (2008)
Forever Fingerprints: An Amazing Discovery for Adopted Children by Sherrie Eldridge (2007)
Over the Moon, An Adoption Tale by Karen Katz (2001)
We Belong Together: A Book About Adoption and Families by Todd Parr (2007)
The Tummy Mummy by Michelle Madrid-Branch and Marin Thurber (2004)
Sam's Sister by Juliet C. Bond and Dawn W. Majewski (2004)
Tell Me Again About the Night I Was Born by Jamie Lee Curtis (2000)

Resources for Adults

Great Answers to Difficult Questions About Adoption: What Children Need to Know by Fanny Herlem (2008)
Promising Practices in Adoption and Foster Care: A Comprehensive Guide to Policies and Practices That Welcome, Affirm and Support Lesbian, Gay, Bisexual and Transgender Foster and Adoptive Parents (3rd ed.) by HRC Foundation's for Children—All Families Initiative (2009)
In On It: What Adoptive Parents Would Like You to Know About Adoption: A Guide for Relatives and Friends by Elisabeth O'Toole (2010)
Twenty Things Adopted Kids Wish Their Adoptive Parents Knew by Sherrie Eldridge (1999)
20 Things Adoptive Parents Need to Succeed by Sherrie Eldridge (2009)

Parenting Your Internationally Adopted Child: From Your First Hours Together Through the
   Teen Years by Patty Cogen (2008)
Children of Open Adoption and Their Families by Kathleen Silber and Patricia Dorner (1990)

DEPLOYMENT: SAYING GOOD-BYE AGAIN

More than 700,000 children have experienced one or more parental deployment. Currently,
about 220,000 children have a parent deployed.

—White House (2011, p. 7)

Gabrielle was getting ready for her 10th birthday party. All of her friends were going to be
there. Her new best friend was Maggie. Maggie had just moved to her street, and the girls
had played together a few times before the party. Maggie's first question after everyone
sang "Happy Birthday" was "Where's your dad?" It was a question that overwhelmed
Gabrielle, and she explained it was just too hard to answer. "My dad had to work today,"
was all she could share. Actually Dad had been working for 8 of the 10 years of her life. He
had been deployed three times. Gabrielle said she felt like he was a stranger, coming home
for short periods of time only to need to leave again.

Gabrielle's story is one of many children living during the period of the Iraq and
Afghanistan conflicts. They are experiencing the deployment of one or both parents that
makes them feel like Mom and Dad are strangers through continuous and ongoing separation.

Admiral Mike Mullen, former chair of the U.S. Joint Chiefs of Staff, addressed the
stress of this period of war, noting "This isn't just about the spouse, this is about kids who
have known nothing but war . . . an entire generation of military families has been dealing
with absent parents" (quoted in Dejesus, 2011).

A RAND study quoted in *We Serve, Too* (2010), "explored how children from military
families are faring with the wartime deployments of their parents . . . The study found that
rates of anxiety among military children—as well as emotional and behavioral difficulties—
are higher than the national averages, and that longer periods of parental deployment
exacerbated these challenges" (National Military Family Association, 2010, p. 2). "A 2010
study reports an 11 percent increase in outpatient visits for behavioral health issues
among a group of 3- to 8-year-old children of military parents and an increase of 18 percent in behavioral disorders and 19 percent in stress disorders when a parent was
deployed" (White House, 2011, p. 7).

When parents are deployed, military kids:

- Become "different" but still "look" the same
- Discover their world turned upside down
- Find usual support systems no longer relevant
- Lack connections to each other
- Are impacted by intensity and frequency of
  media coverage of the Global War on Terrorism.
  (Leonhard, Digby, and Rice, 2005, p. 4)

Talk, Listen, Connect: Sesame Street

Talk, Listen, Connect is Sesame Workshop's multiphase outreach initiative designed to help kids through deployment, homecoming, changes in the family, combat-related injuries, and the death of a loved one. It underscores the impact these issues have on the youngest of children and their difficulty in understanding why mommy or daddy needs to leave home, or how things could be different when they come back. Materials include DVDs, magazines for parents/staff/volunteers, and activity posters for children.

Rosita explains the sentiments of many little ones in a video for military children. She shares how she feels after dad comes home in a wheelchair. "I just wish things could go back to the way they were" (Sesame Workshop, 2011). Materials can be downloaded at http://archive.sesameworkshop.org/tlc/.

OPERATION: MILITARY KIDS

Operation: Military Kids is a Department of Defense outreach program that is a collaborative effort with America's communities to support children and youth impacted by military deployment. The program includes mobile technology labs, camps, and activities to create awareness of the challenges young people face through deployment. The *Operation: Military Kids* program creates a positive youth development experience for girls and boys, with an opportunity to be with other kids in the same situation and to have fun. These children are provided with Hero Packs, packages to thank and salute children with deployed parents for the sacrifice they have given while a parent serves the country.

The website for *Operation: Military Kids* is http://www.operationmilitarykids.org.

Hero Packs

Hero Packs are backpacks that are assembled by youth in 4-H clubs or other youth organizations, and then distributed to military kids when their parent is deployed. Some of the items in the Hero Pack, such as a disposable camera and stationery, are things that young people can use to stay in touch with their deployed parent. Many military youth feel isolated because they do not know anyone else in their same situation. Receiving a Hero Pack lets them know that others in the community recognize their situation.

Hero packs also include a backpack, a "parent pouch" with information on support services, a 4-H stuffed bear, a day planner that can be used as a journal, a storybook called *The Kissing Hand* by Audrey Penn, about a raccoon family facing a separation, and an accompanying raccoon puppet.

The young people who assemble these packs learn about the stresses faced by military youth when their parent is deployed, raising community awareness about situations faced by military families. A key component in the Hero Pack is a handwritten letter by the youth who assemble the Hero Packs, thanking the military youth for their contribution. A lesson plan to use with the Hero Pack assembly is available. The following is a sample letter to a military family child that might be included in the package.

Dear Child,

Thank you for supporting our country. I really appreciate all of the services and sacrifices that you are making while your parent is gone. I made this Hero Pack for you because you are one of my Heroes. Yes, you and your parents are heroes for making such a big contribution to our country. I hope you can use some of the items in this care package to keep in contact with your parent while they are gone . . . Thanks for being a hero! (Leonhard, Digby, and Rice, 2005, p. 11)

Operation Give a Hug

Operation Give a Hug is an organization dedicated to providing comfort to military children who are missing a parent, helping families connect to their units and resources in place to support them, and giving back to the military community. The organization provides military children with special soft dolls that have a photo sleeve face to hold a photo of the parent they are missing (www.ogah.org).

We Serve, Too: National Military Family Association

We Serve, Too. A Toolkit About Military Kids (National Military Family Association, 2010) shares voices and sentiments from children with military families. Some of the children said:

"I hope to one day be as great as him."

"My dad serves in the military and we do, too."

"You move a lot so you have to rely on family."

"I can't wait for my dad to come home from his deployment. It's going to be the best day ever."

"In my family it's a tradition to be in the military."

"It's terrible without my dad. And it would be really hard if he gets hurt or shot or even killed."

The National Military Family Association's Operation Purple program provides a week of camp for military youth with a deployed parent. It offers a free downloadable tool kit for children ages 6 to 11 and one for teens as well (http://www.timetotalk.org/military/pdf/10%20things%20article-NMFA09.pdf). The younger children were asked to list the best and hardest parts of military life in an activity called the Top Ten List. They offer advice about what helps military kids the most. Military kids need people in their community to know what they are going through.

"The best thing you can do for a military kid is know who they are and be there when they need to talk to someone" (National Military Family Association, 2010, p. 2).

Resources for Children

I Miss You! A Military Kids Book About Deployment by Beth Andrews and Hawley Wright (2007)
Night Catch by Brenda Ehrmantrau (2005)
A Paper Hug by Stephanie Skolmoski (2006)
Heroes! Activities for Kids Dealing with Deployment by Susan Weaver (2011)

CONCLUSION

We are powerless to control the losses and catastrophic events our children may need to experience, but by honoring their inner wisdom, providing mentorship, and creating safe havens for expression, we can empower them to become more capable, more caring human beings.

—Goldman (2005)

Each of the many diverse family systems can exist in a kind of pure or idealized form as is described in Chapter 8, "Family Diversity." The many challenges of life in the 21st century, however, often make it difficult if not impossible to prevent disruption and confusion for kids about what is a "normal" family. Our task is to create a paradigm shift that allows children to function constructively within challenging settings.

Eric kissed Mom's picture every night. She was deported to Mexico. Ginger writes Dad a letter. He is in prison. Charlotte plays a song on the piano for her grandmother. She lives in China. Gregory talks with his father via the Internet. He is serving in Iraq. Young people remember by doing. Separation becomes bearable through reaching out in a special way.

The complexities of family issues in this age of modernity force children and adults to practice *creative flexibility* while a new construct of family emerges. This construct embraces loving ties regardless of distance and time . . . through outreach, inclusion, education, and the resilience of the human spirit.

Resources on Separation

Getting Yourself Together When Your Family Comes Apart: Coping With Family Changes by Janet Bender (2004)
Llama Llama Misses Mama by Anna Dewdney (2009)
When I Miss You by Cornelia Maude (2004)
I Don't Want to Go to School: Helping Children Cope With Separation Anxiety by Nancy Pando (2005)
The Kissing Hand by Audrey Penn (2006)
The Sea Cat Dreams by J. R. Poulter (2011)
I Love You All Day Long by Francesca Rusackas (2004)
What Will I Play While You Are Away? by James R. Thomas (2010)

10

ESPECIALLY FOR EDUCATORS

Identify the child
Recognize grief as a cry for help
Find resources
Insist on getting help

Children are the living messages we send to a time we will not see.
—John W. Whitehead, *The Stealing of America* (1983)

WE CAN MAKE A DIFFERENCE

Many educators are frustrated, overwhelmed, and drowning in accountability. Too often they lack immediate resources to help them pull a child through a period of crisis.

While waiting to present a seminar on loss and grief issues to elementary school counselors, one counselor confided an interesting yet typical story.

Joey's mom had died when he was age 7. He was in second grade. An aunt reluctantly took him in. He began having severe attention and learning problems and acting-out behaviors after his mom's death.

This is all too common after such a traumatic loss. In first grade, Joey had been a good student, achieving on grade level in reading and math. He was well liked by students and teachers. For the following two years he had no counseling or psychological help. His disruptive behaviors and poor performance in school were factors leading to his placement in a Level IV learning disabled class.

The counselor sadly relayed the story. She felt defeated that a child had fallen through the cracks of the educational system. Left on this path, he may very well be headed for the penal system next. However, if Identified by the school system as a grieving child, Joey could be provided with needed resources, supports and understandings to meet his loss and grief challenges productively.

Life Is a Process: Loss—Change—Growth

Life is a process of loss, change, and growth. Understanding loss issues can make them more predictable and therefore less frightening. Through grief we can grow in inner and outer strength, and healing can take place.

Educators Face Loss Issues Daily

Educators face loss issues every day in their jobs, the kids with whom they work, and the school districts in which they work. They may ask themselves these questions:

Will I get a raise?
Will I get the promotion?
Will I get my materials?
Will I lose my job?
Will I be accountable to parents, children, and administrators when I walk through the door?
Will I get the respect I need in the classroom today?
Will I achieve my teaching goals with the children?
Will I be a victim of violence in the school?
Will I be sued for hugging a child?
Will I be fired?
Will a student harm me?
Will my personal life be exposed on the Internet?

Children Face Loss Issues Daily

Kids face loss issues every day with teachers, other kids, and their daily life activities and problems. They may ask themselves these questions:

Will I lose the baseball game?
Will my best friend like someone else?
Will the kids pick on me at lunch?
Will my sick mother be OK when I'm at school?
Will they think I'm different because I go to speech class?
Will they make fun of my braces, my skin, my hair, my sex?
Will anyone discover my secrets? (Mom got drunk last night. Dad came into my bed-
    room. The police arrested my brother.)
Will I forget my homework?
Will I be bullied on Facebook?
Will my teacher like me?
Will I fail this grade?
Will I fail a test?
Will I learn today?

Bobby's and Gregory's Stories: A Child's Voice Is Heard

While working as a counselor in a school where the majority of children came from divorced and single-parent homes, I met Bobby, a bright sixth-grader. He had flourished under the love and support of his foster parents during the two years he had lived with them. They adored Bobby, and Bobby adored them. Bobby and I would play chess in my room, and he would speak fondly of his biological mother, but spoke of his foster mother as "Mom."

One day the courts decided that Bobby would be better off going back to his biological mom. *No one asked him how he felt.* Bobby moved back. The devastation of that act wreaked havoc on the emotional and physical well-being of both Bobby and his foster parents. Within a few months, Bobby's grades dropped, his smile dimmed, and his natural mom began drinking again. No one had asked Bobby how he felt, and no one had offered a solution.

Many children like Bobby have been, and still are, in the school system. A child named Gregory broke new ground by coming up with his own solution and making headlines in 1992. Gregory contacted a lawyer on his own and expressed his strong desire to terminate his parents' parental rights and divorce them. This was the first time a child had sued his parents on his own right. Usually an adult, guardian, or friend sues on behalf of the child. Gregory felt his mom and dad had abandoned and neglected him. He wanted the courts to consider children's choices in domestic matters and have children be "treated as people and not as property."

Gregory had found a permanent, stable home and wanted to stay there. His voice *needs to be heard* as part of the legal requirements in our courts. Kids need protection for their rights to participate in divorce and foster care decisions in the judicial system when the parental and governmental systems have not worked for them.

WE CAN SEE THE DAY DIFFERENTLY

We, as educators, need to identify the behaviors, thoughts, and feelings that grief and loss issues bring to the foreground. Our school day is an ongoing kaleidoscope of children working through their many grief processes.

Children acting out or "acting in" are crying for help. These behaviors may be a red flag to adults that a child is working through a grief issue.

We can create a SAFE and feeling environment for kids by turning humiliations into experiences that build self-esteem. So often grief issues have an immediate and direct effect of lowering self-esteem and creating guilt and shame, the underlying forces behind many disruptive behaviors. In encouraging children to talk about loss, we need to have the patience to wait before responding and to think before we act. This lets us:

S   **Seize** the moment. Guide the child to feel safe in communicating, creating an open environment.
A   **Act.** When in doubt, reach out. It works. Kids feel sincerity.
F   **Find** strengths. Every child has them. Children are taught to stuff feelings, and these feelings come out in other ways. If we really knew what was pushing that child to act out, we would never judge him or her.
E   **Establish** a relationship. Talk to children alone. Let them know you are aware of their challenges and that you will be there if they need to talk.

Children will be more open to learning and relating if they are given avenues to express their bottled-up feelings. Their academic, social, and spiritual growth will soar with the release of stored-up hurts.

Teachable Moments

Teachable moments are an important concept for *unplanned* lessons. A teachable moment is a spontaneous mini-lesson inserted into the daily planned activities based on something that has just happened. Its *power* comes from catching the moment and creating a living, dynamic learning situation. Teachable moments can be trauma related or a natural part of the day. It is important to seize these opportunities and not deny their value.

Mrs. Albert, a kindergarten teacher, confided her feelings of fear and inadequacy that held her back from relating in the here and now. Karen, a 5-year-old, had recently experienced the death of her dad. Every time Karen mentioned Daddy, Mrs. Albert ignored her. This went on for three months. The teacher explained that she didn't know what to say, and so she avoided any mention of Karen's dad in the classroom.

Sometimes we can integrate special vocabulary to ease the flow of conversation. Open-ended questions allow the child to remember and verbalize events and feelings. Mrs. Albert could have asked Karen, "What are some of the times you remember best with your dad?" giving Karen an avenue for sharing. Had she asked a closed question such as, "Do you remember some good times with your Dad?" Karen could have easily just answered, "Yes."

Integrating a teachable moment into the classroom can be done easily if a class goldfish dies or if a dead worm is found outside after it rains. As educators, we can:

- Explain it is part of the life cycle.
- Have a funeral for it.
- Bury it.
- Talk about feelings.
- Make a class memory book or memory box.
- Suggest reading *Children Also Grieve* (Goldman, 2005) or *Goodbye Mousie* (Harris, 2004).

Hands-on practical curricula and manuals are available that provide lesson plans specific to each grade level.

Daily Lesson

An example of loss and grief lesson plans might be a first grade having a lesson on understanding the differences between dead and alive. Students can go outdoors and explore the change of seasons. Notice the color of the leaves and the changing temperature and sky. Kids can examine live and dead plants, which could lead them into a discussion of the concept that when we die our bodies stop working.

Discussion

In contrast, a fourth-grade lesson can introduce discussion of loss and that it's OK to have your feelings. Suggested activities include speakers covering topics from losing a sports championship to a house being destroyed by a fire. Girls and boys can brainstorm losses in groups and discuss them, collect newspaper articles on loss, or keep loss journals. *Charlotte's Web* (White, 1952) is a wonderful book to use with children at this age. *The Hurt* (Doleski, 1983) is a book for all ages that illustrates that the hurt grows when we hold on to it, and that "magic" can happen when we let it go. Resource corners in each classroom and in the school library benefit children of all ages.

A good example of integrating a trauma into a teachable moment is that of a caring fourth-grade teacher. The children in her class were talking about nightmares and drawing pictures after hearing on the news about a 7-year-old girl who was brutally attacked by dogs. The class began writing the little girl and even collecting money for a music tape for her.

This teacher had chosen to transform the children's fear into a positive, empowering memory. Art Kirsch, educator and director of Detroit's Kids in Crisis Program, emphasizes that these "emotional inoculations" of teachable moments are a shot in the arm for preparing children for their own next loss. Hopefully, the more comfortable we educators become with these grief and loss issues, the more we can become role models for children to work through their grief. Through education, we can become increasingly aware of our own barriers and can conquer and dispel myths associated with grief.

Elementary, middle, and high school students and teachers can use spontaneous teachable moments as an opportunity for growth and learning. The mass murders by teens in Littleton, Colorado, and the elementary school shooting massacre in Newtown, Connecticut, sent a wave of terror to kids, parents, and educators throughout our country and the world. These poignant events shocked our nation, placing fear, sadness, and compassion in the hearts of many school children. Media covered the gamut of horrific to heroic for our children to see and hear with constancy throughout the days.

Thirteen-year-old Thomas called his mom at work, upset and scared. "I can't believe this is happening," he told her as he watched a terrifying school shooting unfold in real time on TV. I'm scared to go to school tomorrow. A lot of kids are staying home tomorrow, and I want to stay home too!"

Seven-year-old Mara watched the same news on TV and started to cry. "They are going to kill those kids the way they shot Tony (her 14-year-old brother). She ran over to her grandmother, sat in her lap, began sucking her thumb, and holding her tight. Fear, anxiety, and regression occur when events such as teen terrorism and murder in schools are in plain sight for all children to see. These images instill terror in children and rekindle old wounds and regrieving.

Class discussions and assignments can be incorporated into children's learning by using kids' preoccupation with traumatic events or loss as a vehicle to release powerful feelings, reduce danger, and lesson anxiety.

Allowing safe expression of powerful feelings can be a golden opportunity for educators to relate to students in a meaningful way.

Questions

Margaret, a third-grader, was disappointed when she came to school that her teachers didn't even mention the killings at Columbine High School. She wanted to talk about it. "These murders are all that's on my mind," she thought. Alexander was glad his school chose to discuss the school shootings.

The following is a summary of his class discussion led by his teacher, Mr. Harter, and the discussion questions asked:

Do you feel safe at our school?
What do you wish we would do to make school safe?
What do you think about Columbine?
Do you feel you understand what happened?
Is there anything you don't understand?
Would you like to do something to remember the students who died?

Students' reactions were open and varied. "This is so scary. This could happen to us!" Alice explained. "The news is always blaming violence on video games and music. What about the parents, the school, the politicians, gun control?" Joseph responded. Liam added, "I think Columbine is a real eye-opener to everyone across the country to look out for each other and treat people with respect. The kids that murdered were reclusive—bullied a lot."

"What can we do to feel safe and change the violence?" asked Mr. Harter of his class. "Have gun detectors," Sara suggested. Melvin called out, "Have more police and security guards!" Tom said, "Stronger no-bully policies." And Joseph suggested, "Let's just stay home from school." Mr. Harter felt teachers and principals could explain and institute a school policy on no violence and bullying with procedures for students to follow when an incident occurs. He warned, "If children hear a threat, take any threat seriously. Any student who threatens another student's health or well-being will be suspended or expelled. If you hear a threat, you must notify an adult or you will be in jeopardy also."

The following was a poster that 14-year-old Liam made to represent his school's feelings of grief and to commemorate the lives of all the students shot at Littleton. Every child in the school signed the poster.

Sensitive life issues can be used in today's classrooms proactively to enhance student motivation by creating lessons that encourage kids to talk, write, or role-play complex daily situations.

Assignments

Teachers can actively engage young people in a valuable assignment that allows expression and completes an educational task. A sensitive teacher allowed Christopher, a 10th-grade student who was grieving the death of four significant people in his life, to use an English assignment of poetry writing to express his deep feelings. The following is one of these poems about the sudden death of his friend Doug, followed by a heartfelt response by his teacher.

Doug Able (1999)

by Christopher Hawk

You played a bold game of basketball,
Even though you were dizzy and wanted to fall.
You jumped high and shot well,
Which led us to victory at the sound of the bell.

We slapped five and bragged to the other team,
For the game had ended much like a dream.
We left the building and went to the parking lot.
And found the Caravan in the same spot.

We pulled out of the school and rolled over a bump,
A few seconds down the road I heard a large thump.

I turned around to see what fell,
And in the dark it was hard to tell.

I soon realized it was Doug draped over the seat.
I held him up and checked for a beat.
He looked through me as if I were a ghost,
He sat in his seat as motionless as a post.

He was a happy kid that didn't deserve to die.
For he was a friend on whom you could always rely.
He lived for soccer and tried his best,
Which is all you can ask from a kid now at rest.

His English teacher responded with the following note:

These are well-written. I realize that comfort and well-meant words often sound trite, but
I offer them anyway. I truly admire your strength. I hope writing these poems were as much
a comfort to you as they were an enjoyment to me.
50/50 A+

GUIDELINES FOR EDUCATIONAL REFERRALS

Become familiar with local agencies and their programs. They can provide help for children and their families and connect them with community resources. When meeting with parents about the child:

1. Present observations and concerns honestly to both parents if possible. Be clear, organized, and specific. Use a children's loss inventory as a resource. (A sample Children's Loss Inventory Checklist follows.)
2. Find out if the child is or was in counseling, and if the parents are familiar with specific resources. (Samples resources in Chapter 11.)
3. Offer to share information and observations with a person in the community of the parent's choice (clergy member, doctor, etc.).
4. Maintain the privacy of the child. Only talk about the child with resource personnel in other agencies with the parent's permission.
5. Obtain written authorization from a parent or guardian before releasing information. Protect the rights of the child and family. Date your request and specify the person in the agency to whom you are giving information.
6. Suggest several possibilities for help to parents to find what feels right. Let parents schedule the referral appointment.
7. Suggest that the parents follow up with you after their first appointment.
8. Ask the parent to inform you of ways to help the child during this period.
9. Keep a list of significant dates (birth dates or date of loss) that may affect the child throughout school.

Children's Loss Inventory Checklist

A Complete Picture of the Whole Child

Identify Child

Name _____ Age _____ Grade_____
Address _____ Birth date _____
Phone number _____ Today's date _____

Referral Information

Reasons for referral _____
_____
Source for referral _____

Identify Recent Significant Loss

Relationship of deceased to child _____
What are the facts about the loss? (Who, what, where, how) _____
_____
_____

Who told the child? _____
How was he/she told? _____
Date of birth of deceased _____ Date of death of deceased _____

Previous Loss and Grief History

Include significant dates or birth dates involved in previous losses.

Divorce or separation _____ Date _____
Moving _____ Date _____
Friends move away _____ Date _____
Past deaths _____ Who? _____ Date _____
Pet deaths _____ Who? _____ Date _____
Parents changing job _____ Date_____
Parents losing job _____ Date _____
Fire _____ Robbery _____ Date _____
Natural disaster _____ Date_____
Deployment _____ Deportation _____ Other _____ Date _____

Inherited Family Loss

Examples are a grandfather killed in a war or a previous sibling death.
_____
_____

Family Unit

Single parent _____ Divorce _____
Unmarried _____ Adoption _____

Natural parents _____   Blended family _____
Living with grandparent _____
Same-sex parents _____

Family History of Chronic Cultural Loss

Drugs _____   Injuries _____
Crime _____   Unemployment_____

Medical History

Significant parent illness _____
Significant children's illness _____

Previous School History

Grades _____
Progress _____
Participation _____

Assessment History

Standardized tests _____   Date _____
_____
Speech and language evaluation _____   Date _____
_____
Educational assessment _____   Date _____
_____
Psychological evaluation _____   Date _____
_____

Identify Child's Attitude Toward Significant Others

Siblings _____
_____
Parents _____
_____
Friends _____
_____
Pets _____
_____
Self _____

Identify Likes and Dislikes

Interests _____
Likes _____
Dislikes _____
Abilities _____
Likes _____
Dislikes _____

Identify Present Behaviors at School

(Check those that apply)

Disruptive in school _____ Failing grades _____

Inability to concentrate _____ Increased absenteeism _____

Fighting with peers _____ Withdrawn _____

Using bad language _____ Very tired _____

Physical complaints (headaches, stomachaches) _____

Nervousness _____ Other _____

Identify Present Behaviors at Home

(Check those that apply)

Less interaction _____ Sleeplessness _____

Poor eating _____ Bed-wetting _____

Clinging to parents _____ Nightmares _____

Increased perfectionism _____ Crying _____

Talks excessively about loss _____

Fighting with siblings or parents _____

Fear of dark, noise, or robbers _____

Identify Present Peer Behaviors

(Check those that apply)

More arguing _____

Less interest in play dates _____

Less communication with peers _____

Others _____

_____

Recommendations

Team conference _____

In-school individual counseling _____

In-school peer group counseling _____

Referral to counseling agency _____

Referral to medical doctor _____

Referral to support group _____

Testing _____

Follow-Up

Monthly follow-up _____ Source_____ Date_____

Information _____

Suggestions for Parents Seeking Professional Help

When any of the following behaviors are observed in a child, professional intervention may be helpful.

1. Child continually refuses to share thoughts or feelings about loss. *Tommy doesn't cry or talk about his mom's recent death.*
2. Child is extremely clingy to adults. *Tommy screams and cries. He is afraid to go to school and wants to stay home.*
3. Child has been lied to about loss. *Tommy was told his dad died of a heart attack. He overheard his dad had by suicide.*
4. Child threatens to hurt him- or herself. *Tommy tells his best friend that he wants to kill himself.*
5. Child won't socialize. *Tommy quits baseball, soccer, or riding bikes.*
6. Child involved with drugs or alcohol. *Tommy's mom finds marijuana in his room.*
7. Child is cruel to animals or physically abusive to other children. *Tommy repeatedly kicks his dog and throws sticks at him.*
8. Child has had a very difficult relationship to the deceased. *Tommy's deceased dad was an alcoholic who physically abused him.*
9. Child shows extremes in not sleeping or eating. *Tommy has lost 10 pounds in three weeks. He wakes up crying at 2 a.m.*
10. Child is failing school. *Tommy got four F's on his report card.*
11. Child exhibits sudden unexplained change. *Tommy gets suspended from school for continually starting fights with other children.*

Children exhibit normal signs of loss and grief in many ways. It is the extreme behaviors and intensity of feelings and actions that signal outside intervention is needed.

If parents are seeking professional help for their child, you may recommend that they:

1. *Use* word-of-mouth recommendations as a source of referrals. A friend, physician, or guidance counselor can make these referrals.
2. *Seek* out professional mental health associations (social worker, psychology, counseling associations, etc.), which provide referrals for grief therapists.
3. *Meet* with the therapist if possible to help decide whether he or she is right for the child. Counselors or therapists typically work with children using play therapy tools such as art, music, clay, storytelling, and dialogue to facilitate the expression of feeling.
4. *Ask* questions of the counselors or therapists.

How does he or she approach loss and grief issues?
How long are sessions?
What is the cost per session?
How frequently are the parents informed about or included in sessions?
What are the limits of confidentiality?

Confidentiality is an important component of child therapy. If the child has been abused or has thoughts of hurting him- or herself or others, the parent needs to know. Otherwise, the parent needs to understand the therapist-child relationship is separate and unique. The child's thoughts and feelings need to remain private. Then parent and child both gain a sense of respect for this valued relationship.

WE CAN MAKE A DIFFERENCE

We can:

1. Identify the child who is dealing with a specific, significant loss.
2. Recognize the grief and loss issue he or she is working through.
3. Realize his or her behaviors are a cry for help. These behaviors are threatening to the system, yet they can be turned around if identified early.
4. Insist on getting help. How can a child learn in school and enjoy his or her day productively when he or she is carrying overwhelming feelings of grief?
5. Find resources: community, agencies, staff, and peers.
6. Use team conferences as a checks-and-balances system to safeguard a child's right to emotional as well as intellectual help.
7. Develop an intraschool database where counselors can connect children within the same school with specific problems to each other in peer groups.
8. Create an interschool database to connect children in different schools when no children with similar experiences exist within their own schools. They can communicate by computer from long distances in private or in a school counselor's office.
9. Reassure teachers that educators can help. A panicked teacher can't create the environment a child needs to work through the hurt. But a calm and reassuring, sensitive teacher can be a highly healing influence.
10. See the child differently. Expand time. Wait 10 extra seconds to talk. Talk less.

It is important to be with the children and encourage them to tell you where they are and what they need in their process. Have faith and trust in them. They are the only ones that can relay their personal experience. Allow them to explore and express freely.

Resources for Educators

Breaking the Silence: A Guide to Help Children With Complicated Grief Suicide, Homicide, AIDS, Violence, and Abuse, 2nd Ed. by Linda Goldman (2001)
Classroom Crisis: The Teacher's Guide by Kendall Johnson (2004)
Death in the Classroom: Writing About Love and Loss by Jeffrey Berman (2009)
Death and the Classroom by Kathleen Cassini and Jacqueline Rogers (1996)
Dying, Death, and Grief in an Online Universe: For Counselor and Educators by Carla Sofka, Illene Noppe, and Kathleen Gilbert (2012)
Grief Comes to Class: A Teacher's Guide by Majel Gliko-Braden (2004)

Great Answers to Difficult Questions About Death: What Children Need to Know by Linda Goldman (2009)

Helping the Grieving Child in the Classroom by Linda Goldman (2000)

Raising Our Children to Be Resilient: A Guide to Help Children With Traumatic Grief in Today's World by Linda Goldman (2005)

Talking About Death and Bereavement in School: How to Help Children Ages 4–11 by Ann Chadwick (2011)

The Art of Grief: The Use of Expressive Arts in a Grief Support Group by J. Earl Rogers (2007)

What Will We Do? Preparing a School Community to Cope With Crisis by Robert Stevenson (2002)

When Death Impacts Your School: A Guide for School Administrators by the Dougy Center (2003)

CHAPTER

11 /

THE GLOBAL GRIEF TEAM

Friends **Relatives** **Babysitters**
Dads Teachers Sisters **Doctors**
Moms **Community agencies** Brothers
Bus drivers Grief support camps

We are not put on this earth to see through one another . . .
We are put on this earth to see one another through.
—Gloria Vanderbilt, on *Anderson Live*, September 19, 2011

WE'RE IN IT TOGETHER

This millennium presents a revolution of the mind and a transformation of the heart. Never before has it been so apparent that all the inhabitants of this planet are profoundly interconnected and interdependent.

What happens in an earthquake in Japan deeply impacts a child in Kenya. This is a unique paradigm. The economic instability of Greece can catapult global finances in many directions. More and more adults are learning the timeless, essential lesson of life; we must coexist in harmony for the best interest of all. This rapidly emerging common goal appears mandatory.

Our children are the children of the world. They can communicate instantaneously with friends around the globe. Their incredible ease in travel, school, and exploration of other cultures is historically unparalleled. They are truly citizens of the human race.

The tumultuous stress and change of modern life appears for many like living in a world turned upside down. Hopefully enormous change and upheaval is helping to produce a world turned right side up. A world in which the universal child is recognized and honored in all of the losses she or he may experience.

The universal child sees everything. The Internet, TV, Facebook, Twitter, and cell phones open an instantaneous window of experience into world events. Girls and boys text, e-mail, and video chat through a virtual grief community in cyberspace, and engage in online memorials to join with others. Children's direct or vicarious exposure to grief and trauma range from rock concerts streamed globally to collect money for the victims of the Haiti earthquake, to projects in Washington, DC, to send backpacks to the survivors of Hurricane Katrina, to Sesame Street creating online packets and videos for children who have experienced the death of a parent or a loss due to a parent's deployment in the military.

THE CHALLENGE: WHERE DO WE GO FROM HERE?

This is a question that needs to be addressed for all grieving children. We have gained a basic understanding of the child and his or her grief process, and now we need to ask ourselves how we can implement this understanding into modern times. The phrase "It takes a village to raise a child" has become a very popular one. I have found that it takes a village, a community, a nation, and a world to care for and support our grieving children.

The more we, as parents, educators, therapists, clergy, and other caring professionals, can join together in creating a cohesive unit, sharing similar thought forms, supports, resources, and information, the more congruent a child's grieving experience becomes.

Imagine a child's journey through grief as a three-dimensional hologram, where each and every part is as important and representative as the whole. The teacher, the doctor, the babysitter, the guidance counselor, the friend, the clergy, the aunt and uncle, the cousins, the therapist, the relief agency all become a team of like-minded adults and children offering congruency in a world of loss.

Usually when children grieve, their world feels fragmented. The more consistency we can create throughout their lives, the more solid and secure their life will become. Our goal is to create a *global grief team* to meet the needs of our grieving young people.

A GRIEF TEAM MODEL

As we join together, we allow each member to become an advocate, educator, liaison, therapist, and friend working in support and recognition of the grieving child. Throughout the home, the school, the community, the nation, and the world there are support people and organizations available to facilitate the following six tasks of a grief team within a community or extended to global support.

Wyatt Gallery

Grief Team Tasks

Task 1: Work with the surviving parent or guardian.
Task 2: Provide a school advocate for the grieving child.
Task 3: Supply children's grief support groups and camps.
Task 4: Present trainings.
Task 5: Offer preventive and crisis education for children.
Task 6: Create respect for our multicultural and diverse world.

Task 1: Work With the Surviving Parent or Guardian

The community grief team first works with the surviving parent or guardian to create words to use with the children. Caring adults need to understand what the common signs of grief are and how to approach them to reduce anxieties that unconsciously get projected onto the children.

- Educate caring adults on the common signs and symptoms of children's grief.
- Create age-appropriate words to use to open dialogue and grieve freely.
- Identify unresolved grief of the caring adult so it is not unknowingly projected onto children.

Dave was a 6-year-old whose mom had suffered from severe depression all her life. She shot and killed herself in her bedroom closet, leaving Dave, his 10-year old sister, Ellen, and their dad to find her. Dad called me as a grief therapist to "nip any problems in the bud," before any adverse reactions could develop. Dave's dad needed to be educated in the tremendous impact the death of a parent has on a child, and the added shame and shock of such a sudden and brutal death. His awareness needed to be expanded in knowing that grief is a long and ongoing process and cannot be halted or diminished in a few therapy sessions.

When Dave's guidance counselor visited his home after his mom's funeral, he ran up to her, grabbed her hand, and explained "My mom shot herself in the head in her closet in the bedroom. You want to see?" leading her into the room. He repeated this with many of the visitors that came that day. This young child needed to tell his story over and over again—a common sign of grief in children. As the counselor sat down to read Dave and his sister a story about a mom that dies, he jumped up and said, "I don't want to talk about this anymore. It's making me really sad. I want to play!" He ran out of the room. He needed to play, often a way young children respond to and work through their grief.

Ellen responded to the story quite differently, agreeing with the child in the story about some feelings of happiness. "I'm happy like that little girl. That's how I feel. I feel happy. But my dad makes me feel guilty about being happy. He thinks I should be sad, be crying. Sad is a bad feeling because my mom is where she wanted to be. This is what she wanted. If she's happy, I'm happy."

Ellen had lived most of her young life in a suicide watch over her mom, constantly feeling her job was to make her mother happy and rarely succeeding. This overwhelming burden may have been relieved by her mom's death, ending the pressure she had explained to her counselor of "doing the job of keeping my mother happy." It is normal for children to feel a sense of relief of being freed from this complicated situation. Dad had attempted to prescribe how Ellen should feel instead of respecting the dignity of her grieving process.

Parents often don't understand the tremendous impact of their unresolved grief on the child and the secondary loss of parental trust that can arise.

Blake was a 14-year-old whose dad died of suicide on Blake's birthday. Filled with shame, Blake stopped calling his old friends, fearing that if he called them, he would have to tell them that his dad died, and then he would have to tell how his dad died. Blake said his mom was always worried that he was lying to her, doing drugs and alcohol, or getting into trouble with the law. One year later, Blake's mom called and shared for the first time that her husband had left a suicide note, which read:

Dear Margaret,

It is your fault I am killing myself. Do not tell Blake how I died, and remember to keep an eye on Blake because you know suicide runs in our family!!!
    Love,
    Tom

This mom's unacknowledged terror and guilt was unknowingly projected onto her son, creating a huge amount of anxiety for him, because not only had he lost his dad and his friends but also his mother's trust. Had this mom been educated in the signs of complicated grief, she could have illuminated some of the devastation her child experienced.

Task 2: Provide a School Advocate for the Grieving Child

The community grief team provides an advocate for the grieving child in the school system. This advocate makes sure the teacher or counselor will implement the following practices when the child comes back to school after a death and allows the child to be a part of the decision-making process. These practices remain a part of the child's grief experience throughout the year and are continued for another year if necessary.

- Permit the child to leave the room if needed without explanation.
- Suggest the child choose a designated adult to talk with.
- Choose a designated place to go within school as a safe space.
- Allow the child to call home.
- Invite the child to visit the school nurse as a reality check.
- Assign a class helper.
- Create private teacher time.
- Give the child more academic progress reports.
- Modify some work assignments.
- Inform faculty, PTA, parents, and children of loss.

Charlie was a sixth-grader and a star athlete in the intramural basketball game. Many of the parents had gathered to watch their children play. Coach Matt went up to Charlie before the game and asked, "Is your dad here today?" "No," Charlie grumbled. "He had to work." Charlie played his worst game. Coach Matt was unaware that Charlie's dad had died a year before, and there was no written record to communicate this in the school. Had this school system established the practice of using a loss inventory, this lapse in communication may not have had such an upsetting impact on Charlie.

Jesse was a 7-year-old boy whose mom died after a long and debilitating bout with cancer. Mother's Day was two weeks after Mom's death. While kids made Mother's Day cards, someone came to get Jesse out of the room. No one offered the teacher or Jesse the insight to invite him to make a symbolic card for his mom or maybe one for his grandmother instead. This grieving child was made to feel different and isolated by being removed from the class.

Mrs. Morgan, Jesse's teacher, gave an assignment to all the children: "Interview your mom with Mother's Day questions." Jesse came home hysterical. He was terrified his teacher would be furious because he couldn't interview his mom. That same week, the PTA sent a note home with Jesse with this message:

Dear Jesse,
Please give this note to your mom and thank her for her help in the PTA.
Mrs. Smith/PTA President

Jesse wept uncontrollably when he read it. Lack of communication and lack of a central focus that guarantees everyone in the system has an awareness of this death is apparent. Certainly, the PTA did not want to hurt this child, but its miscommunication was devastating.

Task 3: Supply Children's Grief Support Groups and Camps

The Dougy Center: A Center for Grieving Children

The Dougy Center in Portland, Oregon, was founded in 1982 in tribute to Dougy, a young boy who died of an inoperable brain tumor. It has served as an inspiring model for educating more than 160 centers nationally and internationally. The Dougy Center offers a wide variety of workshops and training sessions on helping grieving children as well as educational workshops for those working with grieving children in hospitals, schools, hospices, youth service organizations, and mental health agencies across the nation.

Each summer, the Dougy Center offers the Summer Institute at the Portland facility, a program that presents theory and skill development with hands-on experience running peer-to-peer support groups for grieving children and teens. A new book for grief support groups by the Dougy Center, *Memories Matter* (2012), provides activities for grieving children and teens that can be used in peer support groups very effectively. For more information about the Dougy Center, go to www.dougy.org.

Camp Solace: A Retreat for Grieving Children

Solace Tree, a grief center for children, teens and adults, created a summer camp at Lake Tahoe. The camp was a fun-filled weekend where grieving youth kayaked, played on the beach, completed art projects, learned how to cook, and shared stories of the people they had lost in a special environment that supported their journey through the grieving process. The camp created an environment where young people could gain a new outlook on their grief journey and share with others.

Faith found the Solace Tree through a friend on her high school softball team. Then she found another good friend at Camp Solace. "My father committed suicide a year ago and it really messed me up," she shares. "I was depressed and angry and just not a fun person to be around, and I ended up losing a lot of my friends. AJ had lost her mom through suicide as well, so she knew what I was going through. She's the one who told me about the Solace Tree."

Joined by her mom, Alisha, and her sister, 13-year-old Erika, 16-year-old Faith attended Solace Tree meetings. She says it has helped her deal with her dad's death. "This year at school, I'm a lot happier," she says. "I mingle with more people now and I'm just trying to get out there more." Erika, Faith, and Alisha joined together to plant a tree in their dad's memory.

In her openness to new friends, Faith met Ashley at Camp Solace. "Ashley had the same story as I did; it was awesome meeting her and knowing someone who I have so much in common with," Faith says. "We had never met before because we went to the Solace House on different nights, but she lives near me so we're still able to see each other."

Faith says that camp was another fun experience in this new phase of her life. "It was a lot of fun, just like camp should be, but we also did a lot of special things," she says. Those things include making memory boxes for the people they've lost, along with other art projects. "And we wrote letters to our people," Faith says. "Then we put them in the fire so the message would go up with the smoke. It was just a really comfortable place to share our feelings." Faith plans to volunteer for the Solace Tree when she turns 18 so that she can help others in the same way she has been helped.

One bereaved mother expressed her concern around her bereaved son, who was staying silent and keeping busy and not openly acknowledging or discussing his loss. This mother wasn't sure whether her son was grieving in a healthy manner, and she feared he was delaying his grief.

Solace Tree executive director Emilio Parga responded to this mother's concern by stating, "Believe it or not, he is grieving. He is showing it in other ways—ways that we can't understand because we see them playing, involved in things, staying busy, smiling. In this case, we have learned that grief is something we feel on the inside of our body: heavy heart, stomachaches, fatigue, et cetera, and mourning is grief gone public—for example, tattoos, hair changes, clothing changes. So it's not delayed at all. He is grieving."

What we see on the outside is not always representative of what a teen is experiencing inside. It can be hard to offer support when we do not know what is going on inside. The following images from Solace campers display some of the feelings kids have inside when they are grieving.

TAPS Grief Camp: A Special Camp for Military Children

Since 1994, the Tragedy Assistance Program for Survivors (TAPS) has conducted grief camps for the children of our nation's fallen heroes at military installations across the United States. Military personnel volunteer to participate in the grief camps as mentors and work with skilled group leaders to create a safe place for young children to cope and heal following traumatic losses. Prior to the arrival of the children, the soldiers, marines, airmen, and sailors complete an online course and a day of training to prepare them for the weekend ahead.

To promote healing, the grief camp allots time for special events such as candlelight remembrance ceremonies, picture sharing, and special talk sessions known as circle time. "At circle time, the kids can talk about anything and everything," said Tina Saari, regional director for TAPS. "It's their chance to get together with other kids and realize that they are not the only ones grieving the loss of a parent or sibling."

While in a communal circle at camp, children share memories. Seven-year-old Hannah told stories about her stepfather, a soldier who died during deployment. Her unique story rang with similarity to the stories of the other camp participants, each of whom is coping with the loss of a parent or sibling who served in the military. They display photos of their loved ones for all to see.

As the children and mentors bond through shared loss and newly forged friendship, they often develop a desire to become part of a program that works to heal others who have lost a loved one in service.

Dosti found the TAPS experience to be one of her favorites. "It's such a wonderful camp. We get to stay in cabins. We get our own mentors. Best of all, we get to hang out together as one big group. It's just sad that it only lasts for three days."

"Every year, I tell myself that I am going to grow up and become a TAPS mentor," said Dosti. "It would mean more to me than anything. You can connect to these kids, and them to you. Soon one connection leads to another, and then everybody can connect as a big group." (Adapted from Clarke, Heather "Camp Erin/TAPS Grief Camp: Healing Through Mentoring," *TAPS Magazine* (Fall 2011), 18–19. Photos courtesy of Tragedy Assistance Program for Survivors.)

The Wendt Center's Grief Camp: Forget-Me-Not/Camp Erin DC

Kids love camp! It symbolizes fun, independence, friendships, and playfulness. For over a decade, the Wendt Center for Loss and Healing in Washington, DC, has provided Camp Erin, a weekend grief camp experience to children and adolescents who have experienced the death of a parent, sibling, grandparent, aunt, uncle, or other close relative. Grief can be overwhelmingly painful, isolating, and confusing for young people. Camp provides young people the opportunity to honor and remember their loved ones in a fun, accepting, and child-friendly environment. Layers of healing can occur during the grief camp weekend.

Campers and specially trained volunteers are matched as buddies. Big buddies spend the weekend with campers, moving through all activities together. The relationship provides an individualized support and role model for each camper during the weekend.

The children share their feelings and experiences through dialogue, mutual aid, support, play, and art. These interventions are designed for age-specific needs of the grieving child. A team of trained mental health professionals facilitates all grief-related activities.

Programming outside of the grief groups consists of a blend of traditional camp activities (canoeing, ropes course, campfire, swimming, crabbing) and therapeutic projective workshops, which can include drama, yoga, martial arts, music and drumming, art therapy, dance, and writing. Activities foster self-expression and healthy coping strategies while building bonds with others.

Although Camp Forget-Me-Not/Camp Erin has many therapeutic components, it is not designed as a replacement for therapy but as an enjoyable opportunity to explore grief where a child's self-expression is heard, valued, and honored.

The guiding principles of Camp Forget-Me-Not/Camp Erin DC, adapted from Stephanie Handel of The Wendt Center, include:

1. Normalizing grief for young people and helping them to recognize they are not alone in their grief.
2. Providing a safe and supportive environment for young people to explore their grief.
3. Caring, listening, and acceptance help a child to grieve, thrive, and heal.

Task 4: Provide Trainings

We can't "cure" grief. We can only support healing after a loss by facilitating its safe expression.

Provide support for grieving kids in:

- Children's social living units and guidance curriculums.
- Faculty meetings and PTA workshops.
- Schools and universities that train caring professionals.
- Staff in-service workshops and seminars at the workplace.

The child's grief team must provide trainings for all parents, educators, therapists, physicians, clergy, and other caring professionals in ways to work with children and grief. Many times, the old, inappropriate paradigms about children and grief within the therapeutic community still resurface. A mental health professional once explained, "Everything is loss and grief, we already know this." Each day more and more unique children's grief issues emerge. The enormity of information and resources available on this subject is astounding and is a continuing source of learning and growth for the professional.

One health professional offered advice to parents of grieving children which shocked me. The advice explained how to cure kids from talking about death. The giver of this advice felt his child was asking too many questions about death. He explained a new program he devised for his son. "You are only allowed to ask two questions about death. If you ask a third, that means you need to calm yourself down. To help you calm down you will need to go to your room for 30 minutes." This health care professional explained the child was "cured" within a month. This advice may leave many interested, searching parents feeling confused and misguided. Information like this can potentially shut down the very process we want to bring out into the open.

We need to encourage PTAs to provide workshops for parents preventively, and when a crisis arises. This allows parents to work through their own fears and feelings when their child experiences a loss, and offer words to use and a perspective on grief that can be shared with their children.

School systems and other professional workplaces can provide trainings and in-service courses for all personnel. These trainings heighten awareness of and sensitivity to the normal and complicated signs of children's grief by enhancing ways to approach and work with the children in their system.

Colleges and universities can implement undergraduate and graduate courses to train future educators, therapists, physicians, clergy, and all other caring professionals in practical yet universal ways to work with grieving children. This will prepare professionals for future events they will surely face.

Task 5: Offer Preventive and Crisis Education for Children

- Teachable moments
- Guidance curricula
- Life issues units
- Grief support groups

Children in grief need the support of their peers, for they tend to hide their grief or withdraw from friendships because they feel different. Ten-year-old Michelle's mom died of a sudden heart attack. Six months later, while getting her hair cut, the beautician unknowingly asked Michelle where her mom was that day. "She's home," Michelle replied. Wanting to feel like all the other kids she knows, she said her mom was waiting for her at home. Michelle hated feeling different and yearned to be like the other kids. "I'm not going to tell anyone how much I miss my mother," she explained. "You can tell me." I replied. The following poem was written by Michelle as a way of expressing her special and intimate feelings of missing her mom.

Michelle needed to be educated in the common signs of grief. She needed to know that most kids feel different when a parent dies and that this feeling is common and can be shared. She and other children can benefit from school systems that provide support groups within the school as a base to share similar experiences with peers. Children can make use of the Internet to provide intra- and interschool groups to communicate and maintain peer support. Private chat rooms can be formed to maintain confidentiality.

Schools can also educate children by creating a loss and grief school curriculum that provides preventive information, educational interventions, crisis interventions, and follow-ups for the grieving child throughout his or her school career. This can be incorporated into life issues curricula, guidance curricula, and trainings that help find teachable moments.

Task 6: Create Respect for Our Multicultural and Diverse World

- Honor specific rituals and customs particular to diverse, multicultural groups.
- Develop ways to use a second language in grief work.
- Respect and adapt to the unique belief systems of specific cultures.

Jose was an 8-year-old boy who came to see me one year after his dad, Juan, had capsized his boat while sailing and plunged suddenly to his death. His mom, Maria, and Jose were shocked and devastated, and this first year was a nightmare and blur. Maria spoke not only of the death of her husband but the loss of her rich culture. They spoke Spanish at home, and after Juan died, Jose did not and could not carry on this second language.

Maria yearned for Spanish-speaking people to relate to, and a way to pass this heritage on to her son. We located a Spanish-speaking support group and a memory book for grieving children in Spanish. This book allowed Jose to feel closer to his dad, and more eager to learn the language and the traditions of his culture. Written grief resources translated into other languages are valuable resources for children and families in areas of ethnic diversity.

THE GLOBAL GRIEF TEAM: WHAT WE CAN DO?

Laying the framework for a global grief team is the first step toward action.

Wyatt Gallery

The development of life issues, curricula, and guidance and social living programs is essential. These trainings and curricula include prevention, intervention, and postvention techniques for children, parents, educators, and other caring professionals on issues children experience in today's world. They emphasize resources that match the needs of the grieving child, from birth through the school career, and highlight accountability for loss and grief issues that may greatly impair learning and emotional well-being if not addressed openly.

The next step is to create a broad-based mission statement that will outline the emergence of the children's grief team. This mission statement includes areas of focus on trainings, materials, resources, and supports for children, parents, and professionals within the home, school, community, nation, and world.

Mission Statement

The goal of the global grief team is to create a broad-based program to meet the emotional, social, educational, and spiritual needs of the population of children with loss and grief issues.

Loss and grief issues range from death due to violence or suicide to loss due to sudden trauma, chronic illness, divorce, AIDS, teen pregnancy, imprisonment, alcoholism, drugs, and many other causes. This global grief team focuses on the creation and maintenance of six components under the umbrella of education and mental health.

I have been working with children and families for many years. Twenty years were spent as an elementary teacher and guidance counselor in the public school system. Serving as a liaison to children, teachers, and administrators was coupled with being chair of the School Team, a school-based group used to identify and create learning strategies for children.

This strong educational background, combined with present experience as a grief therapist and educator, allows me to see that many problems identified as "learning disabled," "attention deficit," or just "slow learning" had a direct relationship to emotional well-being and, more specifically, to unresolved grief and trauma.

Experience as a classroom teacher and guidance counselor coupled with therapeutic understandings has profoundly affected my perception of these problems as being anything but isolated, fragmented, and unrelated. In fact, they appear to be a very congruent continuum.

Children with grief and loss issues often manifest the same behavioral signs used to diagnose attention deficit disorder and learning disability—impulsivity, distractibility, and hyperactivity. Kids are often misdiagnosed, leaving them in a learning-disabled track that may provide methylphenidate (Ritalin) or other medications for behavior control and convenience rather than address the underlying issues.

These children need to be seen through a different vision—that of a normal child living and working through many emotional life issues. A new concept of "normal" and "normal learning" must be put into place to meet the needs of today's and tomorrow's kids. They are capable of productive lives and successful learning, but they may be temporarily stuck in blocks of time. If not addressed, children remain permanently locked into silence and repression, and the cost to their own lives and society is immeasurable.

Components of the Global Grief Team

1. Intervention: prevention, education, and crisis response.
2. Information and resources: books, articles, data, and community and national agencies and programs.
3. Trainings: parents, children, educators, therapists, clergy, physicians, and other caring professionals.
4. Supports: children, parents, and professionals.
5. Curricula: life issues, guidance and social living programs, health-related studies.
6. Research: children, grief, early brain development, attachment relationships, learning and esteem.

Many of these components are presently available and in use in some schools. Now we need an appropriate integration—a new and shared paradigm for the parental, educational, psychological, health-related, and spiritual communities. A shared vision of learning, emotional and physical well-being, and personal growth is essential. A child who becomes a burden on the community may also be disowned by family, friends, and schools and then relegated solely to the psychological community. Learning strategies, emotional needs, and community resources must merge as a congruent unit for the common interest and healing of the grieving child.

People of like minds need to join together and produce a working model for parents, educators, mental health professionals, and community, national, and global agencies that meets the emotional, social, and spiritual needs of the children as well as their academic needs. By meeting these needs, we can enhance their capacity to learn and grow as human beings.

HAITI: A GLOBAL GRIEF EXPERIENCE

The 2010 earthquake in Haiti created multiple levels of misfortune for many girls and boys. Children were orphaned, homes and schools destroyed, animals abandoned, and special objects lost. Millions still live in tent cities or on the streets as a result of the devastation and poverty. Daily life can often be a continuing lesson of dealing with frustration, abandonment, and scarcity coupled with multiple levels of loss.

Wyatt Gallery

The Haiti Hope and Healing Project

The Haiti Hope and Healing Project was a collaborative program that included Hope for Humanity, Haitian Union, ADRA Inter-American Division, the Loma Linda University International Behavioral Health Trauma Team, and the Reginald S. Lourie Center for Infants and Young Children.

This project was designed to work with the grieving adults in Haiti with strategies to aid their recovery process so they could help their grieving children to do the same. These grieving adults needed to feel safe and understand and gain mastery of their grief and trauma in order to help the children.

The Training Goals

- Acknowledge the special role of supporting children
- Understand the impact of trauma for children
- Teach earthquake education and emergency preparedness
- Convey attachment theory, brain development, and child principles
- Educate on grief and loss
- Teach techniques for supporting resilience in children
- Build resiliency in caregivers
- Establish a network of support
- Appreciate cross-cultural issues

The challenge was to help people who have experienced overwhelming stress to understand they are not alone. Examples of the international response to distraught communities worldwide were presented. Sharing lessons learned by the world community from other catastrophes such as the 1999 Taiwan earthquake and Hurricanes Andrew and Katrina helped to bring home this point.

Telling the Story: Mastering Overwhelming Experience

An effective exercise with the future child grief supporters was the task of telling "my story." Through words and pictures, adults began to master the terror and helplessness of the trauma by placing their individual experiences into the context of their life. To do this, the participants broke into small groups and remained in these groups throughout the training. Each person was asked to make a drawing of the earthquake, and as one person drew a picture, the next person added to it. The finished drawing was discussed in the small group and reported to the larger group.

This final drawing allowed everyone to see their story in a cultural context with others. In this way, they were learning to help children place their experiences in a cultural context as well.

The Narrative

Another exercise involved projective play. The adults were asked to tell their story through the use of puppets. This is a safe mode of creating a narrative that can be used with children to express emotions with fear.

Puppets

Puppet storytelling also provided experiential learning to allow adults to successfully lead children through the same activity. Adults begin using projective play to tell their story through puppets. They practiced doing this to be prepared for children to share through puppetry and learned how to anticipate children's responses. They were amazed at the healing effect of telling their own story and sharing it with others. The puppet play tapped into the healing power of laughter, spontaneity, and creativity and offered greater mastery over the grief.

The children and adults who had experienced the trauma of the earthquake incorporated much of their experiences through the five senses of vision, touch, hearing, smell, and taste. This visceral imprint needed avenues of expression. Kids saw rubble everywhere. A smell engulfed the city. The residue powder from the concrete could be tasted. Many children heard cries from others. Living through the experience of such a disaster was often experienced through the entire body.

The Rock Garden

A unique rock garden project was used to transform visual reminders. Small groups designed a rock garden, discussed its meaning, and reported to others. The goal was to create rock gardens for classrooms, schools, and/or the community with few resources available as materials. Each person painted his or her story of the earthquake on a chosen rock. They then told their story through the rock. One by one, they shared their rock, and then listened to everyone else share, too.

In this way, they were learning how to gain mastery over the experience and to allow children to do the same.

One woman explained her sadness about the death of her husband. "This is my bleeding heart for my husband who died in the earthquake." Another man shared his gratitude. "This is for all the nations that came to help."

Still another adult echoed the sentiments of the group in their desire to help children. "The colors symbolize that the future is the education of children."

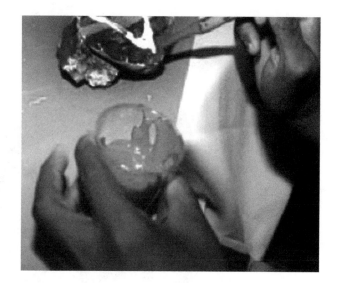

Dr. James Venza, associate executive director of the Lourie Center, is shown holding his rock, which was particularly significant to him and all the participants in the Haiti Hope and Healing Project. He was one of the last to share his story. When he did, the room exploded with spontaneous applause.

The rock simply says, "ALL ARE ONE." This vision of unity and universal compassion exemplifies the goals of this global grief community embraced by everyone.

"All true feeling, deeply lived, may be a source of inspiration" (Venza, Freeman and Buckles, *Haiti Hope and Healing Project*). Difficult and unusual circumstances can be the very ones that inspire all of us to express our best selves.

CONCLUSION: WE ARE ONE

The original *Life and Loss* (1992) and *Life and Loss, Second Edition* (2000), contained chapters on the community grief team. *Life and Loss, Third Edition*, expands this concept. With the explosion of the digital age, the world has become smaller, but the community grief team larger. It has grown to become a global grief team—pushing into conscious awareness the idea that we are all in this life together. Within this new framework, children can express grief and loss, communicate with each other, and support peers in every part of our Earth in fresh and caring ways.

If we can envision each universal child having the support of caring adults . . .

If we share the conviction that we can join together to help our young people everywhere . . .

We can create a light to lead the way through grief with understanding and compassion for all.

NATIONAL AND INTERNATIONAL RESOURCES AND ORGANIZATIONS

Mental health agencies
Funeral service professionals
School psychologists and counselors
Local support groups for children and families
Agencies or programs dealing with specific losses
Student personnel workers
Hospice programs
Pediatricians
Grief camps
Nurses
Clergy
Hotlines

American Association of Suicidology
5221 Wisconsin Ave. NW, #2
Washington, DC 20015
202-237-2280

American Hospice Foundation
2120 L St. NW, Suite 200
Washington, DC 20037
202-223-0204

Association for the Care of Children's Health
7910 Woodmont Ave.
Bethesda, MD 20814
301-654-6549

Association for Death Education and Counseling
111 Deer Lake Rd., Suite 100
Deerfield, IL 60015
847-509-0403

Baton Rouge Crisis Intervention Center
4837 Revere Ave.
Baton Rouge, LA 70808
225-924-1431

Bereavement Services: Resolve Through Sharing
La Crosse Lutheran Hospital/Gundersen Clinic, Ltd.
1900 South Ave., Mailstop Alex
La Crosse, WI 54601
608-775-4747

Boys and Girls Clubs of America
1275 Peachtree St. NE
Atlanta, GA 30309-3506
404-487-5700

Center for Loss and Life Transitions
3735 Broken Bow Rd.
Fort Collins, CO 80526
970-226-6051

Children's Defense Fund
25 E St. NW
Washington, DC 20001-0500
202-628-8787

Children's Hospice International
1101 King St., Suite 131
Alexandria, VA 22314
800-2-4-CHILD

Children With AIDS Project of America
P.O. Box 23778
Tempe, AZ 85285-3778
602-405-2196

Compassionate Friends Inc.
900 Jorie Blvd., Suite 78
Oak Brook, IL 60523
630-990-0010

Cove: Center for Grieving Children
250 Pomeroy Ave., Suite 107
Meriden, CT 06450
203-634-0500

D'Esopo Resource Center
280 Main St.
Wethersfield, CT 06109
860-563-5677

Dougy Center
3909 SE 52nd Ave.
Portland, OR 97206
503-775-5683

Ele's Place
600 W. St. Joseph St., Suite 1-G
Lansing, MI 48933
517-482-1315

Hope for Bereaved, Inc.
(Support Groups and Telephone Help)
4500 Onondaga Blvd.
Syracuse, NY 13219
315-475-4673

Hospice Education Institute
3 Unity Square
P.O. Box 98
Machiasport, ME 04655-0098

207-255-8800
800-331-1620 (computerized hospice link)

Hospice Foundation of America
1710 Rhode Island Ave. NW, Suite 400
Washington, DC 20036
800-854-3402

Inner Source
980 Awald Rd., Suite 200
Annapolis, MD 21403
410-269-6298

Institute for the Advancement of Service
111 S. Columbus St.
Alexandria, VA 22320
703-706-5333

Judge Baker Children's Center
295 Longwood Ave.
Boston, MA 02115
617-232-8390

Kidspeace National Center for Kids in Crisis
1650 Broadway
Bethlehem, PA 18015-3998
800-8KID-123

Kids' Place
2 E. 11th St.
Edmond, OK 73034
405-844-5437

Life and Death Matters
2958 Lamont Rd.
Saanichton, BC
V8M 1W5 Canada
250-652-6781

Lourie Center for Infants and Young Children
12301 Academy Way
Rockville, MD 20852
301-984-4444

Mothers Against Drunk Driving (MADD)
511 E. John Carpenter Freeway, Suite 700
Irving, TX 75062
877-275-6233

National Down Syndrome Society
666 Broadway, Suite 810
New York, NY 10012
800-221-4602

National Family Resiliency Center Inc.
10632 Little Patuxent Pkwy.
2000 Century Plaza, Suite 121
Columbia, MD 21044
410-740-9553

National Hospice Organization
1901 N. Fort Myer Dr., Suite 307
Arlington, VA 22209
703-243-5900

National Military Family Association Inc.
2500 N. Van Dorn St., Suite 102
Alexandria, VA 22303-1601
703-931-4600

New England Center for Loss and Transition
35 Boston St.
Guilford, CT 06437–0292
203-458-1734

Operation Give a Hug
P.O. Box 99519
Lakewood, WA 98496
253-691-9391

Our House Grief Support Center
1663 Sawtelle Blvd., Suite 300
Los Angeles, CA 90025
310-473-1511

Parents of Murdered Children
1739 Bella Vista
Cincinnati, OH 45237
513-242-5683

Parents Without Partners
7910 Woodmont Ave., Suite 1000
Bethesda, MD 20814
800-638-8078

Peacock Foundation
P.O. Box 372
North Hollywood, CA 91603
818-732-0633

Ronald McDonald House
405 E. 73rd St.
New York, NY 10028
212-639-0100

Safe Harbor Program
Abington Health Center
2510 Maryland Rd., Suite 225
Willow Grove, PA 19090
215-481-5983

Share/Perinatal Support Group
St. Elizabeth's Hospital
211 S. Third St.
Belleville, IL 62220
613-346-0509

Share Pregnancy and Infant Loss Center
402 Jackson St.
Saint Charles, MO 63301-6819
636-947-6164

Sudden Infant Death Syndrome Foundation
10500 Little Patuxent Pkwy., Suite 420
Columbia, MD 21044
800-221-SIDS

**Suicide Prevention Education Awareness for
    Kids (SPEAK)**
P.O. Box 36802
Baltimore, MD 21286
410-377-7711

Suicide Prevention Resource Center
43 Foundry Ave.
Waltham, MA 02453-8313
877-438-7772

Survivors of Suicide
Suicide Prevention Center
184 Salem Ave.
Dayton, OH 45406
513-223-9096

TAPS Tragedy Assistance Program for Survivors of the Military
1777 F St. NW, Suite 600
Washington, DC 20006
800-959-TAPS

UNICEF House
3 United Nations Plaza
New York, NY 10017
212-326-7000

William Wendt Center
4201 Connecticut Ave. NW, Suite 300
Washington, DC 20008
202-624-0062

Grief Camps for Children

**Camp Forget-Me-Not/Camp Erin
(Sponsored by The Wendt Center)**
4201 Connecticut Ave. NW, Suite 300
Washington, DC 20008
202-624-0010

Camp Jamie
(Sponsored by the Hospice of Frederick County)
516 Trail Ave.
P.O. Box 1799
Frederick, MD 21702
240-566-3030

Camp New Hope
(Sponsored by Delaware Hospice)
911 S. Dupont Hwy.
Dover, DE 19901
855-672-2200

Camp Solace
(Sponsored by The Solace Tree)
P.O. Box 2944
Reno, NV 89505
775-324-7723

Katerpillar Kids
(Sponsored by Covenant Health)
3001 Lake Brook Blvd.
Knoxville, TN 32909
865-374-0864

TAPS Grief Camp
(Sponsored by Tragedy Assistance Program for Survivors (TAPS)
3033 Wilson Blvd., Suite 630
Arlington, VA 22201
800-959-TAPS

Hotlines

Boys Town Hotline	800-443-3000
Childhelp National Child Abuse Hotline	800-4ACHILD
National AIDS Hotline	800-232-4636
National Center for Missing and Exploited Children	800-843-5678
National Domestic Violence Hotline	800-799-SAFE
National Parent Helpline	855-4APARENT
National Runaway Safeline	800-786-2929 (1-800-Runaway)
National Suicide Hotline	800-273-8255
National Suicide Prevention Lifeline	800-784-2433
Trevor Project Hotline	866-488-7386

CHAPTER

12

LET'S EXPLORE
RESOURCES

Books Videos Manuals

Guides Curricula CD-ROMs

Websites Projects and media

Children are the world's most valuable resource . . . and its best hope for the future.

—John Fitzgerald Kennedy

TODAY'S RESOURCES — A MODERN UPDATE

As caring adults, we are not alone in a world without excellent resources to help grieving children. Many new and useful resources are available for parents, educators, therapists, caregivers, and even children. These resources provide practical ideas and information covering the spectrum of topics of grief and loss issues for young people. They are geared to different ages and different developmental levels, and often stress that ideas designed to prepare and help children through inevitable loss must be age-appropriate.

THE SESAME STREET WORKSHOP: WHEN FAMILIES GRIEVE

When Families Grieve is a project created by Sesame Workshop to reach out in this digital age to grieving children throughout the world. It serves as an example of what can be done on a grand scale to provide information and resources for grieving kids on television and via the Internet, video, and downloadable materials.

The Project

When Families Grieve presents the heartfelt quality of the *Sesame Street* Muppets captured in resources that support families with young children coping with the death of a parent. As part of this outreach initiative, Sesame Workshop created a prime-time television special and two customized, bilingual (English and Spanish) resource kits: one designed to support the specific needs of military families and one designed for the public.

Goals

When Families Grieve materials help families with young children ages 2 to 8 to:

- Reduce the levels of anxiety, sadness, and confusion that children may experience following the death of a parent.
- Provide families with age-appropriate tools to support and comfort children, including ways to talk about death with a young child.
- Reassure children that they are loved and safe. Together with families and friends, they can learn ways of being there for one another and moving forward.

This program recognizes that the death of a parent impacts every aspect of a child's life and that grief encompasses a child emotionally, socially, cognitively, and behaviorally. Young children's emotions may be hard to identify and express, and death can be overwhelming and difficult to understand. *Sesame Street's* grief project was created to meet the needs of adults who many find it difficult to tackle the challenging topic of death in ways that are comforting and developmentally appropriate for a child.

ANNOTATED BIBLIOGRAPHY

Books for Adults

Bertman, Sandra. (1999). *Grief and the Healing Arts.* Amityville, NY: Baywood. This resource shows ways to use healing arts through grief.

Birney, James. (2011). *Parenting From Prison.* Seattle, WA: CreateSpace. This hands-on guide provides support for incarcerated parents.

Burgess, Stacey, Tonia Casselman, and Jennifer Carsey. (2009). *Empowering Children of Incarcerated Parents.* Bel Air, CA: Youthlight. This is a resource for professionals working with children ages 7 to 12 who have a parent in prison.

Chadwick, Ann. (2012). *Talking About Death and Bereavement in School.* London: Jessica Kingsley. This book helps children feel supported with bereavement issues in school.

Coles, Robert. (1991). *The Spiritual Life of Children.* Boston: Houghton Mifflin. This book reflects the inner world of children.

Corr, Charles, Clyde Nave, and Donna Corr. (2008). *Death and Dying: Life and Living* (6th ed.). Beverly, MA: Wadsworth. This book is helpful in working with encounters involving death, dying, and bereavement.

Crosetto, Alice, and Rajinder Garcha. (2012). *Death, Loss, and Grief in Literature for Youth.* Plymouth, UK: Scarecrow Press. This is a thorough and well-done annotated bibliography providing death, loss, and grief literature for youth.

Del Campo, Diane, Robert Del Campo, and Kourtney Vaillancourt. (2012). *Taking Sides: Clashing Views in Childhood and Society* (9th ed.). New York: McGraw-Hill. This book presents current issues children face.

DeSpelder, Lynne, and Albert Strickland. (2010). *The Last Dance: Encountering Death and Dying* (9th ed.). Mountain View, CA: Mayfield. This book presents a comprehensive and readable introduction to the study of death and dying.

Di Ciacco, Janis. (2008). *The Colors of Grief.* London: Jessica Kingsley. This book helps to understand a child's journey thorough loss from birth to adulthood.

Enebrand, Shirley. (2009). *Over the Rainbow Bridge.* Bothell, WA: Book Publishers Network. This is a mom's heartfelt sharing of her son's illness and death.

Fitzgerald, Helen. (2000). *The Grieving Teen.* Beaverton, OR: Touchstone. This is a wonderful guide for parents to work with grieving teens.

Fitzgerald, Helen. (1995). *The Mourning Handbook.* Beaverton, OR: Touchstone. This is a thorough and practical resource for families.

Frankl, Viktor. (2006). *Man's Search for Meaning.* Boston: Beacon Press. This is a powerful account of the author's imprisonment in Nazi Germany and the love that helped him survive his losses.

Furth, Gregg. (2002). *The Secret World of Drawing* (2nd ed.). Toronto: Inner City Books. This is a comprehensive understanding of children's artwork.

Gardner, Howard. (2011). *Frames of Mind: The Theory of Multiple Intelligences* (3rd ed.). New York: Basic Books. Gardner's theory and practical application for school systems is a fresh look at the way children learn.

Gil, Eliana. (2011). *Helping Abused and Traumatized Children.* New York: Guilford Press. This book shares direct and nondirect approaches to help traumatized children.

Gilbert, Richard. (2009). *Finding Your Way After a Parent Dies.* Notre Dame, IN: Ave Maria Press. This is a good resource to help grievers cope with parent death.

Gilbert, Richard. (2012). *Heartpeace.* Omaha, NE: Centering Corporation. This book provides simple and heartfelt help for the bereaved.

Golden, Tom. (2010). *Swallowed by a Snake.* Gaithersburg, MD: Golden Healing. This resource is about the grief process of men in our culture.

Goldman, Linda. (2001). *Breaking the Silence: A Guide to Help Children With Complicated Grief, Suicide, Homicide, AIDS, Violence, and Abuse* (2nd ed.; in English and Chinese). New York: Taylor & Francis. This resource is a guide for parents and professionals to work with children and complicated grief issues.

Goldman, Linda. (2009). *Great Answers to Difficult Questions About Death: What Children Need to Know* (in English, Polish, Korean). London: Jessica Kingsley. This is a guide for caring adults to dialogue with children about death.

Goldman, Linda. (2010). *Great Answers to Difficult Questions About Sex: What Children Need to Know*. London: Jessica Kingsley. This is a guide to help adults dialogue with children on issues surrounding sex.

Goldman, Linda. (1991). *Helping the Grieving Child in School: Opportunities to Help and Enhance Learning*. Bloomington, IN: Phi Beta Kappa International. This is a practical guide to help grieving schoolchildren.

Goldman, Linda. (2005). *Raising Our Children to Be Resilient: A Guide to Help Children With Traumatic Grief in Today's World*. New York: Taylor & Francis. This is a practical guide to help children with traumatic grief and support resilience.

Gonzalez-Mena, Jane. (2006). *50 Early Childhood Strategies for Working and Communicating With Diverse Families*. Columbus, OH: Pearson. This is a practical guide that provides strategies for communication with diverse families.

Granat, Tamar. (2005). *Without You: Children and Young People Growing Up With Loss and Its Effects*. London: Jessica Kingsley. This resource presents the lives of different children who have experiences a loss.

Harpham, Wendy. (2004). *When a Parent Has Cancer: A Guide to Caring for Your Children*. New York: William Morrow Paperbacks. This is a guide to caring for children when a parent has cancer.

Heavilin, Marilyn. (2006). *Roses in December*. Eugene, OR: Harvest House. The author expresses a deep understanding of the grieving process, having experienced the death of three children.

Hedderman, Lori. (2011). *Preparing Your Children for Goodbye*. Seattle, WA: CreateSpace. This is a guidebook for dying parents.

Herlem, Fanny. (2008). *Great Answers to Difficult Questions About Adoption: What Children Need to Know*. London: Jessica Kingsley. This is a useful book in helping adults dialogue with children about adoption.

Hindjuda, Sameer, and Justin W. Patchin. (2008). *Bullying Beyond the Schoolyard: Prevention and Responding to Cyberbullying*. Thousand Oaks, CA: Corwin Press. This book provides information, tools, and strategies to be used in schools regarding issues surrounding cyberbullying.

Holland, John, Ruth Dance, Carole Stitt, and Nic Macmanus. (2005). *Lost for Words: Loss and Bereavement Awareness Training*. London: Jessica Kingsley. This is a clearly written loss awareness training package to help teachers and other educators supporting children through death and loss.

Horsley, Gloria, and Heidi Horsley. (2011). *Open to Hope*. Palo Alto, CA: Open to Hope Foundation. This is a compilation of inspirational stories of healing after loss.

Huntley, Theresa. (2002). *Helping Children Grieve When Someone They Love Dies*. Minneapolis, MN: Augsburg Fortress. This is an easy-to-read resource for caring adults that honestly addresses children's grief.

Ilse, Sherokee. (2008). *Empty Arms*. Maple Plain, MN: Wintergreen. This is a practical book for anyone who has experienced infant death or miscarriage. It offers suggestions and support at the time of loss and future concerns and grief work.

Jeffreys, J.S. (2011). *Helping Grieving People—When Tears Are Not Enough: A Handbook for Care Providers* (2nd ed.). New York: Taylor & Francis. This is an excellent and practical guide for helping the bereaved.

Kübler-Ross, Elisabeth. (1997). *On Death and Dying*. Englewood Cliffs, NJ: Prentice Hall. This is a pioneering book on the subject of death and dying, using real-life situations to create true understanding.

Kushner, Harold. (2004). *When Bad Things Happen to Good People*. New York: Anchor. Following his son's illness and subsequent death, Rabbi Kushner shares his thoughts and feelings of why we suffer.

Lagasse, Mary Helen. (2004). *The Fifth Sun*. Seattle, WA: Curbstone Books. This is a novel about a woman from Mexico and her life journey to raise her children, experience deportation, and attempt to reunite with her family.

Legrand, Louis. (2011). *Healing Grief, Finding Peace*. Naperville, IL: Sourcebooks. This excellent resource provides ways to cope with the death of a loved one.

Losey, Butch. (2011). *Bullying, Suicide, and Homicide*. New York: Routledge. This book is about understanding, assessing, and preventing bullying.

Markell, Kathryn, and Marc Markell. (2008). *The Children Who Lived*. New York: Taylor & Francis. This book uses the *Harry Potter* series to help grieving children.

McCue, Kathleen, and Ron Bonn. (2011). *How to Help Children Through a Parent's Serious Illness: Supportive, Practical Advice from a Leading Child Life Specialist* (2nd ed.). New York: St. Martin's Griffin. This book provides supportive, practical advice on how to help children through a parent's serious illness.

Miller, Alice. (1990). *For Your Own Good* (3rd ed.). New York: Farrar, Straus, and Giroux. Miller explores the repercussions of adults taking over a child's will.

Neimeyer, Robert, Darcy Harris, Howard Winokuer, and Gordon Thornton. (2011). *Grief and Bereavement in Contemporary Society: Bridging Research and Practice*. New York: Routledge. This book bridges a gap between bereavement researchers and practitioners.

O'Toole, Donna, with Cory Jerre. (1988). *Helping Children Grieve and Grow*. Burnsville, NC: Compassion Books. This is a practical guide for any caring adult working with a grieving child.

Rando, Theresa. (2000). *Clinical Dimensions of Anticipatory Grief*. Champaign, IL: Research Press. This book presents theory and practice in working with the dying and their loved ones.

Rogers, J. Earl. (2007). *The Art of Grief: The Use of Expressive Arts in a Grief Support Group*. New York: Routledge. This is a book using expressive arts with grief.

Rosenthal, Howard. (2010). *Favorite Counseling and Therapy Techniques* (2nd ed.). New York: Routledge. This book gathers favorite therapy techniques from 51 well-known therapists.

Ross, Cheri. (2005). *Pet Loss and Children*. New York: Routledge. This is an excellent guide to help adults with pet loss for children.

Schneider, John. (2011). *Finding My Way*. Colfax: WI: Seasons Press. This is a journey of healing and transformation through loss and grief.

Schuurman, Donna. (2004). *Never the Same*. New York: St. Martin's Griffin. This book helps the reader come to terms with the death of a parent.

Silverman, Phyllis. (2012). *A Parent's Guide to Raising Grieving Children*. New York: Oxford University Press. This book helps families rebuild after a death and shares how children experience death; includes supporting research data.

Smith, Harold Ivan. (2004). *When a Child You Love Is Grieving*. Kansas City, MO: Beacon Hill Press. This is an excellent resource to help parents and professionals care for and support the grieving child.

Tavangar, Homa. (2009). *Growing Up Global*. New York: Ballantine Books. This is a resource on raising children to be at home in the world.

Thompson, Rosemary. (2004). *Crisis Intervention and Crisis Management*. New York: Brunner-Routledge. This book presents strategies that work in schools and communities.

Tuzeo-Jarolmen, JoAnn. (2007). *When a Family Pet Dies*. London: Jessica Kingsley. This is a guide to dealing with children's pet loss.

Webb, Nancy Boyd, and Kenneth Doka. (2010). *Helping Bereaved Children* (3rd ed.). New York: Guilford Press. This is a handbook for practitioners on helping the bereaved child.

Webb, Nancy Boyd, and Lenore Terr. (2007). *Play Therapy With Children in Crisis* (3rd ed.). New York: Guilford Press. This is a helpful resource for individual, group and family treatment.

Winokuer, Howard, and Darcy Harris. (2012). *Principles and Practice of Grief Counseling*. New York: Springer. This is a textbook for students on grief counseling.

Wittberger, Pat, and Russ Wittberger. (2004). *When a Child Dies From Drugs*. Emeryville, CA: Alibris. This is a practical guide for parents after a child dies from drugs.

Wolfelt, Alan. (2012). *Loving From the Outside In, Mourning From the Inside Out*. Fort Collins, CO: Companion Books. This book emphasizes that the human capacity to love requires the necessity to mourn.

Wolpert, Ellen. (2005). *Start Seeing Diversity*. St. Paul, MN: Redleaf Press. This is a basic guide to an anti-bias classroom.

Worden, J. William. (2008). *Grief Counseling and Grief Therapy: A Handbook for the Mental Health Professional* (4th ed.). New York: Springer. This is a comprehensive handbook for grief counseling.

CDs, DVDs, and Videos for Children

Boulden, Jim. (2007). *Buddy's Granddad Dies*. Weaverville, CA: Boulden. This is an animated story (CD) about Buddy and the death of his granddad.

Cassavetes, Nick. (2009). *My Sister's Keeper*. Warner Home Video. This is the story of a family living with cancer.

Dougy Center. (2010). *Helping Teens Cope With Death*. Portland, OR: Dougy Center for Grieving Children. This DVD shares the lives of six grieving teens who attended a peer support group at the Dougy Center.

O'Toole, Donna. (1994). *Aarvy Aardvark Finds Hope*. Burnsville, NC: Compassion Books. The grief journey of Aarvy is presented through puppets and music for young children.

Rogers, Fred. (1993). *Mr. Rogers Talks About Living and Dying*. Pittsburgh, PA: Family Com. This is a video for young children on death.

Romain, Trevor. (2008). *Bullies Are a Pain in the Brain*. Sherman Oaks, CA: Porchlight Home Entertainment. This DVD deals with bullying issues for children.

Romain, Trevor. (2008). *What on Earth Do You Do When Someone Dies?* Sherman Oaks, CA: Porchlight Home Entertainment. This DVD for children explores questions children have about death.

Sesame Street. (2008). *Talk, Listen, Connect: Deployment, Homecomings, Changes*. New York: Sesame Street. This kit includes two Sesame Street DVDs, a magazine for adults, and an activity poster for children.

Williams, Vera, and Martha Plimpton. (2009). *A Chair for My Mother and Other Stories CD*. New York: Greenwillow Books. This audio book addresses family loss.

CDs, DVDs, and Videos for Adults

Helping Children Grieve. (2009). Paul D'Arcy and Khris Ford (Actors). Charity Olsen (Director). Brewster: MA: Paraclete Video Productions. This DVD offers helpful information for adults in how to help grieving children.

I Am Because We Are. (2009). Nathan Rissman (Director). New York: Virgil Films and Entertainment. This film explores the lives of children orphaned by AIDS.

A Look at Children's Grief. (2001). Linda Goldman (Presenter). Deerfield, IL: Association for Death Education and Counseling. This is a two-part module CD on children and loss and grief and techniques to use.

LOVE HATE LOVE. (2012). Dana Nachman and Don Hardy (Filmmakers). Sean Pean (Executive Producer). Santa Clara. CA: KTF Film. This film depicts traumatic events children and adults face and their resilience to meet their challenges.

Supporting the Grieving Child. (2012). Portland, OR: Dougy Center. This is a DVD of real families from the Dougy Center sharing their grief journey.

Understanding Suicide, Supporting Children. (2011). Portland, OR: Dougy Center. This is a DVD of real families from the Dougy Center sharing experiences surrounding suicide.

What About Me? Kids and Grief. (2006). Northbrook, IL: Film Ideas. This excellent video uses grieving children telling their experiences with grief.

When a Parent Dies: Supporting the Children. (1998). This is a Community in Crisis Teleconference by Service Corporation International (SCI) and Loma Linda University Medical Center, featuring Martin Luther King III and a national panel of experts on children and grief.

You'll Always Be With Me. (2010). Pam McDonough (Producer). Reno, NV: KNPB Channel 5 Public Broadcasting. This is a video documenting children in grief camp and their grief process.

Young Children on the Home Front: Coming Together Around Military Families. (2008). Washington, DC: Zero to Three. This video helps families with deployment.

Resources for Professionals: Guides, Curricula, and Manuals

Berman, Jeffrey. (2009). *Death in the Classroom: Writing About Love and Loss*. Albany: State University of New York Press. This is a guide for educators to explore literature on bereavement with students.

Bitney, James, and Beverly Title. (2001) *The No-Bullying Program*. Minneapolis, MN: Hazelden/Johnson Institute. This is a curriculum developed for grades K–8 to prevent bully/victim violence in the school.

Boggeman, Sally, Tom Hoerr, and Christine Wallach (Eds.). (1996). *Succeeding With Multiple Intelligences*. St. Louis, MO: New City School. This is a manual for educators teaching through the personal intelligences.

Burns, Donna. (2010). *When Kids Are Grieving: Addressing Grief and Loss in School*, Newbury Park, CA: Corwin Press. This is a resource about grieving children.

Cane, Patricia, and Mary Duennes. (2005). *Capacitar for Kids*. Santa Cruz, CA: Capacitar International. This is a multicultural wellness program for children, schools, and families.

Cassini, Kathleen and Jacqueline Rogers. (1996). *Death and the Classroom*. Burnsville, NC: Compassion Books. This is a teacher's textbook on death in the classroom.

Chadwick, Ann. (2011). *Talking About Death and Bereavement in School: How to Help Children Ages 4–11*. London: Jessica Kingsley. This is a guide for educators to work with children and bereavement.

Cohen, Judith, Anthony Mannarino, and Esther Deblinger. (2012). *Trauma-Focused CBT for Children and Adolescents: Treatment Applications*. New York: Guilford Press. This guide shares information on trauma-focused cognitive-behavioral therapy.

Cunningham, Linda. (1990). *Teen Age Grief (TAG)*. Panorama City, CA: Teen Age Grief. This is an excellent manual for teen grief work.

Dougy Center. (2003). *When Death Impacts Your School: A Guide for School Administrators*. Portland, OR: Dougy Center. This is a resource for school personnel facing a death in the schools.

Gay, Lesbian & Straight Education Network. (2011). *The Safe Space Kit*. New York: GLSEN. This is an excellent guide to being an ally to LGBT students.

Gliko-Braden, Majel. (2004). *Grief Comes to Class: A Teacher's Guide*. Omaha, NE: Centering Corp. This book is meant to help teachers and parents assist bereaved children.

Goldman, Linda. (2001). *Breaking the Silence: A Guide to Help Children With Complicated Grief, Suicide, Homicide, AIDS, Violence, and Abuse* (2nd ed.). New York: Taylor and Francis. This resource for parents and professionals helps children with complicated grief issues.

Goldman, Linda. (2009). *Great Answers to Difficult Questions About Death: What Children Need to Know*. London: Jessica Kingsley Publishers. This resource creates ideas to dialogue with children on topics surrounding death.

Goldman, Linda. (2000). *Helping the Grieving Child in the Classroom*. Arlington, VA: Phi Delta Kappan. This is a practical guide to help grieving children after initial loss and continuing throughout their school career.

Goldman, Linda. (2005). *Raising Our Children to Be Resilient: A Guide to Help Children With Traumatic Grief in Today's World*. New York: Routledge. This is a comprehensive guide to help professional work with children and traumatic grief.

Johnson, Kendall. (2004). *Classroom Crisis: The Teacher's Guide*. Alameda, CA: Hunter House. This book provides techniques for stabilizing students during a crisis.

Klicker, Ralph. (1999). *A Student Dies, a School Mourns. Are You Prepared?* New York: Taylor & Francis. This is a guide to reduce effects of personal loss and suffering in a school community when death occurs.

Lehman, Linda. (2000). *Grief Support Group Curriculum*. New York: Routledge. This is a curriculum for assisting children and teens through the mourning process.

O'Toole, Donna. (1989). *Growing Through Grief*. Burnsville, NC: Compassion Books This is an excellent K–12 curriculum to help children through loss.

Perschey, Mary. (2004). *Helping Teens Work Through Grief* (2nd ed.). New York: Taylor & Francis. This manual explains teen grief and then provides useful activities and resources to use with teens.

Rogers, J. Earl. (2007). *The Art of Grief: The Use of Expressive Arts in a Grief Support Group*. New York: Routledge. This book includes an eight-session curriculum for use with grief support groups.

Salloum, Alison. (2004). *Group Work With Adolescents After Violent Death*. New York: Taylor & Francis. This is an excellent manual for working with teens after a violent death.

Sofka, Carla, Illene Noppe, and Kathleen Gilbert. (2012). *Dying, Death, and Grief in an Online Universe: For Counselor and Educators*. New York: Springer. This book explores opportunities to deal with dying and death in the digital age for educators.

Stevenson, Robert. (2002). *What Will We Do? Preparing a School Community to Cope With Crisis*. Amityville, NY: Baywood. This clear and informative book prepares school personnel to help children cope with death-related topics.

Ward, Barbara. (1995). *Good Grief* (2nd ed.). London: Jessica Kingsley. This manual gives specific classroom lessons for children under age 11.

Book Services

Centering Corporation. Centering Corporation offers a comprehensive grief resource center for publications and trainings on topics of loss and grief. Omaha, NE. 402-553-1200.

Compassion Book Service. Compassion Books provides a wealth of resources and training tools, including books, videos, and cassettes dealing with loss, death, dying, and hope. Burnsville, NC. 800-970-4220.

Living with Loss and Bereavement Publications offers current resources on life's losses. Eckert, CO. 1-888 60-4HOPE.

Self-Esteem Shop. This resource center meets the needs of teachers and mental health professionals. Royal Oak, MI. 248-549-9900.

Western Psychological Services. This is an excellent service for therapists and counselors providing therapeutic tools. Los Angeles, CA. 800-648-8857.

Websites

Open to Hope: Grief and Loss Support On the Web

Open to Hope's website (www.opentohope.com) is an online resource for individuals who have suffered a loss and are seeking support and advice. Gloria Horsley, president, and Heidi Horsley, executive director of the *Open to Hope Foundation*, explain that losing a sibling, a parent, or other loved one when you are a child can be a deeply isolating experience. Some children lose hope.

Providing parents with information about children's grief and helping children find hope again is one of Open to Hope's missions. The following quote by Brandon, a 15-year-old, explains how he felt supported by having this website.

"I lost my only brother in November 2007. It was unexpected and he was only a few months away from his 17th birthday. I'm 15 and none of my friends know what it's like because their siblings are still alive. It hurts to know I'm so alone but it is a relief to know there are others out there in similar situations and others who understand why the little things can be the biggest triggers."

Children and Death

American Hospice Foundation http://www.americanhospice.org/

Association for Death Education and Counseling http://www.adec.org/

Barr-Harris Children's Grief Center http://barrharris.org/

Center for Loss & Life Transition http://www.centerforloss.com/

Children's Bereavement Center, Children's Grief Education Association http://www.childgrief.org

Children's Grief and Loss: Linda Goldman http://childrensgrief.net/

Compassionate Friends http://www.compassionatefriends.org/

Crisis, Grief, & Healing http://www.webhealing.com

D'Esopo Pratt Resource Center http://safeplacetogrieve.com

Elisabeth Kübler-Ross Foundation http://www.ekrfoundation.org/

Fire in My Heart http://www.fireinmyheartjournal.com

GriefNet.org http://www.griefnet.org/

Grief Speaks ww.griefspeaks.com

HelloGrief http://www.hellogrief.org/

Highmark Caring Place http://www.highmarkcaringplace.com

Hospice http://www.hospicenet.org

Kidsaid http://www.kidsaid.com/

Life & Death Matters http://www.lifeanddeathmatters.ca

National Alliance for Grieving Children http://childrengrieve.org/

Peacock Foundation http://peacockfoundation.org/about-us/

Rainbows http://www.rainbows.org/

Reginald S. Lourie Center for Infants and Young Children http://www.louriecenter.org/lc/

Solace Tree: For Grieving Children, Teens and Families http://www.solacetree.org/

UNICEF http://www.unicef.org/about/index.html

Children and Divorce

Banana Splits Resource Center http://www.bananasplitsresourcecenter.org/

Kids in the Middle http://www.kidsinthemiddle.org/

Kids' Turn http://kidsturn.org/kt/

National Family Resiliency Center, Inc. http://www.divorceabc.com/

National Stepfamily Resource Center, Auburn University http://www.stepfamilies.info/

Sesame Street http://www.sesamestreet.org/divorce

Tucson Divorce Recovery http://www.divorcerecovery.net/

Children and Family Issues

Boys and Girls Clubs of America http://bgca.org/Pages/index.aspx

Independent Adoption Center http://www.adoptionhelp.org

Teaching Tolerance http://www.tolerance.org/Welcoming Schools http://www.welcomingschools.org

Children and the Military

Army Community Service: Military Family Life Consultants http://hoodmwr.com/acs/sfrb_mflc.html

Military Kids Connect http://www.MilitaryKidsConnect.org

Military Partnership 2011 http://www.4-hmilitarypartnerships.org/doc13524.ashx4-H

National Military Family Association http://www.MilitaryFamily.org

Operation Give a Hug http://www.operationgiveahug.org

Operation: Military Kids http://www.operationmilitarykids.org

Sesame Street Workshop http://archive.sesameworkshop.org/tlc/

TAPS Tragedy Assistance Program for Survivors in the Military http://www.TAPS.org

Zero to Three http://www.zerotothree.org/military

Children of Incarcerated Parents

Children Left Behind http://www.ChildrenLeftBehind.org

Friends Outside http://www.friendsoutside.org

Get on the Bus http://www.getonthebus.us

Children's Bullying Issues

Anti-Bullying Network http://www.antibullying.net/resourceswwwlinks.htm

Bullying in Schools and What to Do About It http://www.kenrigby.net

Bullying No Way http://www.bullyingnoway.com.au/

Bullying.org http://www.bullying.org/

Gay, Lesbian, & Straight Education Network http://www.glsen.org

National Bullying Prevention Center http://www.pacer.org/bullying

National Child Traumatic Stress Network http://www.nctsn.org/resources/

Pacer Center's Kids Against Bullying http://www.pacerkidsagainstbullying.org

Pacer Center's Teens Against Bullying http://www.pacerteensagainstbullying.org/#/home

Parents, Families, and Friends of Lesbians and Gays http://www.pflag.org

Sesame Street http://www.sesamestreet.org/parents/topicsandactivities/topics/bullying

Stop Bullying http://www.stopbullying.gov

The Trevor Project http://www.thetrevorproject.org

Children's Grief Support Groups and Camps

Comfort Zone Camp http://www.comfortzonecamp.org/

Dougy Center http://www.dougy.org/

Solace Tree for Grieving Children, Teens, and Families http:www.solacetree.org

TAPS Grief Camp for Kids http://www.taps.org

Cultural Connection and Immigration

Art Museum of the Americas Educational Outreach http://museum.oas.org/programs _education.html

Boat People SOS http://www.bpsos.org/mainsite/

Children and Family http://www.globalfundforchildren.org

Latin American Youth Center http://www.layc-dc.org/

Homeless Children

National Association for the Education of Homeless Children and Youth http://www.naehcy .org

National Center for Homeless Education, Publications and Products http://center.serve.org /nche/pr/reading_go.php

National Public Radio http://www.npr.org/2011/11/20/142364493/young-gay-and-homeless -fighting-for-resources

Internet Safety and Cyberbullying

American Academy of Pediatrics, Talking to Kids and Teens about Social Media and Sexting http://www.aap.org/advocacy/releases/june09socialmedia.htm

Bullying in Schools and What to Do About It http://www.kenrigby.net

Cyberbullying Research Center http://www.cyberbullying.org

Cyberbullying: Understanding and Addressing Online Cruelty http://www.adl.org/education

HealthyChildren.org http://www.healthychildren.org/

Middle School Cyberbullying Curriculum www.seattleschools.org/area/prevention/cbms.html

NetSmartz http://www.netsmartz.org/resources/realikfe.htm

A Thin Line http://www.athinline.com

Wired Safety http://www.wiredsafety.org

Pet Death

Association for Pet Loss and Bereavement http://www.aplb.org

Pet Partners (The Delta Society) http://www.deltasociety.org

Rainbow Bridge http://rainbowsbridge.com/hello.htm

Rainbows for All Children http://www.rainbows.org

Recover-From-Grief http://www.recover-from-grief.com

Trauma and Children

American Academy of Experts in Traumatic Stress http://www.schoolcrisisresponse.com

Listen, Protect, and Connect http://www.ready.gov

National Association of School Psychologists http://www.nasponline.org

National Child Traumatic Stress Network http://www.nct snet.org

ANNOTATED BIBLIOGRAPHY FOR CHILDREN

Wyatt Gallery

Books About Death

Brown, Laura, and Marc Brown. (1996). *When Dinosaurs Die.* New York: Little, Brown. This is a practical guide for helping children understand and deal with real concerns and feelings about death. Ages 5–11.

Brown, Margaret Wise. (1995). *The Dead Bird.* New York: HarperCollins. This is a story of four children who find a dead bird, bury it, and hold a funeral service. Ages 4–8.

Ferguson, Dorothy. (2006). *A Bunch of Balloons* (2nd ed.). Omaha, NE: Centering Corporation. This is a resource to help grieving children understand their loss and how it feels after someone dies. Ages 5–8.

O'Toole, Donna. (1988). *Aarvy Aardvark Finds Hope.* Burnsville, NC: Compassion Books. This is a resource of stories of animals that present the pain, sadness, and eventual hope after death. Adult manual available. Ages 5–8.

Penn, Audrey. (2009). *Chester Raccoon and the Acorn Full of Memories.* Terre Haute, IN: Tanglewood Press. This is a story about death for young children. Ages 3–8.

Schwiebert, Pat, and Chuck DeKlyen. (2005). *Tear Soup* (3rd ed.). Portland, OR: Grief Watch. This book addresses the many aspects of grief. Ages 8–12.

Shriver, Maria, and Sandra Speidel. (2007). *What's Heaven?* New York: Golden Books Adult. This book relays a conversation between a young girl and her mom about death. Ages 5–10.

Stickney, Doris, and Robyn Nordstrom (2010). *Water Bugs and Dragonflies: Explaining Death to Young Children*. Pasadena, TX: Pilgrim Press. This is a fable for young children explaining death. Ages 4–10.

Varley, Susan. (1992). *Badger's Parting Gifts*. New York: HarperCollins. Badger was a special friend to all the animals. After his death, each friend recalls a special memory of him. Ages 4 and up.

White, E. B. (2006). *Charlotte's Web*. New York: HarperCollins. Through the eyes of farm animals, life and death are sweetly portrayed. Ages 8 and up.

Books About Death of a Parent

Blume, Judy. (2010). *Tiger Eyes*. New York: Delacorte Books. Fifteen-year-old Davey works through the feelings of his father's murder in a store holdup. Ages 12 and up.

Dennison, Amy, Allie Dennison, and David Dennison. (2003). Minneapolis, MN: Free Spirit. *Our Dad Died: The True Story of Three Kids Whose Lives Changed*. This is the story of three children sharing the death of their dad. Ages 9 and up.

Friedman, Dina. *Playing Dad's Song*. New York: Farrar, Straus and Giroux. This is the story of a dad that died during 9/11. Ages 10 and up.

Geithner, Carole. (2012). *If Only*. This is a sensitive story for young people about grief after a mother's death. New York, NY: York: Scholastic Press. Ages 10 and up.

Hughes, Lynne. (2005). *You Are Not Alone*. New York: Scholastic Paperbacks. Teens discuss life after the loss of a parent. Ages 12 and up.

Kaplow, Julie, and D. Pincus (2007). *Samantha Jane's Missing Smile*. Washington, DC: Magination Press. This is about a girl whose dad dies, and she loses her smile. Ages 5–10.

Krementz, Jill. (1996). *How It Feels When a Parent Dies*. New York: Knopf. Eighteen children (ages 7 to 16) speak openly about their feelings and experiences after the death of a parent. Ages 7 and up.

Lanton, Sandy. (2001). *Daddy's Chair*. New York: Lanton Haas Press. Michael's dad died. The book follows the shivah, the Jewish week of mourning. He doesn't want anyone to sit in Daddy's chair. Ages 5–10.

Nicholis, Sally. (2011). *Seasons of Secrets*. New York: Arthur A. Levine Books. This is a story about a girl whose mom dies, and she then lives with grandparents. Ages 8 and up.

Powell, E. Sandy. (1991). *Geranium Morning*. Minneapolis, MN: Carolrhoda Books. A boy's dad is killed in a car accident and a girl's mom is dying. The children share their feelings within a special friendship. Ages 6 and up.

Rovere, Amy. (2012). *And Still They Bloom*. New York: American Cancer Society. This is a family's journey of loss and healing. Ages 8–12.

Scrivani, Mark. (1996). *I Heard Your Daddy Died*. Omaha, NE: Centering Corporation. This is a book for young children that describes the special feelings they might have when a dad dies. Ages 6–10.

Smith, Hope. (2009). *Mother Poems*. New York: Henry Holt. Through poetry, emotions are shared about the death of a parent. Ages 10 and up.

Vigna, Judith. (1991). *Saying Goodbye to Daddy*. Park Ridge, IL: Albert Whitman. This is a sensitive story about a dad's death and the healing that takes place in the weeks that follow. Ages 5–8.

Books About Sibling Death

Alexander, Sue. (1992). *Nadia the Willful*. New York: Dragonfly Books. Nadia's older brother dies, and she helps her father heal his grief by talking about her brother. Ages 6–10.

Blanford, Cathy. (2010). *My Baby Big Sister*. Seattle, WA: CreateSpace. This is a book for children born subsequent to a pregnancy loss. Ages 4–8.

Deriso, Christine. (2011). *Then I Met My Sister*. Woodbury, MN: Flux. This story describes the challenges a girl faces after the death of her sister. Ages 12 and up.

Erskine, Kathryn. (2011). *Mockingbird*. New York: Puffin Books. This is the story of Caitlin, a little girl with Asperger's syndrome, and her grief after her brother dies. Ages 10 and up.

Forrester, Sandra. (2009). *Leo and the Lesser Lion*. New York: Knopf. This is the story of the tragic death of a brother. Ages 8 and up.

Gryte, Marilyn. (1991). *No New Baby*. Omaha, NE: Centering Corporation. Siblings express feelings about mom's miscarriage in this story. Ages 5–8.

Jackson, Aariane. (2004). *Can You Hear Me Smiling?* Washington, DC: Child and Family Press. This is the story of a child grieving the death of her sister. Ages 8 and up.

Johnson, Joy, and Marv Johnson. (1982). *Where's Jess?* Omaha, NE: Centering Corporation. This book for young children address questions and feelings kids have when a sibling dies. Ages 4–7.

Pitcher, Annabel. (2012). *My Sister Lives on the Mantelpiece*. New York: Little, Brown Books. This is the story of a 10-year-old whose twin sister dies. Teens.

Reagan, Jean. (2009). *Always My Brother*. Gardiner, ME: Tilbury House. This is the story of a boy and his grief after his brother dies. Ages 6 and up.

Schwiebert, Pat. (2007). *Someone Came Before You*. Portland, OR: Grief Watch. This resource explains to young children a sibling's death before they were born. Ages 4–9.

Temes, Roberta. (1992). *The Empty Place*. Far Hills, NJ: Small Horizons. This is a story about a third-grade boy whose older sister dies. Ages 5–9.

Books About a Friend's Death

Berenstain, Stan. (2007). *The Berenstain Bears Lose a Friend*. New York: HarperFestival. The family realizes their friend Goldie the goldfish died. Ages 4 and up.

Blackburn, Lynn. (1991). *The Class in Room 44*. Omaha, NE: Centering Corporation. The children in Room 44 share their feelings of grief when their classmate, Tony, dies. Ages 6–10.

Cohen, Janice. (1987). *I Had a Friend Named Peter*. New York: William Morrow. Betsy's friend Peter dies suddenly. She learns through parents and teachers that Peter's memory can live on. Ages 5–10.

Gootman, Marilyn. (2005). *When a Friend Dies*. Minneapolis, MN: Free Spirit. This is a book for teens about grieving and healing when a friend dies. Teens.

Kaldhol, M., and O. Wenche. (1987). *Goodbye Rune*. New York: Kane-Miller. This is a story about the drowning death of a girl's best friend and how parents can help. Ages 5–12.

Kübler-Ross, Elisabeth. (2004). *Remember the Secret*. New York: Tricycle Press. This is the imaginative story of love and faith of two children and their experience with death. Ages 5–10.

Loth, Sebastian. (2010). *Remembering Crystal*. New York: NorthSouth. This is a story about a friend that dies. Ages 3 and up.

Park, Barbara. (1996). *Mick Harte Was Here*. New York: Yearling. This is a chapter book about a boy who dies and how it affects the life of the kids who knew him. Ages 8–13.

Stickney, Doris. (2009). *Water Bugs and Dragonflies: Explaining Death to Young Children*. Cleveland, OH: Pilgrim Press. Stickney tries to explain the death of a 5-year-old neighborhood child. Ages 5–10.

Books About Grandparent Death

Burrowes, Adjoa. (2008). *Grandma's Purple Flowers*. New York: Lee & Low Books. This is the story of the death of a grandma and the memories that keep her alive. Ages 4 and up.

Castellucci, Cecil. (2010). *Grandma's Gloves*. Somerville, MA: Candlewick Press. This is a story about a little girl and her grandmother that died. Ages 5 and up.

Goldman, Linda. (2005). *Children Also Grieve: Talking About Death and Healing* (in Chinese and English). London: Jessica Kingsley. This is an interactive storybook about the death of a grandparent. Ages 5 and up.

Holden, L. Dwight. (1989). *Gran-Gran's Best Trick*. New York: Washington, DC: Magination Press. This book deals directly with cancer. It follows the treatment, sickness, and death of a grandparent. Ages 6–12.

Krishnaswami, Uma. (2007). *Remembering Grandpa*. Honesdale, PA: Boyds Mills Press. Daysha helps her grandmother in grieving after her grandfather dies. Ages 7 and up.

Levy, Janice. (2007). *I Remember Abuelito: A Day of the Dead Story* (in English and Spanish). New York: Albert Whitman. This is a story about the Day of the Dead and remembering grandfather. Ages 7 and up.

Liss-Levinson, Nechama. (1995). *When a Grandparent Dies*. Woodstock, VT: Jewish Lights. This is a kid's own remembering workbook for dealing with shivah and the year beyond a death. Ages 8–13.

Liss-Levinson, Nechama, and Molly Baskette. (2006). *Remembering My Grandparent*. Woodstock, VT: Skylight Paths. This is a children's workbook for remembering a grandparent that died in the Christian tradition. Ages 7 and up.

Pascuzzo, Margaret. (2009). *Anton Loses a Friend*. Bloomington, IN: Trafford. This is a story about Anton and his grandfather that died. Ages 6–10.

Ryan, Victoria. (2002). *When Your Grandparent Dies*. St. Meinrad, IN: Abbey Press. This is a guide for young children grieving the death of a grandparent. Ages 5–9.

Soetoro-Ng, Maya. (2011). *Ladder to the Moon*. Somerville, MA: Candlewick Press. This is the story of a girl wanting to know about her grandmother. Ages 4 and up.

Books About the Death of a Pet

Biale, Rachel. (2004). *My Pet Died*. Berkeley, CA: Tricycle Press. This is a memory book for young children who have experienced the death of a pet. Ages 4–8.

Burleigh, Robert. (2010). *Good-bye Sheepie*. Tarrytown, NY: Marshall Cavendish Childrens. This is the story of Owen and his dog, Sheepie, who gets very old and dies. Ages 8–11.

Cochran, Bill. (2007). *The Forever Dog*. New York: HarperCollins. This is the story of a young boy saying good-bye to his dog that died. Ages 4–8.

Cohen, Miriam. (2008). *Jim's Dog Muffins*. New York: Star Bright Books. Jim's dog, Muffins, is killed, and everyone in his first-grade class is sad and tries to help him feel better. Ages 4–8.

Demas, Corinne. (2009). *Saying Goodbye to Lulu*. New York: Little, Brown Books for Young Readers. This is the story of a little girl and how she feels about the death of her dog Lulu. Ages 5–10.

Goldman, Linda. (in-press 2014). *Lucy Let's Go: Helping Children Love a Pet Through Death and Dying*. This is an interactive story and memory book to help kids cope with a sick pet or their death. Omaha, NE: Centering Corporation. Ages 5–10.

Harris, Robie. (2004). *Goodbye Mousie*. New York: Aladdin. This is a wonderful book about saying good-bye to a pet mouse that dies. Ages 4–10.

Heegaard, Marge. (2001). *Saying Goodbye to Your Pet*. Minneapolis, MN: Fairview Press. This is an activity book for children to learn to cope with pet loss. Ages 5–10.

Liss-Levinson, Nechama. (2007). *Remembering My Pet*. Woodstock, VT: Skylight Paths. This is a workbook for children to remember their pet. Ages 8 and up.

Meagher, David. (2009). *Zach and His Dog*. Bloomington, IN: AuthorHouse. This is a story about bonding, loving, and loss involving pets for children. Ages 6–11.

Rogers, Fred. (1998). *When a Pet Dies*. New York: Puffin Books. This is a first experience book using photographs and words to show what we can do and feel when a pet dies. Ages 4–7.

Sanford, Doris. (1986). *It Must Hurt a Lot*. Portland, OR: Multnomah Press. A boy learns to express his emotions and hold memories after his dog is killed. Ages 4–10.

Smith, Maggie. (2003). *Desser the Best Ever Cat*. New York: Dragonfly. This is a simple story about a little girl's love for her cat. Ages 3–8.

Stein, Sarah. (1974). *About Dying*. New York: Walker. This is a classic book with simple text and photographs to help young children understand death, including a discussion for adults about children's feelings. Ages 3–6.

Viorst, Judith. (1987). *The Tenth Good Thing About Barney*. New York: Atheneum. This is the classic story of a pet cat that dies and how we can use funerals and other ways of commemorating with children. Ages 4–8.

Walsh, Barbara. (2011). *Sammy in the Sky*. Somerville, MA: Candlewick Press. This is the story of a little girl's love for her hound dog Sammy. Ages 4–9.

Weaver, Susan. (2010). *Forever Friend*. Herndon, VA: Rainbow Reach. This is an activities book for kids who have had a pet die. Ages 5–10.

Wild, Margaret. (2011). *Harry and Hopper*. New York: Feiwel and Friends. This is the story of Harry and how he feels after his dog Hopper dies. Ages 2–7.

Books About Hospice and Dying

Baber, Beth. (2011). *My Life by Me: A Kid's Forever Book*. Washington, DC: Magination Press. This is a personal memory book for terminally ill children. Ages 9–12.

Carney, Karen, and William Pilkington. (1995). *Everything Changes, but Love Endures*. Wethersfield, CT: D'Esopo-Pratt Resource Center. This wonderful storybook for young children clearly explains hospice. Ages 5–10.

Flynn, Jessie. (1994). *Hospice Hugs*. Louisville, KY: [Jessie Flynn's Center for Living. This is a book for young children that explains hospice. Ages 3–7.

Mills, Joyce. (2004). *Gentle Willow: A Story for Children About Dying* (2nd ed.). Washington DC: Magination Press. This is a book about children who may not survive their illness. Ages 4–8.

Thompson, Christine. (2012). *Scarlett Says Good-Bye*. New York: United Healthcare Services. Scarlet learns to say good-bye to a loved one in hospice. Ages 5–10.

Yolen, Jane. (2011). *The Day Tiger Rose Said Goodbye*. New York: Random House. This is a story of the last days with a dying cat. Ages 4–9.

Books About Death Through War and the Military

Barnett, Brandon. (2010). *A Salute to Our Heroes*. Dudley, MA: Mascot Books. This is a book for children about the U.S. Marines. Ages 4 and up.

Bunting, Eve. (1992). *The Wall*. Navarre, FL: Sandpaper. Through illustrations and a story, this book tells about a father and son's visit to the Vietnam Veterans Memorial and the impact of war on their lives. Ages 5–8.

Coerr, Eleanor. (2004). *Sadako and the Thousand Paper Cranes*. New York: Puffin Books. This is a true story about a Japanese girl who is dying from her exposure to radiation from the bomb at Hiroshima. Her hope is symbolized in her paper cranes. Ages 8–13.

Dennis, Brian. (2009). *Nubs: The True Story of a Mutt, a Marine and a Miracle*. New York: Little, Brown Books. This is the story of a bond of a soldier and his dog in Iraq. Ages 10 and up.

Lee, Marlene. (2005). *The Hero in My Pocket*. Boyds, MD: Early Light Press. This book helps military families cope with grief. Ages 6 and up.

McDaniel, Lurlene. (1992). *When Happily Ever After Ends*. New York: Bantam Books. This is a story about a girl whose dad killed himself after the Vietnam War. Ages 10 and up.

Scillian, Devin. (2011). *H Is for Honor*. North Mankato, MN: Sleeping Bear Press. This is a military family alphabet book. Ages 6–12.

Memory Books and Workbooks on Death for Children

Beeney, Susan, and Jo Anne Chung. (2005). *A Kid's Journey of Grief* (official TAPS ed.). Long Beach, CA: Vision Unlimited. This is an activity book for children of military families who have experienced a death.

Flynn, Jesse. *Kids Cope With Grief Memory Kit*. Louisville, KY: Jessie Flynn's Center for Living. This helpful kit for children includes special books, crayons, stickers, a picture frame, and activities. Ages 3 and up.

Goldman, Linda. (1998). *Bart Speaks Out on Suicide*. Los Angeles: WPS. This is an interactive workbook for young children who have had someone die from suicide. Ages 5 and up.

Goldman, Linda. (2005). *Children Also Grieve: Talking About Death and Healing*. London: Jessica Kingsley. This is an interactive storybook for children to cope with death. Ages 5 and up.

Haasl, Beth, and Jean Marnocha. (1999). *Bereavement Support Group Program for Children*. New York: Taylor & Francis. This is a step-by-step workbook for children (with leader manual) to use in a bereavement group. Ages 8–13.

Heegaard, Marge. (1996). *When Someone Very Special Dies*. Minneapolis, MN: Woodland Press. This is an excellent workbook that uses artwork and journaling to allow children to work through their grief. Ages 7–12.

Kilgore, Tanya. (2011). *The Grief Recovery Kit*. Austin, TX: Aepisaurus. This is a young person's guide through the journey of grief. Teens.

Lindholm, Amy, and Donna Schuurman. (2007). *After a Death: An Activity Book for Children*. Portland, OR: Dougy Center. This is a workbook for children who have experienced a death. Ages 6 and up.

O'Toole, Donna. (1995). *Facing Change*. Burnsville, NC: Compassion Books. This is an excellent guide and workbook for preteens and teens. Ages 11 and up.

Pargo, Emilio. (2007). *Love Never Stops*. [Omaha, NE: Centering Corporation. This is an engaging memory book for children. Ages 4–7.

Rogers, Fred. (1991). *So Much to Think About*. Pittsburgh, PA: Family Communications. This resource provides activities for young children when someone they love has died. Ages 5–8.

Traisman, Enid Samuel. (1992). *Fire in My Heart: Ice in My Veins*. Omaha, NE: Centering Corporation. This is a wonderful workbook for teenagers to explore thoughts and feelings and record grief memories. Teens.

Books About Life Cycles

Adams, John. (2007). *The Dragonfly Door*. Maple Plain, MN: Feather Rock Books. This is a story for young children about the life cycle. Ages 5–10.

Buscaglia, Leo. (1982). *The Fall of Freddie the Leaf*. Thorofare, NJ: Charles B. Slack. The story of the changing seasons as a metaphor for life and death. Ages 4–8.

Gerstein, Mordica. (1987). *The Mountains of Tibet*. New York: Harper & Row. This is a story of a woodcutter's journey from the mountains of Tibet through the universe of endless choices and back to his home again. Ages 7 and up.

Goble, Paul. (1993). *Beyond the Ridge*. New York: Aladdin Books. This book captures the essence of the Native American belief system on dying and death and the great circle of life. Ages 5–10.

Hoban, Tana. (1971). *Look Again*. New York: Macmillan. This book of photographs illustrates to children that we can't always know the larger picture when we see only one small part. Ages 4–7.

Mellonie, Bryan, and Robert Ingpen. (1983). *Lifetimes: The Beautiful Way to Explain Death to Children*. New York: Bantam Books. This book explains the ongoing life cycle of plants, animals, and people. Ages 3–10.

Munsch, Robert. (1995). *Love You Forever*. Ontario, Canada: Willow-dale, Firefly Books. This is a beautiful book for adults and children alike about the continuance of love throughout life. All ages.

Silverstein, Shel. (2004). *The Giving Tree* (40th anniversary ed. with CD). New York: HarperCollins. This is a beautiful story of love and the life cycle. Ages preschool and up.

Wood, Douglas, and Chang-Khee Chee. (2007). *Old Turtle*. New York: Scholastic Press. This fable captures the message of peace on earth and oneness with nature. Ages 6 and up.

Books About Aging Grandparents

de Paola, Tomie. (2000). *Nanny Upstairs and Nana Downstairs*. New York: Puffin Books. This is the story of a young boy's struggle to say good-bye to grandparents. Ages 4–8.

dePaola, Tomie. (2006). *Now One Foot Now the Other*. New York: Puffin Books. This is a story about a grandfather's stroke and how it affects his grandchildren. Ages 4–8.

Miles, Miska. (1985). *Annie and the Old One*. New York: Little, Brown Books. A Navaho girl's aging grandmother gets ready to die. The girl attempts to undo the weaving of a rug to stop this dying process. Ages 6–12.

Velasquez, Eric. (2010). *Grandma's Gift*. London: Walker Children's. This is the story of a boy and his grandma and their special bond. Ages 5 and up.

Books About Alzheimer's Disease

Nelson, Vacinda. (1988). *Always Grandma*. New York: South China. This is a story of a grandmother who develops Alzheimer's disease and her grandchild who learns to hold memories of her when she was healthy. Ages 5–8.

Shriver, Maria. (2004). *What's Happening to Grandpa?* New York: Little, Brown Books. This story speaks to young children about Alzheimer's disease and other forms of memory loss. Ages 5–10.

Van Den Abeele, Veronique. (2007). *Still My Grandma*. Grand Rapids MI: Eerdmans Books. This story is for young children about a grandma with Alzheimer's disease. Ages 4–8.

Books About Adult Illness

American Cancer Society. (2002). *Because . . . Someone I Love Has Cancer: Kids' Activity Book*. Atlanta, GA: American Cancer Society. This book helps support children when a loved one has cancer. Ages 6 and up.

Colburn, Cherie. (2010). *Our Shadow Garden*. Houston, TX: Bright Sky Press. This is a beautiful book about a grandmother too ill to work on her beloved garden. Ages 5–9.

Filigenzi, Courtney. (2009). *Let My Colors Out*. Atlanta, GA: American Cancer Society. This beautifully illustrated book assures children of cancer patients that they are not alone and helps them express feelings. Ages 4–8.

Glader, Sue. (2010). *Nowhere Hair*. Mill Valley, CA: Thousand Words Press. This book explains cancer and chemotherapy to children. Ages 4–9.

Goodman, Michael B. (1991). *Vanishing Cookies*. Mississauga, ON: Arthur Jones Lithographing. This is a book that talks honestly about a parent's cancer treatment. Ages 6–13.

Greenfield, Nancy, and Ralph Butler. (2005). *When Mommy Had a Mastectomy*. Savage, MD: Bartleby Press. This is a book for young children about cancer and mastectomy. Ages 4–8.

Heegaard, Marge. (1991). *When Someone Has a Very Special Illness*. Minneapolis, MN: Woodland Press. This workbook addresses feelings when a parent is sick. Children can illustrate it themselves. Ages 6–12.

Henley, Sue. (2013). *Cancer in Our Family* (2nd ed.). Atlanta, GA: American Cancer Society. This is a guide to help children cope with a parent's illness. All ages.

Kohlenberg, Sherry. (1994). *Sammy's Mommy Has Cancer*. New York: Washington, DC: Magination Press. This is a book written by a real mom and her son who lived with cancer. Ages 4–8.

Lewis, Alaric. (2005). *When Someone You Love Has Cancer: A Guide to Help Kids Cope*. St. Meinrad, IN: One Caring Place. This book helps children cope with cancer. Ages 5–9.

McVicker, Ellen, and Nanci Hersh. (2006; Spanish ed. 2011). *Butterfly Kisses and Wishes on Wings: When Someone You Love Has Cancer . . . A Hopeful, Helpful Book for Kids*. Self-published. This book gives kids words to talk about cancer. Ages 5–10.

Moore-Malinos, Jennifer. (2008). *Mom Has Cancer!* New York: Barron's Educational Series. This is a book to help young children cope with a mom having cancer. Ages 4–8.

Nystrom, Caroline. (1994). *Emma Says Goodbye.* Batavia, IL: Lion. Emma's aunt has a terminal illness, and Emma comes to visit with her. Ages 8–14.

Books About Children's Illness

Carney, Karen. (1998). *Barlay and Eve: What Is Cancer Anyway?* Wetherfield, CT: D'Esopo Resource Center. This is a simple and clear explanation of cancer for young children. Ages 4–8.

Gaynor, Kate. (2008). *The Famous Hat.* New York: Special Stories. This is a storybook to help children with childhood cancer and treatment. Ages 5–10.

Heegaard, Marge. (2003). *Beyond the Rainbow.* Minneapolis, MN: Fairview Press. This is a workbook for children in the advanced stages of a serious illness. Ages 5–10.

Heegaard, Marge. (2003). *Living Well With My Serious Illness.* Minneapolis, MN: Fairview Press. This is a workbook for children who have been diagnosed with a serious illness. Ages 5–10.

Maple, Marilyn. (1992). *On the Wings of a Butterfly.* Seattle, WA: Parenting Press. A butterfly becomes a friend to Lisa, a child dying of cancer. Lisa shares her fears of dying. Ages 5–10.

Mays, Lydia, and Barbara Meyers. (2011). *The Long and the Short of It: A Tale About Hair.* Atlanta, GA: American Cancer Society. This is a story about two girls who are friends, and one has cancer. Ages 7–11.

Peters, Dylan. (2009). *Tic Talk: Living with Tourette Syndrome.* Chandler, AZ: Little Five Star. This is a 9-year old boy's story of living with Tourette syndrome. Ages 8–12.

Schultz, Charles M. (2002). *Why, Charlie Brown, Why?* New York: Ballantine. The story about Charlie's friend Janice, who has leukemia, and what happens when a friend is very ill. Ages 5–10.

Sileo, Frank, and Martha Gradisher. (2006). *Toilet Paper Flowers.* Albuquerque, NM: Health Press. This is a story for children about Crohn's disease. Ages 8 and up.

Books About Organ Donation and Tissue Transplant

Carney, Karen. (1999). *Precious Gifts: Katie Coolican's Story: Barklay and Eve Explain Organ and Tissue Donation.* Wethersfield, CT: D'Esopo Resource Center. This resource explains the issues around organ donation to young children. Ages 4–8.

Ellsworth, Loretta. (2010). *In a Heartbeat.* London: Walker Children's. This is about a 14-year-old who received a heart transplant. Ages 12 and up.

Flynn, Jesse. (1996). *A New Heart for Hannah.* Louisville, KY: Accord. This is a book written for very young children about organ donors. Ages 4–7.

Wood, Ramona. (2004). *Now Caitlin Can.* San Diego, CA: ABC Press. This is a story about a donated organ that helps a child get well. Ages 4–9.

Books About AIDS

Fassler, David. (1991). *What's a Virus, Anyway?* Burlington, VT: Waterfront Press. This children's book explains concepts about the AIDS virus. Ages 5–9.

Hausherr, Rosemare. (1989). *Children and the AIDS Virus.* New York: Clarion Books. This informative book for older and younger children tells and shows through pictures the world of AIDS. Ages 5 and up.

Johanson, Paula. (2007). *HIV and AIDS.* New York: Rosen. This is a book for young people coping in a changing world with issues on HIV and AIDS. Ages 13 and up.

Merrifield, Margaret. (1998). *Come Sit by Me.* Markham, ON: Fitzhenry and Whiteside. This is a useful book for parents and teachers to educate young children on the facts about AIDS. Ages 4–8.

Moutoussamy-Ashe, Jeanne. (1993). *Daddy and Me*. New York: Alfred Knopf. This is a wonderful photo story of Arthur Ashe and his daughter, Camera, sharing life with his illness. Ages 4 and up.

Sheinmel, Courtney. (2010). *Positively*. New York: Simon & Schuster. This is the story of a little girl and her mother diagnosed as HIV-positive. Ages 9–13.

Sparks, Beatrice (Editor), and Anonymous Teenager. (2004). *It Happened to Nancy*. New York: HarperTeen. This is a true story about a teenager and AIDS. Ages 13 and up.

Tinsley, Helen. (2012). *Me and My Grandma*. Cherry Hill, NJ: Nefu Books. This is a story for children about AIDS. Ages 10 and up.

Weiner, Lori, Philip Pizzo, and Aprille Best. (1996). *Be a Friend*. Park Ridge, IL: Albert Whitman. This is an excellent book sharing children's voices with HIV. Ages 7–11.

Wolf, Bernard. (1997). *HIV Positive*. New York: Dutton Children's Books. An excellent resource for children; includes photographs and honest explanations about HIV and AIDS. Ages 8–13.

Books About Asthma

Lynette, Rachel. (2009). *How to Deal With Asthma*. New York: PowerKids Press. This book helps kids deal with asthma. Ages 7 and up.

Moore-Mallinos, Jennifer, and Marta Fabrega. (2007). *I Have Asthma*. New York: Barron's Educational Series. This is a story about a child who suffers from asthma. Ages 4–8.

Books About Weight Disorders and Eating Issues

Miller, Edward. (2008). *The Monster Health Book: A Guide to Eating Healthy, Being Active and Feeling Great for Monsters and Kids!* New York: Holiday House. This book presents healthy choices to children about eating. Ages 7–12.

Nelson, Tammy. (2008). *What's Eating You?: A Workbook for Teens with Anorexia, Bulimia, and other Eating Disorders*. Oakland, CA: Instant Help. This is a workbook for teens with anorexia, bulimia, and other eating disorders. Ages 13 and up.

Rabe, Tish. (2001). *Oh the Things You Can Do That Are Good for You!* New York: Random House. This is a book for children about staying healthy and feeling good about body image. Ages 4–11.

Rockwell, Lizzy. (2009). *Good Enough to Eat*. New York: HarperCollins. This is a kid's guide to food and nutrition. Ages 4–9.

Books About Childhood Diabetes

Anderson, Karri. (2012). *I Have Diabetes*. Seattle, WA: CreateSpace. This is a children's book about juvenile diabetes. Ages 2 and up.

Betschart-Roemer, Jean. (1995). *It's Time to Learn About Diabetes: A Workbook on Diabetes for Children*. New York: Wiley. This is an easy-to-understand workbook for children to help them manage diabetes. Ages 6–12.

Gaynor, Kate. (2008). *The Bravest Girl in School*. New York: Special Stories. This is a story about diabetes and taking insulin. Ages 5–10.

Gosselin, Kim. (2004). *Taking Diabetes to School* (3rd ed.). Plainview, NY: JayJo Books. This book tells about a child with diabetes and his sharing at school. Ages 4–9.

Books About Autism and Asperger's Syndrome

Bishop, Beverly. (2011). *My Friend With Autism*. Arlington, TX: Future Horizons. This is a book about autism with a CD of coloring pages. Ages 7–11.

Grossberg, Blythe. (20120. *Asperger's Rules*. Washington, DC: Magination Press. This book describes how children make sense of Asperger's syndrome at school and with friends. Ages 9–13.

Peete, Holly, Ryan Peete, and Shane Evans. (2010). *My Brother Charlie*. New York: Scholastic Press. This is the story of a boy with autism. Ages 7–12.

Robbins, Lynette. (2009). *How to Deal With Autism*. Logan, IA: PowerKids. This is a book to help children deal with autism. Ages 7–11.

Tourville, Amanda. (2010). *My Friend Has Autism*. Mankato, MN: Picture Window Books. This is a book about a child who has a friend with autism. Ages 5–9.

Wine, Angela. (2005). *What It Is to Be Me!* Fairdale, KY: Fairdale. This is a children's book about Asperger's syndrome. Ages 5–10.

Book About Sibling Abduction

U.S. Department of Justice. *What About Me?* Washington, DC: U.S. Department of Justice. This is a book for children about coping with sibling abduction. Ages 12 and up.

Books About Down Syndrome

Bouwkamp, Julie. (2006). *Hi, I'm Ben . . . And I've Got a Secret!* Rochester Hills, MN: Band of Angels. This story is about Ben, a boy with Down syndrome. Ages 5 and up.

Moore-Mallinos, Jennifer. (2008). *My Friend Has Down Syndrome*. New York: Barron's Educational Series. This book helps children to understand Down syndrome. Ages 4 and up.

Pitzer, Margerie. (2004). *I Can, Can You?* Bethesda, MD: Woodbine House. This is a board book of photographs of babies and toddlers with Down syndrome during their day. Ages 2 and up.

Woloson, Eliza. (2003). *My Friend Isabelle*. Bethesda, MD: Woodbine House. This is a sweet story about a friend who has Down syndrome. Ages 4 and up.

Books About Moving

Blume, Judy. (2010). *Are You There God? It's Me Margaret*. Bel Air, CA: Ember. Margaret has to face moving and beginning a new life. Ages 9 and up.

Civardi, Anne. (2005). *Moving House*. Worcester, UK: Usborne Books. This is a story about a boy's first moving experience. Ages 3–7.

Glasser, Debbie, and Emily Schenck. (2011). *New Kid, New Scene*. Washington, DC: Magination Press. This is a guide to help kids with moving and switching schools. Ages 8–13.

Johnson, Angela. (1995). *The Leaving Morning*. New York: Orchard Books. This is a book about the feelings a family goes through during a move, and everything and everyone they need to say good-bye to. Ages 4–8.

Maisner, Heather. (2004). *We're Moving*. New York: Kingfisher. This story is to help children that are moving. Ages 4–8.

Penn, Audrey. (2007). *A Kiss Goodbye*. Terre Haute, IN: Tanglewood Press. This is a story for young children about moving. Ages 3–8.

Books About Divorce

Andre, Katherine. (2009*). I Don't Want to Choose*. Peoria, IL: Kindred Spirits. This book for middle school kids shares feelings of choosing one parent over the other. Ages 10–13.

Dessen, Sarah. (2011). *What Happened to Goodbye*. New York: Viking Juvenile. This is a story about parents' bitter divorce and making a new life. Ages 12 and up.

Fassler, David, Michele Lash, and Sally Ives. (1988). *Changing Families*. Burlington, VT: Waterfront Books. This is advice for parents and children coping with divorce, remarriage, and new families. Ages 4–12.

Hardwick, Charlotte. (2008). *Dear Judge (Kid's Letters to the Judge)*. Livingston, TX: Palehorse. This book shares letters to judges about divorce. Ages 5–11.

Heegaard, Marge. (1996). *When Mom and Dad Separate*. Bloomington, MN: Woodland Press. This is a workbook for children exploring thoughts and feelings about separation and divorce. Ages 6–12.

Krementz, Jill. (1988). *How It Feels When Parents Divorce*. New York: Knopf. Children describe how the divorce of their parents has affected them. Ages 8–13.

Levins, Sandra, and Bryan Langdo (2006). *Was It The Chocolate Pudding? A Story for Little Kids About Divorce*. Washington, DC: American Psychological Association. This book shares the challenges of divorce for children. Ages 4 and up.

Masurel, Claire. (2003). *Two Homes*. Somerville, MA: Candlewick Press. This is a very positive story about divorce and having two homes. Ages 4–8.

Ricci, Isolina. (2006). *Mom's House, Dad's House for Kids*. Beaverton, OR: Touchstone. This is a story about feeling at home in one home or two. Ages 5–10.

Rogers, Fred. (1996). *Let's Talk About Divorce*. New York: G. P. Putnam. This is a beautiful book with photographs explaining divorce to young children. Ages 5–8.

Schmitz, Tamar. (2008). *Standing on My Own Two Feet: A Child's Affirmation of Love in the Midst of Divorce*. New York: Price Stern Sloan. Addison is a little boy whose parents are going through divorce. Ages 3 and up.

Stern, Zoe, and Evan Stern (2008). *Divorce Is Not the End of the World: Zoe's and Evan's Coping Guide for Kids*. New York: Tricycle Press. This book helps kids cope with divorce. Ages 10 and up.

Books About Remarriage

Heegaard, Marge. (1993). *When a Parent Marries Again*. Minneapolis, MN: Woodland Press. This excellent resource is for children and the many complicated feelings involved when a parent remarries. Ages 5–10.

Hugo, Lynn. (2005). *Jessica's Two Families*. Ferrisburg, VT: New Horizon Press. This is a book to help children cope with blended households. Ages 4–9.

Levins, Sandra, and Bryan Langdo. (2009). *Do You Sing Twinkle?* Washington, DC: Magination Press. This is a story about remarriage and new family. Ages 3–8.

Moore-Mallinos, Jennifer, and Marta Fabrega. (2006). *Daddy's Getting Married*. New York: Barron's Educational Series. This book allows children to discuss a parent remarrying. Ages 5–10.

Rogers, Fred. (2001). *Let's Talk About Stepfamilies*. New York: Puffin Books. This is an excellent discussion for young children on the topic of stepfamilies. Ages 5–10.

Books About Adoption

Bartlett, Therese. (2001). *When You Were Born in Vietnam*. St. Paul, MN: Yeong & Yeong. This is a memory book for children adopted from Vietnam. Ages 5–10.

Curtis, Jamie Lee. (2000). *Tell Me Again About the Night I Was Born*. New York: HarperCollins. This little book creates a wonderful dialogue about adoption. Ages 4 and up.

Girard, Linda. (1989). *We Adopted You, Benjamin Koo*. Niles, IL: Albert Whitman. Benjamin is a 9-year-old boy from another country. He tells of how he adjusted to adoption and a culturally blended family. Ages 7–11.

Heegaard, Marge. (2007). *Adopted and Wondering*. Minneapolis, MN: Fairview Press. This resource helps children draw out feelings about adoption. Ages 6–12.

Katz, Karen (2001). *Over the Moon, an Adaption Tale*. New York: Henry Holt. This is a reassuring story about a family's journey in adoption. Ages 4–10.

Lewis, Rose. (2007). *Every Year on Your Birthday*. New York: Little, Brown. This is the story of a Chinese child that was adopted. Her mother helps her remember her Chinese home and family on her birthdays. Ages 4–10.

Parr, Todd. (2007). *We Belong Together: A Book About Adoption and Families*. New York: Little, Brown Books for Young Readers. This is a book for adopted children and their parents. Ages 4–8.

Peacock, Carol. (2000). *Mommy Far, Mommy Near*. Morton Grove, IL: Albert Whitman. This adoption story is about a little girl from China. Ages 5–10.

Richmond, Marianne. (2008). *I Wished for You: An Adoption Story*. Columbia Heights, MN: Marianne Richmond Studios. This story shares a discussion on becoming a family with adoption. Ages 2 and up.

Rosove, Lori. (2001). *Rosie's Family: An Adoption Story*. Ottawa, ON: Asia Press. This is a wonderful resource—a story told by a dog on the complexities of adoption in today's diverse families. Ages 4–8.

Books About Homelessness

Bromley, Anne. (2010). *The Lunch Thief*. Gardiner, ME: Tilbury House. This is the story of a little boy who has lost everything in a fire and is stealing lunches because he's hungry. Ages 8–12.

Carmi, Glora. (2006). *A Circle of Friends*. New York: Star Bright Books. This is a story about a boy who shares his snack with a homeless man and inspires goodwill. Ages 4–8.

Grimes, Nikki. (2010). *Almost Zero: A Dyamonde Daniel Book*. New York: Putnam Juvenile. This is a story of a young girl that grows compassion and creates a clothing drive for another child who has lost everything in a fire. Ages 7–11.

Gunning, Monica. (2004). *A Shelter in Our Car*. San Francisco: Children's Book Press. This is the story of a young girl and her mom who are forced to live in their car because Mom can't find a job. Ages 6–11.

Landowne, Youome. (2005). *Selavi, That Is Life*. El Paso, TX: Cinco Puntos Press. This is a story of hope about a boy who finds himself homeless in Haiti. Ages 6–12.

McDonald, Janet. (2010). *Chill Wind*. New York: Farrar, Straus and Giroux. This story tells of a teenage mom and what happens when welfare payments run out. Ages 12 and up.

Trottier, Maxine. (1997). *A Safe Place*. Morton Grove, IL: Albert Whitman. To escape her dad's abuse, a little girl and her mom find refuge in a shelter. Ages 5–9.

Books About Bullying

Anthony, Michelle. (2010). *Little Girls Can Be Mean*. New York: St. Martin's Griffin. This story shares relational bullying with young girls. Ages 6–11.

Cohen-Posey. (1995). *How to Handle Bullies, Teasers and Other Meanies*. Highland City, FL: Rainbow Books. This resource help kids with bullying issues. Ages 8–13.

Dismondy, Maria. (2012). *Spaghetti in a Hot Dog Bun*. Bel Air, CA: Maria Dismondy. This book inspires children to have courage to be who they are. Ages 6–11.

Homzie, Hillary. (2009). *Things Are Gonna Get Ugly*. New York: Aladdin Mix. This is a story about a girl's experience in middle school with the popular clique. Ages 10 and up.

Kaufman, Gershen, and Lev Raphael. (1990). *Stick Up for Yourself*. Minneapolis, MN: Free Spirit. This guide helps kids feel personal power. Ages 8–12.

Leader, Jessica. (2010). *Nice and Mean*. New York: Aladdin. This is a story of a middle school girl forced to work on a project with a mean girl. Ages 9–13.

Lovell, Patty. (2001). *Stand Tall, Molly Lou Melon*. New York: Putnam. This is a story about a little girl standing up against bullying. Ages 4–8.

Ludwig, Trudy. (2011). *Better Than You*. New York: Knopf. This is a story about how being friends with a braggart can feel hurtful. Ages 6–11.

Ludwig, Trudy. (2010). *Confessions of a Former Bully*. Berkeley, CA: Tricycle Press. This book tells of the transformation of a bully and consequences faced. Ages 7–11.

Ludwig, Trudy. (2006). *Just Kidding*. Berkeley, CA: Tricycle Press. This is a story of emotional bullying among boys. Ages 6–11.

Ludwig, Trudy. (2005). *My Secret Bully*. Berkeley, CA: Tricycle Press. This is the story of relational aggression. Ages 6–11.

McCain, Becky, and Todd Leonardo. (2001). *Nobody Knew What to Do*. Park Ridge, IL: Albert Whitman. This is a story about bullying. Ages 6–11.

Munson, Derek. (2000). *Enemy Pie*. San Francisco: Chronicle Books. This book teaches children a sweet lesson in friendship. Ages 5–9.

Moss, Peggy. (2004). *Say Something*. Gardiner, ME: Tilbury House. This is a book about the power of the bystander. Ages 4–9.

O'Neill, Alexis. (2002). *The Recess Queen*. New York: Scholastic Press. This is the story of a bully at recess. Ages 4–8.

Romain, Trevor. (1997). *Bullies Are a Pain in the Brain*. Minneapolis, MN: Free Spirit. This is a book for children to address the topic of bullies. Ages 7–11.

Senn, Diane, and Susan Bowman. (2007). *Bullying in the Girl's World*. Chapin, SC: Youthlight. This is a schoolwide approach to girl bullying. Ages 8–12.

Sornson, Bob, and Maria Dismondy. (2010). *The Juice Box Bully*. Northville, MI: Ferne Press. This book empowers kids to stand up for others. Ages 5–10.

Books About Emotional Abuse

Davis, Diane. (2010). *Something Is Wrong in My House*. Seattle, WA: Parenting Press. This is a book about parents fighting, ways to cope with violence, and how to break the cycle. Ages 8–12.

Heegaard, Marge. (2005). *When Adults Hurt Children*. Minneapolis, MN: Fairview Press. This book helps children heal from abuse. Ages 6–12.

Loftis, Chris. (1997). *The Words Hurt*. Far Hills, NJ: New Horizon Press. This story tells about a young boy trying to cope with the trauma of verbal abuse. Ages 4–8.

Watts, Gillian. (2009). *Hear My Roar*. Toronto: Annick Press. This is a story about family violence. Ages 6–11.

Books About Sexual Abuse

Carter, Lee. (2002). *It Happened to Me*. Oakland, CA: New Harbinger. This is a teen's guide to overcoming sexual abuse. Ages 13 and up.

Girard, Linda. (1984). *My Body Is Private*. Morton Grove, IL: Albert Whitman. This book provides age appropriate ways for children to distinguish between good touching and unwanted touching. Ages 6–11.

King, Kimberly. (2008). *I Said No! A Kid-to-Kid Guide to Keeping Your Private Parts Private*. Weaverville, CA: Boulden. This book shares healthy boundaries for kids talking about their private parts. Ages 4–8.

Lowery, Linda. (2008). *Laurie Tells*. Laredo, TX: MaxBooks. This is a sensitive story about a girl who is sexually abused by her father. Ages 8–13.

Sanford, Doris. (1986). *I Can't Talk About It*. Portland, OR: Multnomah Press. Annie talks to an abstract form, Love, about her sexual abuse, and begins to heal and trust. Ages 8–13.

Sanford, Doris. (1993). *Something Must Be Wrong With Me*. Sisters, OR: Questar. This is a sensitive story about a young boy's journey with sexual abuse. Ages 5–10.

Starishevsky, Jill. (2009). *My Body Belongs to Me*. New York: Safety Star Media. This book establishes boundaries for young people. Ages 3 and up.

Books About Suicide

Cammarata, Doreen. (2009). *Someone I Love Died by Suicide*. Jupiter, FL: Limitless Press. This is a story for children who have had someone die by suicide. Ages 7–11.

Dougy Center. (2001). *After a Suicide*. Portland: OR: Dougy Center. This is an activity book about suicide for kids. Ages 6–11.

Garland, Sherry. (1994). *I Never Knew Your Name*. New York: Ticknor & Fields. A young boy tells the story of a teenage boy's suicide. Ages 5–10.

Goldman, Linda. (1998). *Bart Speaks Out on Suicide*. Los Angeles: WPS. This is a clear and honest memory book and interactive storybook that creates words to use to discuss the topic of suicide with young children. Ages 5–12.

Kukliln, S. (1994). *After a Suicide: Young People Speak Up*. New York: G. P. Putnam. This book is a great teen resource with stories by teens that have experienced a suicide. Teens.

Requarth, Margo. (2008). *After a Parent's Suicide: Helping Children*. Sebastopol, CA: Healing Hearts Press. This resource explains suicide to older children. Teens.

Rubel, Barbara. (2009). *But I Didn't Get To Say Goodbye* (2nd ed.). Portland, OR: Griefwork Center. This story tells about an 11-year-old coping with suicide. Ages 11 and up.

Books About Depression

Andrews, Beth. (2002). *Why Are You So Sad?: A Child's Book about Parental Depression*. Washington, DC: Magination Press. This is a child's book about parental depression. Ages 5–9.

Chan, Paul. (2006). *Why Is Mommy Sad? A Child's Guide to Parental Depression*. Mission Viejo, CA: Current Clinical Strategies. This is a child's guide to parental depression. Ages 5–9.

Schab, Lisa. (2008). *Beyond the Blues*. Bel Air, CA: Instant Help. This is a workbook to help teens overcome depression. Ages 13 and up.

Books About Abandonment and Foster Care

Gilman, Jan. (2009). *Murphy's Three Homes. A Story for Children in Foster Care*. Washington, DC: Magination Press. This is a story represents children in foster care. Ages 3 and up.

Levy, Janice. (2004). *When Kids Can't Live With Their Parents*. Washington, DC: Magination Press. This is the story of kids who can't live with their parents and are in foster care. Ages 6–11.

Lowery, Linda. (1995). *Somebody Somewhere Knows My Name*. Minneapolis, MN: Carolrhoda Books. Grace and her brother are abandoned by their mother and stay at a shelter. Ages 8–13.

Nelson, Julie. (2007). *Families Change*. Minneapolis, MN: Free Spirit. This is a book for children experiencing termination of parental rights. Ages 4–8.

Nelson, Julie. (2005). *Kids Need to Be Safe*. Minneapolis MN: Free Spirit. This is a book for children in foster care. Ages 4–9.

Wilgocki, Jennifer, Marcia Wright, and Alissa Geis. (2002). *Maybe Days*. Washington, DC: Magination Press. This is a book for children in foster care. Ages 4–9.

Books About Violence

Bentrim, William. (2010). *Mommy's Black Eye: Children Dealing With Domestic Violence*. Seattle, WA: CreateSpace. This is a children's book that addresses domestic violence. Ages 5–9.

Cohen, Janice. (1994). *Why Did It Happen?* New York: Morrow Junior Books. This is a good resource for children on neighborhood violence. Ages 5–10.

Humphreys, Catherine, Ravi Thiara, Audrey Mullender, and Agnes Skamballis. (2006). *Talking About Domestic Abuse: A Photo Activity Workbook to Develop Communication Between Mothers and Young People*. London: Jessica Kingsley. This is an activity book for children and families that have experienced domestic violence. Ages 9 and up.

Lee, Ilene, and Kathy Sylwester. (2011). *When Mommy Got Hurt*. Oakland, CA: Storymine Press. This story tells about a child witnessing domestic violence. Ages 2–7.

Lester, Julius. (2003). *When Dad Killed Mom*. Boston: Graphia. This is the story of a family where the father kills the mother and goes to jail. Ages 12 and up.

Loftis, Chris. (1997). *The Boy Who Sat by the Window*. Far Hills, NJ: New Horizon Press. This is an excellent book for young children about a boy who gets murdered and the cycle of violence surrounding his death. Ages 6–12.

Moser, Adolph. (2001). *Don't Be a Menace on Sundays! The Children's Anti-Violence Book*. Kansas City, KS: Landmark Editions. This book addresses a violent world and violent feelings kids may have. Ages 9 and up.

Verdick, Elizabeth, and Marieka Heinlen. (2012). *Hands Are Not for Hitting*. Minneapolis, MN: Free Spirit. This is a board book for young children that expresses violence is never OK. Ages 2 and up.

Watts, Gillian, and Ben Hodson. (2009). *Hear My Roar*. Richmond Hill, ON: Annick Press. This is a story of family violence. Ages 6 and up.

Books About Homicide

Dougy Center. (2002). *After a Murder*. Portland, OR: Dougy Center. This is a workbook for grieving kids after they are touched by murder. Ages 6–11.

Reisfeld, Randi, with H. B. Gilmour. (2012). *What the Dog Said*. New York: Bloomsbury USA Children. This is the story of a little girl whose dad was a police officer and was killed. Ages 10 and up.

Books About Trauma

Chara, Kathleen. (2005). *A Safe Place for Caleb*. London: Jessica Kingsley. This is an interactive book for kids and teens on early trauma. Ages 8 and up.

Holmes, Margaret. (2000). *A Terrible Thing Happened*. Washington, DC: Magination Press. This is a book for children who have witnessed violence or trauma. Ages 4–9.

Palmer, Libbi. (2012). *The PTSD Workbook for Teens*. Oakland, CA: Instant Help. This book presents effective skills for healing trauma. Ages 13 and up.

Shuman, Carol. (2003). *Jenny Is Scared*. Washington, DC: Magination Press. This is a story about a child afraid of scary events. Ages 4–8.

Books About Natural Disaster

Balcetis, Mat, Connie Johnk, Eugene Oliveto, Joy Johnson, Nancy Crump, Sharon Greelee, and David Walker. *After the Storm*. Omaha, NE: Centering Corporation. This is a workbook for children who have experienced severe weather. Ages 5–10.

Burgan, Michael. (2011). *Surviving Earthquakes*. North Mankato, MN: Heinemann-Raintree. This is a book of children's true stories on surviving earthquakes. Ages 8 and up.

Wyatt Gallery

Raum, Elizabeth. (2011). *Surviving Floods*. North Mankato, MN: Heinemann-Raintree. This is a book of children's true stories on surviving floods. Ages 8 and up.

Williams, Vera. (1984). *A Chair for My Mother*. New York: Mulberry Books. After a fire destroys their home, Rosa, her mom, and grandmother save their money for a big chair to share. Ages 5–10.

Books About Deportation

De Guzman, Michael. (2011). *Growing up Rita*. Seattle, WA: CreateSpace. Twelve-year-old Rita's mom is illegally living in America. After an immigration raid, she searches to find her mother. Ages 12 and up.

Lagasse, Mary. (2004). *The Fifth Sun*. Willimantic, CT: Curbstone Books. This is a story of an immigrant who struggles for a better life and is deported. Teens.

Books About Drugs and Alcohol

Black, Claudia. (1997). *My Dad Loves Me, My Dad Has a Disease*. Denver, CO: MAC. This is a workbook for children of alcoholics to help them better understand alcoholism and their feelings about it. Ages 6–14.

Hastings, Jill, and Marion Typpo. (1994). *An Elephant in the Living Room*. Center City, MN: Hazelden. This is a workbook for children about alcoholism. Ages 8–12.

McClellan, Marilyn. (2004). *The Big Deal About Alcohol*. Berkeley Heights, NJ: Enslow. This is a book addressing teen drinking. Ages 12 and up.

Rogers, Vanessa. (2012). *A Little Book of Drugs*. London: Jessica Kingsley. This activity book explores drug issues with young people. Ages 13 and up.

Sanford, Doris. (1984). *I Know the World's Worst Secret*. Portland, OR: Multnomah Press. A girl talks about her alcoholic mom. Ages 8–13.

Taylor, Clark. (1994). *The House That Crack Built*. San Francisco, CA: Raincoast Books. This book presents a familiar nursery rhyme that tells about drugs. Ages 4 and up.

Books About Dads

Braun, Sebastian. (2004). *I Love My Daddy*. New York: HarperCollins. This book shares the special bond between father and child. Ages 4–8.

Katz, Karen. (2007). *Daddy Hugs*. New York: Little Simon. This books shares the love between father and child. Ages 1 and up.

Loomis, Christine, and Jackie Urbanovic. (2004). *The Ten Best Things About My Dad*. New York: Cartwheel. This book talks about how special dads are. Ages 4–8.

Macnaughton, Tina. (2008). *My Daddy and Me*. Intercourse, PA: Good Books. This is a board book about dads for young children. Ages 2 and up.

Ritchie, Alison. (2007). *Me and My Dad!* Intercourse, PA: Good Books. This is a special book about dads. Ages 2 and up.

Books About Moms

American Girl Editors. (2008). *Just Mom and Me*. Middleton, WI: American Girl. This book is filled with ideas for things mothers and daughters can do together. Ages 8 and up.

Dee, Barbara. (2011). *Trauma Queen*. New York: Aladdin. This is the story of a girl embarrassed by her overly dramatic mom. Ages 9–13.

Gaylord, Laurel. (2004). *I Love My Mommy Because . . . .* New York: Dutton Juvenile. This is a story about the reasons a child loves her mom. Ages 1 and up.

Glassman, Peter, and Tedd Arnold. (2001). *My Working Mom*. New York: HarperTrophy. This is a story about a working mom. Ages 3 and up.

Jacobs, Meredith, and Sofie Jacobs. (2010). *Just Between Us*. San Francisco: Chronicle Books. This is a no-stress journal for girls and their moms. Ages 9 and up.

Macnaughton, Tina. (2008). *My Mommy and Me*. Intercourse, PA: Good Books. This is a story about children and their moms. Ages 2 and up.

Ritchie, Allison. (2009). *Me and My Mom*. Intercourse, PA: Good Books. This is a special book about moms. Ages 2 and up.

Books About Incarcerated Parents

Bender, Janet. (2003). *My Daddy Is in Jail*. Chapin, SC: Youthlight. This is a story, discussion guide, and small group activities resource. Ages 5–10.

Dychesm, Richard. (2010). *Doogie's Dad*. Berryville, AR: Children Left Behind. This story is about children whose dad is in prison and they get to visit him. Ages 5–9.

Hickman, Martha. (1990). *When Andy's Father Went to Prison*. Niles: IL: Albert Whitman. Andy's dad was arrested for stealing and went to prison. Andy copes with his feelings of shame and abandonment while his dad's away. Ages 5–9.

Spanne, A., N. McCarthy, and L. Longhine. (2010). *Wish You Were Here*. New York: Youth Communication. This is a book about teens writing about parents in prison. Teens.

Walker, Jan. (2010). *An Inmate's Daughter* (Kindle ed.). Norris, MT: Raven. This is a story of Jenny and how she feels having a parent in prison. Ages 10–13.

Books About Technology

Collins, Suzanne, and Mike Lester. (2005). *When Charlie McButton Lost Power*. New York: Puffin Books. This is a story about Charlie, a little boy who loves his computer so much and has to deal with no power. Ages 4–8.

Leavitt, Jacalyn, and Sally Linford. (2006). *Faux Paws: Adventures in the Internet*. Indianapolis, IN: Wiley. This is a storybook and CD-ROM for young children to teach them to protect themselves on the Internet. Produced by iKeepSafe.org. Ages 5–9.

Jacobs, Thomas. (2010). *Teen Cyberbullying Investigated*. Minneapolis, MN: Free Spirit. This book covers more than 50 actual court cases involving young people and cyberbullying and the real dangers and legal consequences. Teens.

Ostow, Micol. (2011). *What Would My Cell Phone Do?* New York: Penguin Books. Sixteen-year-old Aggie loses her cell phone, her lifeline, after a move and begins an online search for it. Teens.

Books About Deployment

Andrews, Beth, and Hawley Wright. (2007). *I Miss You! A Military Kid's Book About Deployment*. Amherst, NY: Prometheus Books. This is a book that talks to children about deployment. Ages 6–10.

Christiansen, Rebecca, and Jewel Armstrong. (2007). *My Dad's a Hero*. Tarentum, PA: Word Association. This is a book about a dad in the military. Ages 4–9.

Ehrmantraut, Brenda. (2005). *Night Catch*. Aberdeen, SD: Bubble Gum Press. This is a book about a father and son staying connected during deployment. Ages 5–10.

Hardin, Melinda. (2010). *Hero Dad*. New York: Scholastic Press. This is the story about a military dad. Ages 3–8.

LaBelle, Julie, and Christina Rodriguez. (2009). *My Dad's Deployment: A Deployment and Reunion Activity Book for Young Children*. St. Paul, MN: Elva Resa. This is an activity book for children with a deployed dad. Ages 4–8.

Skolmoski, Stephanie. (2006). *A Paper Hug*. Self-published. A little boy gives his dad the best gift before he leaves for military service. Ages 5–8.

Weaver, Susan. (2011). *Heroes! Activities for Kids Dealing With Deployment*. Breinigsville, PA: Rainbow Reach. This is an interactive workbook for children experiencing someone close to them being deployed. Ages 5–10.

Books About Immigration

Choi, Yangsook. (2001). *The Name Jar*. New York: Dragonfly Books. This is the story of a Korean girl, Unhei, and her assimilation in a new country. Ages 5–10.

Fassler, David, and Kimberly Danworth (1992). *Coming to America: The Kids Book of Immigration*. Burlington, VT: Waterfront Books. Help for children to explore feelings on immigration. Ages 4–12.

Hanel, Rachael (2009). *Mexican Immigrants in America*. North Mankato, MN: Capstone. This is an interactive history adventure about Mexican immigrants. Ages 6–12.

Lai, Thanhha. (2011). *Inside Out and Back Again*. New York: HarperCollins. This book of poetry tells the journey of an escaped Vietnamese family. Ages 10 and up.

Lewis, Rose. (2010). *Orange Peel's Pocket*. New York: Abrams. A 5-year-old Chinese American finds out about China, the place where she was born. Ages 5–10.

Mak, Kam. (2001). *My Chinatown*. New York: HarperCollins. This is a book of one year in poems about growing up in Chinatown. Ages 4–11.

Polacco, Patricia. (2001). *The Keeping Quilt*. New York: Aladdin Paperbacks. This is a story about six generations of families and how they carry their heritage. Ages 6–11.

Recortvits, Helen. (2003). *My Name Is Yoon*. New York: Frances Foster Books. This is a story about a little Korean girl learning to live in America. Ages 5–9.

Robinson, Anthony, and Annemarie Young. (2010). *Gervelie's Journey*. London: Frances Lincoln Children's Books. This is a refugee diary about having to leave one's country to be free. Ages 8 and up.

Warren, Andrea. (2008). *Escape From Saigon*. New York: Square Fish. This book tells how a Vietnam War orphan became an American boy. Ages 10 and up.

Weber, Valerie. (2007). *This Is My Story: I Come From Ukraine*. New York: Weekly Reader. This is a story of a little boy's emigration from Ukraine. Ages 6–11.

Yaccarino, Dan. (2011). *All the Way to America*. This is the story of an Italian family's journey to America. New York: Alfred A. Knopf. Ages 5–9.

Books About Attention Deficit Hyperactivity Disorder

Gavin, Mathew, and Sandra Ferraro. (2001). *Otto Learns About His Medicine*. Washington, DC: Magination Press. This is a story about children with ADHD. Ages 4 and up.

Quinn, Patricia, and Judith Stern. (2012). *Putting on the Brakes: Understanding and Taking Control of Your ADD or ADHD* (3rd ed.). Washington, DC: Magination Press. This guide helps children understand ADHD. Ages 8–13.

Books About Dyslexia

Janover, Caroline. (2004). *Josh: A Boy With Dyslexia*. Bloomington, IN: iUniverse. This is a story about Josh and his feelings about having dyslexia. Ages 8–12.

Moore-Mallinos, Jennifer. (2007). *It's Called Dyslexia*. New York: Barron's Educational Series. This story helps children cope with dyslexia. Ages 5–11.

Books About Magical Thinking

Blackburn, Lynn. (1991). *I Know I Made It Happen*. Omaha, NE: Centering Corporation. This book presents many circumstances in which kids feel guilty and responsible for making things happen. Ages 5–8.

Flynn, Jessie. (1994). *It's Not Your Fault*. Lexington, KY: Accord. This book for young children discusses the magical thinking of feeling responsible for the death of a person. Ages 3–7.

Rappaport, Doreen. (1995). *The New King*. New York: Dial Books. A wonderful book about a boy who becomes king after his father dies. He uses magical thinking to try and bring his father back to life. Ages 6–12.

Books About Linking Objects

Bernardo, Susan. (2012). *Sun Kisses, Moon Hugs*. Encino, CA: Inner Flower Child Books. This book helps children to see that everything in nature can be a linking object in remembering love. Ages 4–10.

Karst, Patrice. (2000). *The Invisible String*. Camarillo, CA: DeVorss. This simple story reminds children that they are never alone and can be connected with a very special string made of love. Ages 5–10.

McLaughlin, Kirsten. (2001). *The Memory Box*. Omaha, NE: Centering Corporation. This is a story about a memory box to remember a grandfather. Ages 4–8.

Polacco, Patricia. (2001). *The Keeping Quilt*. New York: Aladdin. This is a story of a quilt that reminds a family of their home in Russia. Ages 4 and up.

Poulter, J.R., and Sarah Davis. (2008). *Mending Lucille*. Sydney: Lothian. This is a wonderful book about the healing impact of a linking object after a death, such as the doll Lucille. Ages 5–10.

Books About Feelings

Berry, Joy. (2010). *Let's Talk About Feeling Jealous*. New York: Joy Berry Books. This book helps children understand that jealousy is normal. Ages 3–7.

Berry, Joy. (2010). *Let's Talk About Needing Attention*. New York: Joy Berry Books. This book helps children understand their need for attention. Ages 3–7.

Buron, Karl. (2006). *When My Worries Get Too Big*. Shawnee Mission, KS: Autism Asperger. This book for children presents ways for them to recognize and work with anxiety and worry. Ages 5–9.

Burns, Ellen. (2009). *Nobody's Perfect*. Washington, DC: Magination Press. This is a story for children about perfectionism. Ages 7–12.

Cook, Julia. (2006). *My Mouth Is a Volcano*. Chattanooga, TN: National Center for Youth Issues. This book discusses the social nuance of polite conversation, not interrupting, and when to stop talking. Ages 4–8.

Cook, Julia. (2012). *Wilma Jean the Worry Machine*. Chattanooga, TN: National Center for Youth Issues. This story is about childhood anxiety. Ages 7–11.

Doleski, Teddi. (1983). *The Hurt*. Mahwah, NJ: Paulist Press. The wonderful story about a little boy who keeps all of his hurt inside, until the hurt grows so big it fills his room. When he shares his feelings, the hurt begins to go away. All ages.

Goldblatt, Rob. (2004). *The Boy Who Didn't Want to Be Sad*. Washington, DC: Magination Press. This is a story about a boy who doesn't want to be sad and tries to run away from his sadness. Ages 5–9.

Huebner, Dawn. (2006). *What to Do When You Worry Too Much*. Washington, DC: Magination Press. This is a kid's guide to overcoming anxiety. Ages 6–12.

Johnson, Lindan. (2005). *The Dream Jar*. Boston: Houghton Mifflin. This is a story about a girl who turns a bad dream into a good one. Ages 5–9.

Lichtenheld. Tom. (2007). *What Are You So Grumpy About?* New York: Little, Brown Books. This book helps children to change a grumpy mood. Ages 5–9.

Mayer, Mercer. (2005). *There Are Monsters Everywhere*. New York: Dial. This is a story about childhood concerns. Ages 4–9.

Meiners, Cheri. (2010). *Cool Down and Work Through Anger*. Minneapolis, MN: Free Spirit. This book presents constructive ways for children to deal with anger. Ages 4–8.

Parr, Todd. (2005). *The Feelings Book*. New York: LB Kids. This is a board book for young children about feelings. Ages 4–8.

Steig, William. (2011). *Spinky Sulks*. New York: Square Fish. Spinky is angry and begins to sulk. No one can make him stop. Ages 4–8.

Viorst, Judith, and Ray Cruz. (2009). *Alexander and the Terrible Horrible No Good Very Bad Day*. New York: Atheneum Books. Alexander has a day where everything goes wrong. Everyone can relate to this. Ages 4–8.

Weaver, Susan. (2011). *Worry Busters*. Herndon, VA: Rainbow Reach. This is an activity book for kids who worry too much. Ages 5–11.

Wolff, Ferida, and Harriet Savitz. (2005). *Is a Worry Worrying You?* Terre Haute IN: Tanglewood Press. This is a helpful book for children who worry. Ages 5–10.

Books About Inspiration and Resilience

Aslan, Chrisopher. (2008). *Wenda the Wacky Wiggler*. Vancouver, BC: Benjamin Brown Books. This is the story of a girl who has the courage to dance to her own music. Ages 5–11.

Curtis, Jamie Lee, and Laura Cornell. (2006). *Is There Really a Human Race?* New York: HarperCollins. A little boy questions how we can make this world a better place. Ages 5–10.

Greive, Bradley. (2007). *Teaspoon of Courage for Kids: A Little Book of Encouragement for Whenever You Need It*. Kansas City, KS: Andrews McMeel. This book offers children encouragement through life. Ages 10 and up.

Hallinan, P. K. (2006). *A Rainbow of Friends*. Nashville, TN: Ideals Children's Books. This is an easy-to-read book about celebrating differences and the uniqueness of others. Ages 3–8.

Leaf, Munro. (2011). *The Story of Ferdinand*. New York: Viking Juvenile. This is a classic story of a peaceful bull named Ferdinand. Ages 3 and up.

Muth, Jon. (2005). *Zen Shorts*. New York: Scholastic Press. Three classic Zen stories are presented with inspiration through beautiful watercolor and ink illustrations. Ages 5–12.

Obama, Barack. (2011). *Of Thee I Sing*. New York: Knopf. This is a letter from Barack Obama to his daughters about his heritage and their multicultural world. Ages 5–11.

Paterson, Katherine. (2011). *Brother Sun, Sister Moon*. San Francisco: Handprint Books. This book demonstrates respect, love and wonder for the world we inhabit through the words St. Francis used to celebrate life. Ages 5–10.

Robinson, Anthony, and Annemarie Young. (2010). *Gervelie's Journey: A Refugee Diary*. London: Francis Lincoln Children's Books. This is the true story of a young child fleeing militia attacks and civil war in West Africa. Ages 8 and up.

Sabin, Ellen. (2004). *Hero*. New York: Watering Can Press. This is a book that helps children learn lesson from the people they admire. Ages 6–11.

Stepanek, Mattie. (2001). *Heartsongs*. New York: VSP Books. Mattie was a poet and peacemaker who inspired many. Children of all ages.

Waber, Bernard. (2002). *Courage*. Boston: Houghton Mifflin. This is a wonderful book sharing moments of courage for children. Ages 5–10.

Books About Same-Sex Parents

Brannen, Sarah. (2008). *Uncle Bobby's Wedding*. New York: G. P. Putnam. This is a story about Uncle Bobby marrying his boyfriend. Ages 5–10.

De Haan, Linda, and Stern Nijland (2000). *King and King*. Berkeley, CA: Tricycle Press. This is the story of two men that have a relationship. Ages 5–10.

Ferro, Ursula (2007). *Mother's Day on Martha's Vineyard*. West Tisbury, MA. Marti Books. This story is about a child's life on Martha's Vineyard with her two moms. Ages 6–11.

Polacco, Patricia. (2009). *In Our Mothers' House*. New York: Philomel. This is the story of children with two mothers. Ages 5–11.

Richardson, Justin, and Peter Parnell. (2005). *And Tango Makes Three*. New York: Simon & Schuster. This is the story of two male penguins that start a family. Ages 5–9.

Snow, Judith. (2004). *How It Feels to Have a Gay or Lesbian Parent*. New York: Harrington Park Press. This is a book for kids with gay parents. Ages 9 and up.

Books About All Different Kinds of People and Families

Adamson, Heather. (2008). *Families in Many Cultures*. North Mankata, MN: Capstone Press. This is an easy-to-read book describing all kinds of families. Ages 4–8.

Diggs, Taye. (2011). *Chocolate Me!* New York: Feiwel and Friends. This is a story for young children about feeling good about the color of your skin. Ages 3–8.

Global Fund for Children. (2006). *Global Babies*. Watertown, MA: Charlesbridge Publishing. This is a picture book of global babies. Ages 1–7.

Kilodavis, Cheryl. *My Princess Boy*. New York: Aladdin. This is a mom's story about a young boy who loves to dress up. Ages 4–8.

King, Dedie. (2010*). I See the Sun in China*. Hardwick, MA: Satya House. This is a book written in English and Chinese depicting the old and new culture in China. Ages 4–8.

Lin, Grace. (2001). *Dim Sum for Everyone*. New York: Dragonfly Books. A child describes the various dishes of dim sum she enjoys in Chinatown. Ages 4–8.

Muth, Jon. (2002). *The Three Questions*. New York: Scholastic Press. This is an inspiring children's story based on a story by Leo Tolstoy. All ages.

Parr, Todd. (2003). *The Family Book*. New York: Little, Brown. This is a book that shows all kinds of families. Ages 2–7.

Rotner, Shelly, and Sheila Kelly. (2009). *Shades of People*. New York: Holiday House. This book speaks to children's feelings on different shades of skin. Ages 4–8.

Scott, Kathyrn. (2011). *All of the Pieces That Make Me, Me*. Lexington, KY: CreateSpace. This is a story of Miyoko, who traces her background and discovers that appearance comes from many world cultures. Ages 5–9.

Thomas, P. (2003). *The Skin I'm In*. New York: Barron. This is a first look at racial discrimination for very young children. Ages 4–7.

Books About New Siblings

Alexander, Martha. (2006). *When the New Baby Comes, I'm Moving Out*. Watertown, MA: Charlesbridge. A boy is angry with his mom for preparing for a new baby. Ages 4–7.

Blume, Judy. (2007). *Superfudge*. New York: Puffin Books. Peter, a sixth-grade boy, learns his mom is having a baby and wonders how he will survive it. Ages 7 and up.

Boyd, Lizi. (1992). *Sam Is My Half Brother*. New York: Puffin Books. Hessie is afraid that her new half-brother, Sam, will get all the love and attention. This book stimulates discussion on stepfamilies. Ages 4–8.

Cole, Joanna. (2010). *I'm a Big Sister*. New York: HarperFestival. This is a story about a little girl who shares her new baby in the house.

Fuller, Rachel (2009). *My New Baby*. Auburn, ME: Childs Play International. This is a board book for children expecting a new baby in the family. Ages 1–6.

Gaydos, Nora. (2010). *I'm a New Brother*. Norwalk, CT: Innovative Kids. This book helps children share about becoming a big brother. Ages 4–8.

Books About Cremation

Carney, Karen. (1997). *Our Special Garden: Understanding Cremation*. Wethersfield, CT: D'Esopo-Pratt Resource Center. This is a beautifully done book for young children that creates words to use on the important topic of cremation. Ages 3–7.

Service, Robert. (2006). *The Cremation of Sam McGee*. Toronto: Kids Can Press. This is a story for children about cremation. Ages 9 and up.

Smith, Walter. (2007). *Grandad's Ashes*. London: Jessica Kingsley. This is a book about scattering Grandad's ashes. Ages 4–9.

Books About Funerals, Memorial Services, and Rituals

Abue. (2012). *Silly Gilly Gil*. Nannup, Western Australia: MPS Press, Pick-a Woo Woo. This is a book about Grandpa Harley's funeral. Ages 5–9.

Ancona, G. (1993). *Pablo Remembers*. New York: Lothrop, Lee & Shepard. This book has interesting photographs explaining the Mexican fiesta of the Day of the Dead. Ages 6–10.

Balter, Lawrence. (1991). *A Funeral for Whiskers*. Hauppauge, NY: Barron's Educational Series. Sandy's cat dies, and she find useful ways to commemorate. Ages 5–9.

Carney, Karen. (1997). *Barclay and Eve Sitting Shiva*. Wethersfield, CT: D'Esopo-Pratt Resource Center. This resource for young kids explains the customs involving the Jewish practice of shivah. Ages 3–7.

Cooney, Doug. (2003). *The Beloved Dearly*. New York: Aladdin. This is a story about a boy who starts a funeral service for neighborhood pets. Ages 8 and up.

Levy, Janice. (2007). *I Remember Abuelito: A Day of the Dead Story* (in English and Spanish). New York: Albert Whitman. This is a story about the Day of the Dead and remembering a grandfather. Ages 7 and up.

Lowery, Linda. (2004). *Day of the Dead*. Minneapolis, MN: Carolrhoda Books. This book explains rituals and customs involving the Day of the Dead. Ages 7–11.

Mundy, Michaelene. (2009). *What Happens When Someone Dies?* St. Meinrad, IN: Abbey Press. This is a child's guide to death and funerals. Ages 4–8.

Schaefer, Lola. (2011). *Arlington National Cemetery*. North Mankato, MN: Heinemann-Raintree. This book tells the story of Arlington National Cemetery. Ages 6–12.

Techner, D., and J. Hirt-Manheimer. (1993). *A Candle for Grandpa: A Guide to the Jewish Funeral for Children and Parents*. New York: UAHC Press. This is a children's resource on Jewish funerals and burials. Ages 7–12.

Wiles, Deborah. (2005). *Each Little Bird That Sings*. New York: Harcourt Children's Books. This is a book about a special aunt's funeral. Ages 8–12.

Winsch, Jane. (1995). *After the Funeral*. New York: Paulist Press. This book for young children shares possible feelings they have after a funeral. Ages 4–7.

Books About Separation

Bender, Janet. (2004). *Getting Yourself Together When Your Family Comes Apart: Coping With Family Changes*. Chattanooga, TN: National Center for Youth Issues. This is a resource for children facing family change caused by many life events. Grades 7–10.

Dewdney, Anna (2009). *Llama Llama Misses Mama*. New York: Viking Juvenile. Little Llama finds it hard to say good-bye. Ages 3–8.

Maude, Cornelia (2004). *When I Miss You*. Park Ridge, IL: Albert Whitman. This book addresses separation anxiety that many young children have. Ages 4–8.

Pando, Nancy (2005). *I Don't Want to Go to School: Helping Children Cope With Separation Anxiety*. Pearland, TX: New Horizon Press. This is a book about coping with leaving a parent. Ages 4–8.

Penn, Audrey (2006). *The Kissing Hand*. Terre Haute, IN: Tanglewood Press. This is a story for any child temporarily separated from a loved one. Ages 4–10.

Poulter, J.R. (2011). *The Sea Cat Dreams*. Australia: Mustang, OK: Tate Publishing. The theme of this beautifully illustrated book is change and how it impacts children. Ages 5–10.

Rusackas, Francesca (2004). *I Love You All Day Long*. New York: HarperCollins. This story comforts children in realizing a parent's love stays with them whether they are together or apart. Ages 3–8.

Sloan, Christopher. (2002). *Bury the Dead*. Washington, DC: National Geographic. This is a book about tombs, corpses, mummies, skeletons, and rituals. Ages 12 and up.

Thomas, James R. (2010). *What Will I Play While You Are Away?* Seattle, WA: CreateSpace. This book helps kids when parents go away. Ages 5–9.

Books About Good-byes

Hanson, Regina. (2005). *A Season for Mangoes*. New York: Clarion. This book shares the rich culture of Jamaica in saying good-bye and memorializing. Ages 5–10.

Marler, Jerilyn. (2012). *Lily Hates Goodbyes*. Portland, OR: Quincy Companion Books. This is a book for military kids coping with deployment. Ages 5–10.

Penn, Audrey. (2007). *A Kiss Goodbye*. Terre Haute, IN: Tanglewood Press. Chester has to say good-bye to his old home. Ages 3–8.

Rivett, Rachel. (2010). *Are You Sad, Little Bear?* Oxford, UK: Lion Hudson. This is a book about learning to say good-bye. Ages 4–8.

Verick, Elizabeth. (2008). *Bye-Bye Time*. Minneapolis, MN: Free Spirit. This is a book for young children having difficulty saying good-bye. Ages 1–5.

Viorst, Judith. (1992). *The Good Bye Book*. New York: Aladdin Books. This is the story of a child left unwillingly with a babysitter. Ages 4–7.

Your children are not your children. They are the sons and daughters of life's longing for itself . . .
You are the bows from which your children as living arrows are sent forth.

—Kahlil Gibran, *The Prophet*

References

AARP, The Brookdale Foundation Group, Casey Family Programs, Child Welfare League of America. Children's Defense Fund, and Generations United. (n.d.). GrandFacts: National Fact Sheet for Grandparents and Other Relatives Raising Children. Retrieved from http://www .aarp.org/content/dam/aarp/relationships/friends-family/grandfacts/grandfacts-national.pdf

American Academy of Child & Adolescent Psychiatry. (2011). Facts for Families: The Adopted Child. Retrieved from http://www.aacap.org/cs/root/facts_for_families/the_adopted_child

Angela Schwindt Quotes. (n.d.). *Quotes.net*. Retrieved June 20, 2013, from http://www.quotes .net/quote/17418.

Bernstein, Nell. (2005). *All Alone in the World: Children of the Incarcerated*. New York: New Press.

Blackmore, Charlene. (2013, July 12). Direct Conversation. Omni Youth Service Family Preservation Clinical Supervisor. Buffalo Grove, IL: Omni Youth Service.

Blackmore, Charlene. (2013, July 12). Direct Conversation. Omni Youth Service Family Preservation Clinical Supervisor. Buffalo Grove, IL: Omni Youth Service.

Bloomfield, Harold, and Leonard Felder. (1986). *Achilles Syndrome*. New York: Random House.

BPSOS Boat People SOS. (2011). Who We Are. Retrieved from http://www.bpsos.org/mainsite /about-us.html

Burnaby, Kathy Lynn. (2011, May 18). How to Keep Your Child Safe Online. Retrieved from http://issuu.com/pmcommunity/docs/bbywed20110518 p. 14–15.

Caldwell, Alicia and Jim Kuhnhenn. (2012, June 15). New Obama Policy Will Spare Some from Deportation. *Associated Press*. http://news.yahoo.com/obama-policy-spare-deportation-172548797.html

California Department of Corrections and Friends Outside. (n.d.). How to Explain . . . Jails and Prisons . . . to Children: A Caregiver's Guide. Retrieved from http://friendsoutside.org/ resources.htm

Cass, Connie, and Stacy A. Anderson. (2011, September 27). *Poll: Young People Say Online Meanness Pervasive*. *Associated Press*. Retrieved from http://news.yahoo.com/poll-young-people-online-meanness-pervasive-070854585.html

Children's Defense Fund. (2013, March). Each Day in America. Retrieved from http://www .childrensdefense.org/child-research-data-publications/each-day-in-america.html

Children's Defense Fund. (2010, September 3). Marion Wright Edelman's Child Watch Column: "Gun Violence and Children: Have We No Shame or Respect for Child Life?" Retrieved from http://www.childrensdefense.org/newsroom/child-watch-columns/child -watch-documents/gun-violence-and-children.html

Children's Defense Fund. (2011). The State of America's Children, 2011. Washington, DC. Retrieved from http://www.childrensdefense.org/child-research-data-publications/state-of-americas-children-2011/

Clark, Heather (Fall 2011), *"Camp Erin/TAPS Grief Camp: Healing Through Mentoring,"* Washington, DC: TAPS Magazine, 18–19.

Common Sense Media. (2009, June 18). 35% of Teens Admit to Using Cell Phones to Cheat. Retrieved from http://www.commonsensemedia.org/about-us/news/press-releases/35-teens -admit-using-cell-phones-cheat

Conger, Cristen. (2011, July 21). What Is the DREAM Act? Retrieved from http://people .howstuffworks.com/dream-act.htm

Cooper, Anderson, and Gloria Vanderbilt. (September 19, 2011). Anderson Live. *The Story of My Mom: Gloria Vanderbilt*. Season 1, Episode 6. New York: Telepictures Productions.

Dallaire, D. H. (2007). Incarcerated Mothers and Fathers: A Comparison of Risks for Children and Families. *Family Relations*, *56*(5), 440–453.

Dejesus, Ivey. (2011, February 11). Joint Chiefs of Staff Chairman Mike Mullen to U.S. Army War College: The Military Must Look After Its Families. Retrieved from http://www.pennlive .com/midstate/index.ssf/2011/02/joint_chiefs_of_staff_chairman_1.html

Doleski, Teddi. (1983). *The Hurt*. Mahwah, NJ: Paulest Press.

Dougy Center. (2012). *Memories Matter*. Portland, OR: Dougy Center.

Dr. Seuss. (1954). *Horton Hears A Who!* New York: Random House Books for Young Readers.

Eberling, Carol, and David Eberling. (1991). *When Grief Comes to School*. Bloomington, IN: Bloomington Educational Enterprises.

Edelman, Marion. (2011, August 19). Marion Edelman's Child Watch Column: "Bounced Checks From America's Bank of Opportunity." Retrieved from http://www.childrensdefense .org/newsroom/child-watch-columns/child-watch-documents/bounced-checks-from-americas-bank-of-opportunity.html

Eike, Nancy (1992). Personal Conversations. Past Director Northwest Suburban Child Protective Network. Buffalo Grove: Illinois. Omni Youth Services.

Falcone, Michael. (2009, February 13). 100,000 Parents of Citizens Deported over 10 Years. *New York Times*. Retrieved from http://www.nytimes.com/2009/02/14/us/14immig.html

Foley, Elise. (2012, June 15). Obama Administration to Stop Deporting Younger Undocumented Immigrants and Grant Work Permits. *Huffington Post*. Retrieved from http://www.huffingtonpost .com/2012/06/15/obama-immigration-order-deportation-dream-act_n_1599658.html

Fox, Sandra. (1988). *Good Grief: Helping Groups of Children When a Friend Dies*. Boston: New England Association for the Education of Young Children.

Frohnmayer, John. (1994). Music and Spirituality: Defining the Human Condition. *International Journal of Arts Medicine*, *3*(1), 26–29. Retrieved from http://www.mtabc.com/page.php?141

Frost, Sue, and Randy Adams. (2009–2012). *Memphis*. Kennedy Center Theatre.

Get on the bus: Uniting children with their mothers and fathers in prison. (2009). *About Us*. Retrieved from http://www.getonthebus.us/about-us.php

Gibran, Kahlil. (1951). *The Prophet*. New York: Alfred A. Knopf.

Gliko-Braden, Majel. (2004). *Grief Comes to Class: A Teachers Guide*. Omaha, NE: Centering Corporation.

Goldman, Linda. (2000). *Life and Loss: A Guide to Help Grieving Children* (2nd ed.). New York: Taylor and Francis.

Goldman, Linda (2001). *Breaking the Silence: A Guide to Help Children With Complicated Grief, Suicide, Homicide, AIDS, Violence, and Abuse* (2nd ed.). New York: Taylor and Francis.

Goldman, Linda. (2005). *Children Also Grieve: Talking About Death and Healing*. London: Jessica Kingsley.

Goldman, Linda. (2009). *Great Answers to Difficult Questions About Death: What Children Need to Know*. London: Jessica Kingsley.

Goldman, Linda. (2010). *Great Answers to Difficult Questions About Sex: What Children Need to Know*. London: Jessica Kingsley.

Goldman, Linda. (in press-2014). *Lucy Let's Go: Helping Children Love a Pet Through Death and Dying*. Omaha, Nebraska: Centering Corporation.

Gorman, Gregory H., Matilda Eide, and Elizabeth Hisle-Gorman. (December 8, 2010). Wartime Military Deployment and Increased Pediatric Mental and Behavioral Health Complaints Pediatrics. *Pediatrics*, *126*(6), 1058–1066. Retrieved from http://pediatrics.aappublications.org/ content/126/6/1058.full.pdf

Grall, Timothy. (2007). Custodial Mothers and Fathers and Their Child Support: 2009 (2011). *U.S. Census Bureau, 2009*. Retrieved from www.census.gov/prod/2011pubs/p60-240.pdf

Gray, Keturah. (2006, September 12). How Mean Can Teens Be? *ABC Primetime*. Retrieved from http://abcnews.go.com/Primetime/Story?id=2421562&page=1#.UGuDIxxK6is

Gutnik, Aviva, Robb, Michael, Takeuchi, Lori, and Jennifer Kotler. (2010). *Always Connected: The New Digital Media Habits of Young Children*. New York: Joan Ganz Cooney Center at Sesame Workshop.

Harris, Robie. (2001). *Goodbye Mousie*. New York: Margaret McElderry.

Heegaard, Marge. (2007). *Adopted and Wondering: Drawing Out Feelings*. Minneapolis, MN: Fairview Press.

Hindjuda, Sameer, and Justin W. Patchin. (2008). *Bullying Beyond the Schoolyard: Prevention and Responding to Cyberbullying*. Thousand Oaks, CA: Corwin Press.

Hoban, Tana. (1971). *Look Again*. New York: Macmillan.

Holladay, Jennifer. (2010). Cyberbullying: The Stakes Have Never Been Higher for Students—or Schools. *Teaching Tolerance*, Number 38, Fall: 43–46.

Jackson, Edgar. (1973). *Coping with the Crises in Your Life*. Northvale, NJ: Aronson, Jason Inc.

James, Elijah (2009, March 25) citing Fagan, Patrick and Robert Rector, *Children of Divorce The Shocking Statistics*. Retrieved from http://elijahjames.articlesbase.com/divorce-articles/children-of-divorce-theshocking-statistics-833765.html#ixzz1YVvVmOBS

Jones, Audrey. 2013. Current Divorce Statistics Lovetoknow divorce. Retrieved from http://divorce.lovetoknow.com/Divorce_Statistics

Justice Strategies. (2011, January 12). Children on the Outside: Voicing the Pain and Human Cost of Parental Incarceration. Retrieved from http://www.justicestrategies.org/sites/default/files/publications/JS-COIP-1-13-11.pdf

Kaiser Family Foundation. (2010, January 20). Daily Media Use Among Children and Teens Up Dramatically From Five Years Ago. Retrieved from http://kff.org/disparities-policy/press-release/daily-media-use-among-children-and-teens-up-dramatically-from-five-years-ago/

Kosciw, Joseph and Elizabeth Diaz. (2008). Involved, Invisible, Ignored: The Experiences of Lesbian, Gay, Bisexual and Transgender Parents and their Children in Our Nation's *K*-12 Schools. *GLSEN*. Retrieved from http://www.gsanetwork.org/files/resources/GLSEN-Involved InvisibleIgnored.pdf

Kreider, Rose M. (2007). Living Arrangements of Children: 2004. *Current Population Reports*, pp. 70–114. Washington, DC: U.S. Census Bureau.

Kübler-Ross, Elisabeth (Ed.). (1975). *Death: The Final Stage of Growth*. Englewood Cliffs, NJ: Prentice-Hall, Inc.

Lai, Thanhha. (2013). *Inside Out and Back Again*. New York: HarperCollins.

Leonhard, Dona, Janel Digby, and Jessica Rice. (2005). Lesson Plan for Making Hero Packs: A Service-Learning Project for the Operation: Military Kids Initiative. *U.S. Army Child and Youth Services*. Retrieved from http://operationmilitarykids.ohio4h.org

Lindbergh, Anne Morrow. (1940). *The Wave of the Future*. Orlando, FL: Harcourt, Brace.

Mak, Kam. (2001). *My Chinatown: One Year in Poems*. New York: HarperCollins.

McClam, Tricia, and Mary Varga. (2011). Connecting College Students and Grieving Children. *ADEC Forum*, 37(4), 31, 33.

McDonough, Patricia. (2009, October 26). TV Viewing Among Kids at an Eight-Year High. Neilsen *Newswire: The Nielsen Company*. Retrieved from http://www.nielsen.com/us/en/news wire/2009/tv-viewing-among-kids-at-an-eight-year-high.html

McLaughlin Kirsten, and Adrienne Rudolph. (2001). *The Memory Box*. Omaha, NE: Centering Corporation.

Melhem, Nadine, Monica Walker, Grace Moritz, and David Brent. JAMA and Archives Journals. (2008, May 5). Antecedents and Sequelae of Sudden Parental Death in Offspring and Surviving Caregivers. *Pediatric Adolescent Medicine, 162*(5), 403–410. Retrieved from http://archpedi.jamanetwork.com/article.aspx?articleid=379503

Morgan, David. (2011, September 13). Number of Poor Hit Record 46 Million in 2010. *Reuters.* Retrieved from http://www.reuters.com/article/2011/09/13/us-usa-economy-poverty-idUSTRE78C3YV20110913

Movement Advancement Project, Family Equality Council, and Center for American Progress. (2011). *All Children Matter: How Legal and Social Inequalities Hurt LGBT Families* (Condensed Version), 1–34. Foreword by Child Welfare League of America (CWLA). Retrieved from http://www.lgbtmap.org/file/all-children-matter-condensed-report.pdf

National Military Family Association. (2010). *We Serve, Too. A Toolkit About Military Kids.* Retrieved from http://www.militaryfamily.org/publications/community-toolkit/

National Parenting Center. (2011). *Seal of Approval Winner: Moody Monster Manor.* Retrieved from http://tnpc.com/search/tnpcarticle2.asp?rec=7214

Nelson, Vacinda. (1988). *Always Grandma.* New York: South China.

Nicholson, Lucy. (2012). Father's Day in Prison. *Reuters.* Retrieved from http://www.reuters.com/news/pictures/slideshow?articleId=USRTR33NO1#a=1

Oaklander, Violet. (1969). *Windows to Our Children: Gestalt Therapy for Children.* New York: Center for Gestalt Development.

O'Keefe, Gween Schurgin, and Kathleen Clarke-Pearson. (published online March 28, 2011). Clinical Report—The Impact of Social Media on Children, Adolescents, and Family. *Pediatrics, 127*(4), 800–804. Retrieved from http://hcfgkc.org/sites/default/files/documents/The-Impact-of-Social-Media-on-Children-Adolescents-Families.pdf

O'Toole, Donna. (1989). *Growing through Grief: A K-12 Curriculum to HELP Young People through All Kinds of Loss.* Burnsville, NC: Mt. Rainbow.

Parke, R., and K.A. Clarke-Stewart. (2002). Effects of Parental Incarceration on Young Children. *Washington, DC: U.S. Department of Health and Human Services.* Retrieved from http://aspe.hhs.gov/hsp/prison2home02/parke&stewart.pdf

Pastor, P.N., and C.A. Rueben. (2008). Diagnosed Attention Deficit Hyperactivity Disorder and Learning Disability: United States, 2004–2006. National Center for Health Statistics. *Vital Health Statistics, 10*(237), 1–15.

Paventi, J. (2010). Social Security Benefits for Children of Deceased Parents. Retrieved from http://www.livestrong.com/article/226549-social-security-benefits-for-children-of-deceased-parents/

Portnoy, S. M. (2008). The Psychology of Divorce: A Lawyer's Primer, Part 2: The Effects of Divorce on Children. *American Journal of Family Law, 21*(4), 126-134. Retrieved from http://www.portnoyassociates.com/resources/articles/psychology2.html

Recorvits, Helen and Gabi Swiatkowska. (2003). *My Name is Yoon.* New York: Farrar, Straus and Giroux.

Reitmayer, Erynn Elizabeth. (2010). When Parents Get Deported Citizen Children Fight to Survive. *Latino America: Grappling With Immigration, Status and Identity in 2010.* Retrieved from http://asu.news21.com/2010/children-of-deported-parents/

Riley, Sheila. (2008, December 29). Seattle Schools Share Cyberbullying Prevention Curriculum. Retrieved from http://www.hotchalk.com/mydesk/index.php/editorial/121-class.

Rogers, Fred. (2005). *Life's Journey According to Mr. Rogers: Things to Remember Along the Way.* New York: Hyperion.

Rogers, J. Earl. (2007). *The Art of Grief: The Use of Expressive Arts in a Grief Support Group.* New York: Routledge.

Rosove, Lori. (2001). *Rosie's Family: An Adoption Story.* Ontario, Canada: Asia Press.

Rotner, Shelley and Sheila Kelly (2010). *Shades of People*. New York: Holiday House.

Rubenstein, Judith. (1982). Preparing a Child for a Goodbye Visit. *Journal of the American Medical Association*, 247(18): 2571–2572.

San Francisco Children of Incarcerated Parents Partnership. (2012). Children of Incarcerated Parents: Bill of Rights. Retrieved from http://friendsoutside.org/resources.htm#Bill-of-Rights

Sanford, Doris. (1986). *I Can't Talk About It*. Portland, OR: Questar, Multnomah Press.

Schirmer, Sarah, Ashley Nellis, and Marc Mauer (February, 2009). Incarcerated Parents and Their Children: Trends 1991–2007. *Washington, DC: Sentencing Project Research and Advocacy for Reform*, 1–12. Retrieved from http://www.sentencingproject.org/doc/publications/publications/inc_incarceratedparents.pdf

Sesame Workshop. (2011). Arming Military Families With Love, Laughter, and Practical Tools for Deployment. Retrieved from http://www.sesameworkshop.org/what-we-do/our-initiatives/military-families/?o=90&c=featured

Silverstein, Shel. (1974). *Where the Sidewalk Ends*. New York: HarperCollins.

Sorkin, Aaron (screenplay writer) and David Fincher (director). (2010). *The Social Network*. Culver City, CA: Columbia Pictures.

St. George, Donna. (2011, September 6). Bullying Tied to Lower Test Scores in Va. High Schools. *Washington Post*. Retrieved from http://articles.washingtonpost.com/2011-09-05/local/35276007 _1_strength-or-popularity-dewey-cornell-student-behavior

Trim, Diane. (2009, February 16). Cyberbullying: Seattle Public School's Online Lessons. Inside the Schools, Madison, Wisconsin: Magna Publishers.

Vargas, Jose Antonio. (2012, May 24). Shadow Americans. *Time*, 34–44.

Venza, James, Kimberly Freeman and Beverly Buckles. (2010, September). Child training session. Presentation for the Haiti Hope and Healing Project, Port-au-Prince, Haiti.

Webb, Nancy Boyd (2002). *Helping Bereaved Children: A Handbook for Practitioners*. New York: Guilford Press.

Weedn. Flavia (from an idea by) and Doug Haverty. (2004). *Flavia and the Dream Maker: Musical*. Dramatic Woodstock, IL: Publishing Company. P. 23.

Weiner, Lori. (September, 1991). Women and Human Immunodeficiency Virus: A historical and personal psychological perspective. *Social Work*, 36(5), 375–378.

Weitz, Chris. (2011). *A Better Life*. Universal City, CA: Summit Entertainment.

White, E. B. (1952). *Charlotte's Web*. New York: Harper & Row.

Whitehead, John. (1983). *The Stealing of America*. Westchester, IL: Crossway Books.

White House. (2011, January). Strengthening Our Military Families: Meeting America's Commitment. Retrieved from http://www.whitehouse.gov/sites/default/files/rss_viewer/strengthening_our_military_families_meeting_americas_commitment_january_2011.pdf

Wolfelt, Alan. (1983). *Helping Children Cope with Grief*. Muncie, IN: Accelerated Development Inc.

Yen, Hope. (2012, May 17). Census: Minorities Now Surpass Whites in U.S. Births. *Sarasota Herald-Tribune*. Retrieved from http://www.heraldtribune.com/article/20120517/WIRE/12051 9627/2416/NEWS?template=printpicart

About the Author

Linda Goldman has a fellow in thanatology (FT) degree in death, dying, and bereavement, an MS degree in counseling, and a master's equivalency in early childhood education. Linda is a Licensed Clinical Professional Counselor (LCPC) and a National Board for Certified Counselors (NBCC). She worked as a teacher and school counselor for almost 20 years. Currently she has a private grief therapy practice in Chevy Chase, Maryland. She works with children, teenagers, families with prenatal loss, and grieving adults. Linda shares workshops, courses, and trainings on children and grief and trauma and teaches as adjunct faculty in the Graduate Program of Counseling at Johns Hopkins University. She has also taught on the faculty at the University of Maryland School of Social Work/Advanced Certification Program for Children and Adolescents and has lectured at many other universities and organizations—including Penn State University, Buffalo School of Social Work, University of North Carolina, the National Transportation Safety Board, and the National Changhua University of Education in Taiwan—as well as numerous schools systems throughout the United States. She teaches a course on Working With LGBT Youth at Johns Hopkins Graduate School, the University of Maryland School of Social Work, and the Child Welfare Administration. She has written many articles, including *Healing Magazine*'s "Helping the Grieving Child in School" (2012), "The Bullying Epidemic" (2005), "Creating Safe Havens for Gay Youth in Schools" (2006), and "Parenting Gay Youth" (2008). Some of her articles on children and grief and trauma have been translated into Chinese for the Suicide Prevention Program of Beijing. She appeared on the radio show *Helping Gay Youth: Parents Perspective* (2008) and has testified at a hearing before the Maryland Joint House and Senate Priorities Hearing for Marriage Equality (2007) and the Maryland Senate Judicial Proceedings Committee for the Religious Freedom and Civil Marriage Protection Act (2008).

Linda has worked as a consultant for the National Head Start Program and National Geographic and was a panelist in the national teleconference When a Parent Dies: How to Help the Child. She has appeared on *The Diane Rehm Show* to discuss children and grief and Dan Rodricks's Baltimore NPR show *Midday* to discuss gay youth. She was named by *Washingtonian* magazine as one of the top therapists in the Maryland–Virginia–Washington, DC area (1998) and again named by the *Washingtonian* as a therapist to go to after the terrorist attacks in 2001. She has served on the board of the Association for Death Education and Counseling (ADEC), the advisory boards of Suicide Prevention Education Awareness for Kids (SPEAK), RAINBOWS for Our Children, the academic advisory board of McGraw-Hill's *Annual Editions: Dying, Death, and Bereavement*, and the advisory board of the Tragedy Assistance Program for Survivors (TAPS) as children's bereavement advisor. Linda is the recipient of the 2003 ADEC Clinical Practice Award.

Linda Goldman is the author of *Life and Loss: A Guide to Help Grieving Children* (first edition, 1994; second edition, 2000; third edition, 2014), Taylor & Francis. Her second book is *Breaking the Silence: A Guide to Help Children With Complicated Grief* (first edition, 1996; second edition, 2002; Chinese edition, 2000). Her other books include *Bart Speaks Out: An Interactive Storybook for Young Children on Suicide* (1998), WPS Publishers; a Phi Delta Kappan International fastback, *Helping the Grieving Child in the School* (2000); a Chinese edition of *Breaking the Silence: A Guide to Help Children With Complicated Grief* (2002); the Japanese edition of *Life and Loss: A Guide to Help Grieving Children* (2005); *Raising Our Children to Be Resilient: A Guide for Helping Children Cope With Trauma in Today's World* (2005); a children's interactive story and memory book *Children Also Grieve: Talking About Death and Healing* (2005); a Chinese translation of *Children Also Grieve* (2007); and *Coming Out, Coming In: Nurturing the Well Being and Inclusion of Gay Youth in Mainstream Society* (2008). She has also authored contributing chapters in resources including *Loss of the Assumptive World* (2002), *Annual Death, Dying, and Bereavement* (2001–2013), *Family Counseling and Therapy Techniques* (1998), and *The School Services Sourcebook: A Guide for School-Based Professionals* (2006; second edition, 2012). She has also written two books to be included in the series *Great Answers to Difficult Questions About Death* (2009; Polish translation, 2012; Korean translation, 2013) and *Great Answers to Difficult Questions About Sex* (2010).

Linda also created a CD-ROM titled *A Look at Children's Grief* (2001) published by ADEC, and she was a part of ADEC's 2009 webinar series, Children and Grief. Her op-ed "Cut out Guns, Bullying" appeared in the *Baltimore Sun* in March 2001. She was an important part of the *Washington Post* article, "How to Talk to Kids About Suicide," and has participated in other interviews for articles in the media, including the *Washington Post*, the *Los Angeles Times*, *USA Today*, the *New York Times*, the *Boston Globe*, the *Wall Street Journal*, the Associated Press, *Seventeen* magazine, ABC News, and *US* magazine.

Linda contributed in many ways after 9/11. She authored the chapter about children, "Talking to Children About Terrorism," in *Living With Grief: Coping With Public Tragedy*, published by the Hospice Foundation of America in 2003. She contributed to the *Journal for Mental Health Counselors* in its special 2004 grief issue with her article "Grief Counseling with Children in Contemporary Society." She was an active member of the TAPS response team at the Pentagon Family Assistance Center; conducted workshops about children and grief at the TAPS National Military Survivor Seminars in 2002, 2004, 2005, 2006, and 2010; and authored articles including "Helping Children With Grief and Trauma" (2002/2003) and "Fostering Resilience in Children: How to Help Kids Cope With Adversity (2005) in *TAPS Journal* and "Children Coping With a Military Death (2008), also in *TAPS Journal*.

Linda contributed on the Public Broadcasting Service program on children and grief titled *Keeping Kids Healthy*, which aired in October 2006, and the program *You'll Always Be With Me* on KNBP Channel 5 Public Broadcasting in 2010. She consulted with Sesame Street for its program and materials on *Children and Grief* and *Children and the Military* (2010). She also is the recipient of the Tenth Global Concern of Human Life Award 2007.

E-mail: Linda.goldman@verizon.net
Website: www.childrensgrief.net

Index